THE
ECONOMICS
OF TRAVEL
AND TOURISM

2ND EDITION

ADRIAN BULL

LONGMAN

An imprint of
Addison Wesley Longman

Addison Wesley Longman Australia Pty Ltd
95 Coventry Street
South Melbourne 3205 Australia

Offices in Sydney, Brisbane and Perth and associated companies throughout the world.

Edited by Debbi Barnes
Designed by Lauren Statham
Typeset by Done To Perfection
Set in M Plantin 10.5/12.5 pt
Cover designed by Rob Cowpe
Produced by Addison Wesley Longman Australia Pty Ltd
Printed in Malaysia through Addison Wesley Longman China Ltd, VVP

National Library of Australia
Cataloguing-in-Publication data

Bull, Adrian.
    The economics of travel and tourism.

    2nd edn.
    Bibliography.
    Includes index.
    ISBN 0 582 80731 X

    1. Tourist trade. I. Title.

338.4791

CONTENTS

Introduction

There are few human activities which can simultaneously attract academic attention from economists, geographers, environmental scientists, psychologists, sociologists, political and management researchers. Tourism is one.

Each of these disciplines has its own view to contribute to the study of an activity which accounts for an increasing call on global resources and use of people's time. As a result, three approaches have developed to the study of tourism.

The first is the *business studies* approach, which clearly regards travel and tourism as an industry, or set of industries, requiring management and operational skills appropriate to enterprise needs. So for example we have texts on retail travel practice, on front office operations, and so on, culminating in specialised applications of management and marketing to the whole sector.

The second approach is basically *holistic*. More academic than the first approach, scholars attempt to provide a multi-disciplinary view of tourism activity, perhaps with the objective of striving to develop a self-standing theory of tourism. Distinguished scholars such as Alberto Sessa (1984) have sought to build such a methodology, although they admit that a lack of research implies a week theoretical framework. Nonetheless, we are surely feeling our way towards a 'touristic corpus of knowledge', based perhaps on regarding tourism as a system or system set (e.g. Kaspar 1986).

Thirdly, it is possible to have a *discipline-based* approach to study. Using, say, a social science such as economics or geography as a theory base, we can attempt to identify what is significant or special about travel and tourism compared with other activities. Undoubtedly there is the danger of ignoring aspects of activity which do not relate directly to the basic discipline, but perhaps that simply pressures scholars to re-evaluate the scope of their own discipline. A reductionist rather than holistic approach may not give us a pleasing view of the whole house, but enables an understanding of how the floor, walls and roof function.

Economics in travel and tourism

This text takes mainly the third approach. Although it would be foolish to take no notice of environmental, marketing or behavioural contributions, it is essentially based in economic theory. Writers such as H Peter Gray (1970, 1982 and 1984) broke published ground by identifying some of the central issues in tourism to which economic analysis can contribute.

Tourism has some distinct characteristics which I hope will show in this text. Resource immobility, capacity constraints, seasonality, and consumers' inability to experience the product before purchase are some of the hallmarks (Aislabie 1988). As an industry it also tends to have a far wider impact on host economies than many other industries.

Since we are dealing with the *economics* of travel and tourism activity, much of this book is concerned with commercial marketplaces. The bulk of commercial payments in tourism are for travel and accommodation, so there is a concentration on these areas, especially in the first, generally microeconomic, half of the book. The second half broadens out into the macroeconomic picture of tourism's role within national economies, and examines some specific problems such as unpriced services, the environment and multinational enterprise.

This text is designed for those who have some familiarity with economics, preferably having completed at least a first year university or college course. It does not attempt to specialise in the travel and tourism activity of any one country, but seeks to draw examples globally. Where there is nothing specially distinctive about tourism in relation to an economic concept, little will be said. Equally, references are constrained to those which most readily expand on topics covered. Readers without a background in economics are advised to refer to any good basic text first, especially to cover microeconomic concepts such as opportunity cost, utility, or economies of scale.

Acknowledgments

I should like specifically to thank: Peter Chapman of Complete Travel and Paul Macrae of Southern Cross Galileo for computerized information; John Tisdell of the University of Queensland for help in linear programming; Professor Clem Tisdell of the University of Queensland for his constructive comments; and those in the travel and tourism industry, students and colleagues who have helped with information, advice and encouragement. Any deficiencies in the text are my own.

Preface to the 2nd edition

Since the first edition of this text appeared in 1991, travel and tourism worldwide has continued to represent an increasing percentage of economic activity, albeit with disruptions caused by events such as the 1991 Gulf War. The World Tourism Organisation and World Travel and Tourism Council estimate that international tourism expenditures/receipts were worth US$330 billion in 1993, and will be worth US$550 billion or more, at 1993 prices, by 2005. It is estimated that international tourism employs some 127 million people. No-one has reliably valued domestic tourism, but it is fair to assume that its addition would at least double the above figures.

This edition contains some new elements, such as a number of case studies to encourage empirical study of concepts presented in the text. In addition, it updates and expands on some of the topics in the first edition. Thanks are due to the many commentators who have supplied valid criticisms and helpful suggestions. In particular, I should like to thank Mark Hopf of Harvey World Travel for current travel information, and Professor Neil Leiper of Southern Cross University and Professor Stephen Smith of the University of Waterloo for their valuable comments.

CHAPTER 1

Resources in tourism

▦ Tourism concepts

Any examination of the economics of travel and tourism requires definitions of the subject, and its components, which are suitable for economic analysis. By and large such definitions are *technical*, and will be discussed later. However, it is also important to look at tourism *conceptually*, in order to set the scene for a deeper understanding of the subject than the mere technicalities.

Tourism is neither a phenomenon nor a simple set of industries. It is a human activity, which encompasses human behaviour, use of resources, and interaction with other people, economies and environments. It also involves physical movement of tourists to locales other than their normal living places. Although most tourism around the world is a form of recreation, thus implying use of an individual's discretionary time, some tourism is inevitably linked with obligations, such as business or health requirements.

Whilst it is not the place of this text to summarise and explore the many definitions attempted by various writers, no single, satisfactory conceptual definition has been universally agreed upon. It is generally agreed, however, that travel and tourism includes:

- tourist needs and motivations
- tourism selection behaviour and constraints
- travel away from home
- market interactions between tourists and those supplying products to satisfy tourist needs
- impacts on tourists, hosts, economies and environments.

Economics plays a role in many of these areas, particularly where there is a need to analyse market forces relating demand by tourists to supply of 'products', and in analysing economic impacts and measures to control tourism's effects. It is also important to interrelate economics with the sociology, psychology and geography of tourism on the one hand; on the other hand economics plays a role in planning, management and marketing in travel and tourism organisations and destinations.

◼ Working definitions in travel and tourism

Whilst the concepts above provide the rationale for studies in travel and tourism economics, we need technical or working definitions in order to provide identifiable, and preferably measurable, variables with which to undertake analysis. For statistical purposes, the most widely accepted baseline definitions for international visitors were first agreed to by the United Nations Conference on International Travel and Tourism, in Rome in 1963. Visitors were divided into:

Tourists—*temporary visitors to a country staying at least 24 hours, for the purposes of leisure or business; and*
Excursionists—*temporary visitors staying in a country less than 24 hours, for the same purposes, but excluding transit passengers.*

Despite later amendments, these definitions still substantially form the core of travel and tourism definitions.

Leisure tourism is normally held to include travel for recreation or holiday, sport, health, religion or study. The majority of the world's tourists are vacationers, but one could still include here visiting sports teams or Muslims on pilgrimage to Mecca.

Business tourism can include business people travelling, presumably on expenses, convention delegates, and those visiting friends or relatives (VFR). Business travellers are generally less numerous than vacationers, but usually spend more per head, whilst VFR travel is very important to particular countries.

Most countries apply an upper limit length of stay, such as three months, on their definitions of 'international tourist', and this may be related to the length of tourist visas or other permits granted. It is also possible to use most of the above framework to define 'domestic tourists', although there is a problem in deciding how far a person must travel away from home to be regarded as a tourist or an excursionist. Diplomats are not counted as tourists (nor, presumably, would military personnel be considered tourists if diplomacy should break down!). It is also intuitively simple, and correct, to exclude those who travel to a destination in order *primarily* to undertake employment paid by organisations based in the destination. Whilst a student travelling for a working holiday might be classed as a tourist, an expatriate foreign worker would not. This implies that a tourist *generally* brings money earned at home to spend at a destination—which is an important point in analysing tourism's contribution to an economy.

We must now introduce some further, subsidiary definitions. A *destination* may be a country, region or city to which visitors travel as their main objective. They may only visit a single destination, or travel on a multi-destination tour. A *transit point* or *stopover* is a point which, usually for transport or connection reasons, may be visited, but not as a main objective of travel. The country, region or city where visitors normally live is often known as a *generator* or *generating area*; to a destination, this will be the market.

◼ The tourism industry and its products

In the travel and tourism marketplace it follows that the tourism industry, or industries, consists of any organisations supplying goods and services to those people now defined as tourists and excursionists, as part of their 'tourist requirements'. This is bound to encompass a whole mass of organisations, the majority of which are likely to be involved in passenger carriage (or travel), accommodation and amenities or attractions. In addition, however, there are specific and supporting organisations, such as tourist information centres, souvenir manufacturers and retailers, or brochure distribution companies.

Because of this complex range, it is useful to attempt to classify the industry into sectors. One such classification (Holloway 1989) produces:

- *carriers*—in any form of transport for tourist travel
- *accommodation*
- *man-made attractions*—which could also include the managed areas of natural attractions
- *private sector support services*
- *public sector support services*
- *'middlemen'*—such as tour wholesalers and travel agents.

By their nature, the majority of organisations in travel and tourism are concerned primarily with their own individual product, and probably at best with the marketplace represented within their sector. When asked what their 'product' is, most hoteliers will reply 'accommodation', most agents 'travel services', and so on. Thus, in their view, whilst admitting to being within the travel and tourism industry, most will not claim to be supplying a product called tourism. Indeed, some businesses—such as restaurants in tourist areas—may be selling principally to tourists, so are part of the tourism industry, whereas others supplying a similar *physical* product, but to non-tourists—such as restaurants in city business districts—are not really part of the tourism industry (Leiper 1993).

This immediately creates a problem in any economic analysis of the field, in that the products felt to be supplied by members of the industry are not necessarily the same as those products perceived to be in demand by consumers. Tourists on the whole are likely to have a more global concept of the travel and tourism product which they are buying than are individual suppliers. This problem has been considered by a number of writers (for example Chadwick 1981, Murphy 1985).

To compound the difficulties, the end benefits which many tourists seek may not be tradeable products at all. For example, one tourist may really wish to purchase the chance to sit on a sunny beach for a week, to obtain the end benefits of total relaxation, restored well-being and a good suntan. Another simply demands the opportunity for a face-to-face business meeting in order to close a sales contract for his or her company. In neither case are these tourists really seeking to buy tradeable products, but rather a *dream*, *total experience*, *activity* or *business opportunity*.

As travel and tourism organisations develop, and their marketing becomes more sophisticated, they are tending to operate more from a consuming tourist's point of view in, say, putting together inclusive tour packages or promoting non-tradeable end benefits rather than their own individual products. However, in whole areas of tourism there is still a mismatch between product perceptions on different sides of the market. This problem will be given attention later.

■ Resources

It is normal for economists to divide resources into those which are considered *free* (that is, they are in such abundance that there is no need for any mechanism to allocate them to users) and those which are *scarce* (where their supply in general is limited in respect to their actual or potential demand). Scarce resources may be further subdivided, typically (Norton 1984) into:

- Natural resources—*land, minerals, water, biological*
- Labor resources—*human work, and 'enterprise'*
- Capital resources—*man made enhancement of other resources.*

Most economic study is then concerned with production and allocation decisions about these scarce resources.

Decisions about resource allocation are made at many levels of society. A country may adopt a political system which provides the *methodology* for resource allocation, such as market pricing in a capitalist economy, or central planning in a fully communist one. Within that system, national or regional decisions allocate resources between industries, and between economically productive and non productive uses. For example, a government, industries and pressure groups may negotiate over a tract of land which may be available for mining, or agriculture, or tourist use (alternative industries), or to remain as a natural habitat (economically non productive). At an industry level, individual firms compete for resources which have been more or less bound to that industry. For example hoteliers and restaurateurs may compete using attractive remuneration packages to get good chefs—a 'skilled food production labour resource'.

Even within a productive operation, there will be competing demands on scarce resources and a need to determine their allocation: should a National Tourist Office spend all its available advertising budget on a promotional video, or a mixture of brochures and posters, or on something else?

The ways in which outcomes of these decisions are determined are central concerns of economic study, both in general and in relation to specific activities. So one of tourism economics' main areas of study must deal with these questions:

- What resource allocation mechanisms apply in generating areas and at destinations?
- How does tourism compare with other activities or industries in competing for scarce resources?
- What competition for resource use, as well as for markets, is there between suppliers in travel and tourism?
- Are there significant opportunity costs involved in using particular resources for tourism use?
(The cost of using resources for tourism is the lost opportunity of being able to use those resources for the 'next best' alternative.)

These are all *positive* rather than *normative* questions; that is, they address actuality rather than what we think *should* happen. Inevitably, though, this text will at times be concerned with value judgments, as tourism has become such an important influence across many societies and economies.

■ Travel and tourism resources

From the earlier definitions and consequent discussion, two main problems immediately appear:

- As there is frequently a mismatch between producer and consumer perceptions of what constitutes the tourism 'product', there may be conflict in ideas of which resources are properly involved.
- Many of the resources likely to be in demand for tourism are public goods, or even free resources.

Whilst it may be argued that in today's world there are really very few, if any, free resources left (virtually any human activity makes demands on this world such that someone at sometime will have to pay for it), undoubtedly the demand for tourism involves a substantial amount of public goods. These may be defined as existing facilities which are under-utilised, where an individual may make use of them without reducing the amount of the facilities available to others. This is a situation of *zero opportunity cost* (Samuelson 1989). If a family takes a camping vacation by car at an off-season period, they may use the road network, public or national parks, beaches, and they may 'consume' scenery by looking at it or taking photos, without impinging in any way on other people. Of course, if the same family were to travel in peak season, there might be considerable opportunity costs, from traffic congestion, overcrowding at destinations and spoilt views.

Travel and tourism suppliers will also use combinations of the same scarce resources that other producers use. There have been various attempts to list and categorise those resources which are statistically significant in travel and tourism (Murphy 1985, Stabler 1988, Peters 1969, Wahab 1975), which are summarised in figure 1.1.

Figure 1.1   Significant resources for travel and tourism

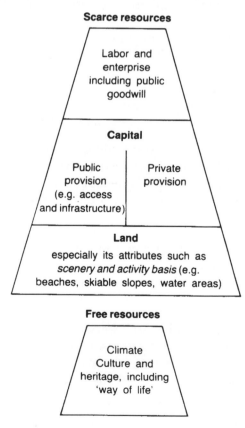

Scarce resources

Labor and enterprise including public goodwill

Capital

Public provision (e.g. access and infrastructure)

Private provision

Land
especially its attributes such as *scenery and activity basis* (e.g. beaches, skiable slopes, water areas)

Free resources

Climate Culture and heritage, including 'way of life'

Figure 1.1 demonstrates that tourism frequently is built upon a basis of free resources, with (in most economies) a mixture of publicly and privately used scarce resources superimposed. Thus there is a combination to form what tourists may perceive as the 'product' they are consuming, and what suppliers are producing.

Some writers have used the terms *resource-basis* and *user-orientation* to identify types of tourism product, particularly destinations and their attractions (Burkart and Medlik 1981). Resource-based products tend to be those unique attractions created by nature or past human activity, whereas user-oriented ones are more widely spread and are likely to have been created specifically for tourist use.

Examples of resource-based products could be: mountains, exotic wildlife in its natural habitat, or Roman ruins; and of user-oriented products: sports stadia or convention centres. However, most successful tourism products are neither entirely of one type nor the other. For downhill skiing, a mountain requires specific tourist-oriented capital investment in runs, lifts and lodging as well as the natural slope, and a successful convention centre benefits from being located in a scenically or culturally interesting place.

■ Resource combinations

Given that travel and tourism products draw on resources or factors of production for their existence, a further question which must later be explored is the relationship between resources used and output produced. Economists term this relationship the *production function*. Examination of production functions enables an understanding not only of the total amount of scarce resources required to make a product, but also of the alternative ways in which these resources may be combined. Classical theory holds that at a given state of technology, and other things being equal, resource use depends on the marginal productivity of each resource, and its price or reward.

In travel and tourism generally, some resources are unique or so individual that they are irreplaceable. To offer a similar or identical tourist experience to visiting the Grand Canyon or Eiffel Tower would be either impossible or uneconomic. Such resources are usually those at the base of the 'tree' in figure 1.1. Attempts have been made to substitute capital for land— for example in Townsville, Australia a shore side complex duplicates wonders of the Great Barrier Reef—but most 'base' resources are more or less fixed.

Other, less rare, resources may be used and varied in combination to bring about a productively efficient solution. Some of the analytical techniques involved, such as neoclassical production theory and activity analysis, will be explored more closely in a later chapter, but it is evident at even a simple level that some firms in travel and tourism constantly seek optimal resource combinations. For example, a standard 'international-style' hotel such as Holiday Inn is likely to operate a property in the United States or Europe with a staff-to-guest ratio of perhaps 1:2 or even 2:5. In a lower-wage Asian country a similar property's ratio may be 1:1 or higher. The high-wage American or European property is likely to have a much more substantial investment in capital equipment, from automatic rather than attended elevators to self-service guest laundry and labour-saving food production equipment.

Many travel and tourism organisations face these choices in resource use, and because there is such a wide range both of productive sectors and types of involved, there are rarely any definitive solutions as to what are the 'best' resource combinations. Tourism in this respect is very different from, say, the global steel industry, which through maturity and competitive rationalisation has a much more consistent pattern of production from firm to firm and country to country.

We can, however, identify some common threads in travel and tourism *relative* to other activities. First, tourism at destinations often makes considerable use of land, or more particularly the *facilities* or *attributes* of land. 'Land' here includes landform, flora and fauna, water space and landscape scenery, as well as purely spatial needs. Sometimes tourism is in serious conflict with other users, as when in a congested harbour area small yachts and windsurfers may get in the way of commercial shipping. (In this instance, any 'zoning' of activities enforced by authorities brings in opportunity costs of those activities chosen.) Elsewhere there may be little or no conflicting alternative use—a surfing beach, or remote picturesque wilderness area with no worthwhile mineral resources may be of interest only to tourism.

Secondly, much of the travel and tourism *industry*, both at generating areas and destinations, is relatively *labour intensive*. Partly this is historic, as traditions in hospitality and ancillary areas have been based on principles of domestic service. Today's luxury hotel still has a staffing structure drawn from grand private homes of the last century, and staff-to-room or staff-to-guest ratios are still seen as an acceptable proxy measurement of quality. The importance of *service* is frequently stressed, whether in luxury hotels, a travel agency, on an airline or in a souvenir shop. Evidence suggests that most tourists prefer personal contact and service rather than automated or self-service systems—unless there are significant trade-offs such as lower prices or compensatory 'freedom' benefits. Despite this, technological advances are of course shifting relative efficiencies of capital and labour in tourism in such a way that many parts of the industry are becoming less labour-intensive, particularly in 'back-of-house' (non tourist contact) functions such as automated reservations and ticketing.

Thirdly, tourism calls upon a resource possessed by tourists themselves, namely time. Unlike the purchaser of household goods, a tourism consumer must give up scarce time as well as money. Like money, time has an opportunity cost: that is, the other things which have to be given up in order to travel. Unlike money, which is paid in exchange for services and goods provided, time is merely used up. Most of this is leisure time which people use willingly for tourism, as the opportunity cost of other activities is low (Hawes 1974), but much of it may be very reluctantly spent, especially on mundane travel and waiting for public transport. When opportunity costs are sufficiently high, consumers may take a shorter trip, or none at all, or expend other resources to reduce time taken. Successful sales of transatlantic Concorde services, together with helicopter transfers, sold at premium first class fares, are proof of this.

■ Controlling and rewarding resource use

In market economies, and even in most centrally-planned ones, some form of pricing mechanism is normal to help allocate scarce resources. In capitalist economies, resources may be owned by private individuals or corporations, who will provide them for productive use in exchange for the best money price, other things being equal. Economists term such resources *factors of production* and the money prices for their use *rewards*. Thus land provided for productive use earns rental or royalties, labour earns wages or salaries, capital earns interest, and enterprise earns profit as a reward. In addition, governments may insist on some control over resource use for social welfare or non-economic ends—this is most marked in communist economies, where the state owns some or all resources itself anyway.

It has been frequently found that factors of production in travel and tourism do not earn the best possible reward. In other words, it may be possible to earn higher rewards in other industries or at least there are comparable factors in other industries earning higher rewards. Why is this? Some of the underlying analysis will be dealt with more fully in chapters 7 and 8, but we may briefly identify some reasons:

- Tourism and travel has the reputation of being a relatively 'clean and pleasant' industry in which to work or invest, so that

    a) it attracts more resource suppliers than a less well-perceived industry, so competition keeps reward prices down;
    b) resource suppliers trade off some monetary return for non-pecuniary considerations. For example, a chef may happily work for less money in a pleasant beach resort than in an industrial catering job in a big city.

- Setting up in the industry is often seen, perhaps erroneously, as simple and requiring few skills other than the oft-claimed 'ability to get along with people'. It is therefore attractive to those retiring from or leaving other jobs and investments, to buy into a bar, guest house or travel business for example. If their finances are already sound, income from travel and tourism is not expected to be optimal, merely useful.

- Travel and tourism is frequently highly seasonal, offering rewards that are competitive with other industries for only some of the time.
- Destination products are often in locations which are of little use to other industries, so competition for resource use is minimal and hence rewards are low.

In addition to this, many governments are extending controls over tourism and its use of resources, for economic, social and environmental reasons. The controls may be direct, such as straight prohibition on development or rationing of access to foreign exchange in order to purchase imported equipment; or they may be indirect, such as imposing special taxation or influencing development from the demand side. In any event, governments around the world have recognised the importance of travel and tourism as a human activity, and as with any other activity, they want to keep it in order.

Study questions

1 Find, from textbooks or policy statements, any three definitions of tourism. Do they agree? If not, why do you think not?
2 Explain in your own words the discrepancy between consumers' and producers' views of tourism as a product.
3 Classify the resources needed to operate a winter sports resort.
4 What is meant by the 'opportunity costs' of tourism? Show how these may be linked to seasonal patterns of tourism.
5 In what ways does tourism use resources differently from other sectors of the economy?
6 Why are rewards for resource use in tourism often low? Find some examples of wage rates in tourism in your locality, and compare them with rates for similar, but nontourism, jobs.

Tourist types

■ The importance of segmentation

In almost any industry, those suppliers who take a strong marketing-oriented approach to their business are concerned with understanding their customers and their needs, in order to deliver products to them most effectively. For a few industries, customers may all be relatively similar, with similar needs—*homogeneous*. However, in most cases suppliers are faced with a variety of customers, each with different needs, who could be satisfied in different ways by the purchase of a specific product.

In this context we may treat tourism as an industry, or rather a set of industries, providing a set of products where the customers are tourists. This is a rather narrower view of tourism than that discussed in Chapter 1, but will serve initially to help understand the economic context of the activity.

By identifying different types of customer, marketers hope to classify them into *market segments*—a process called *segmentation*. This enables marketers to establish common reasons for purchasing a product within each market segment, common consumer behaviour and common responses to marketing activity. It then becomes possible to target market segments with particular products and to market them in individual ways. This is precisely what most successful suppliers of tourism products do.

In addition, we have a very specific economic interest in segmentation within tourism, since various types of tourist (market segments) operate under different economic constraints, and make different economic contributions as the result of their tourism activity. Some types of tourist are much more valuable to destinations and suppliers than others, and so more effort may be expended to attract them. Tourism organisations, particularly governments, may also develop economic or other policies which do not affect all tourists equally.

So there are two main reasons to study segmentation of tourist types:

- as a rationale for differentiated marketing
- to examine varying economic constraints and contributions, and formulate policy based on behavioural or psychological economics (Katona 1975).

This said, the *method* of segmentation becomes important. It is possible to segment types of tourist in many different ways, but the method chosen is only meaningful if it permits some useful conclusions to be made about marketing and economics. In particular, tourist 'classes' must be relatively homogeneous internally in respect to economic factors, and there must be relatively worthwhile differentiation between classes in the same respect.

Three methods of segmentation are very useful here:

- segmentation by purpose of travel
- psychographic (or cognitive-normative) segmentation
- interactional segmentation.

■ Segmentation by purpose of travel

Most published statistics in tourism use some form of standardised typology of tourists similar to that outlined in Chapter 1, which looks at purpose of travel as the main segmentor. A typical breakdown of segments might be as in Figure 2.1:

Figure 2.1   Types of tourist by purpose of travel

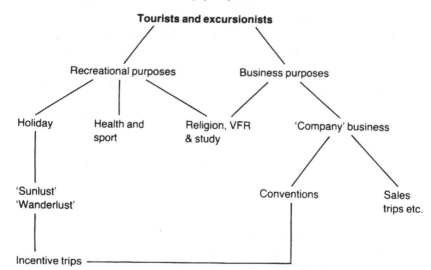

Many statistical series do not distinguish any further than the first division, between recreational and business tourism, although some single out VFR travel (visits to friends and relatives) separately.

In relation to the economics of demand, recreational travel and visits to friends and relatives can mostly be seen as *final demand*—that is, travel undertaken for its own ends, its own satisfaction. Business travel on the other hand is mostly a *derived demand*, a demand for services which may be necessary inputs in the course of producing other goods or services. Business travel is a service analogous to capital goods; recreational travel to consumer goods. Whilst tourists themselves make the purchasing decision for recreational travel and are subject to personal economic constraints, business travel decisions are largely institutionalised, and constrained by corporate economics, including tax deductibility in many economies.

At the lower levels of Figure 2.1, there are some interesting segment-ational differences. Travel for study and religion, and to some extent health and sport, often carries a degree of obligation, as does VFR travel. Tourists making a trip for these reasons will treat their purchase as satisfying basic needs, whereas a holiday is more often thought of as a discretionary item in a consumer's budget. We might therefore expect that general holiday demand is more income elastic, and we will investigate this in the next chapter. The terms 'sunlust' and 'wanderlust' were coined (Gray 1970) to distinguish between those whose main purpose is to escape and relax, often on a beach in the sunshine, and those who may be drawn to destinations offering new sightseeing or cultural experiences. In the latter case, the tourism 'products' in demand are more specific than in the former, and factors affecting demand rather different.

Incentive travel has a rather special place. Whilst it is purchased as business travel, it is normally given (to a business's employees or agents for example) as a reward for some achievement or work target. As such it must be a worthwhile reward, and is likely to be ostentatious as a product. Incentive tourists are welcomed by destinations and travel and tourism organisations, as their per capita expenditure is usually very high.

Table 2.1 shows an example of a comparison between the spending of different groups, and illustrates the value to a destination of attracting the 'right' tourist.

Table 2.1 Estimated average per capita expenditure per day by tourists in Australia, 1992-93

	$A
• Holidaymakers	75
• VFR	38
• Business tourists	147
• Others	63

Source: Australia, Bureau of Tourism Research, International Visitor Survey

Table 2.1 of course takes no account of length of stay, nor tells us exactly which goods and services were purchased by each type of tourist, but gives a clue to the importance of business tourists to a destination.

■ Psychographic segmentation

Practical segmentation, especially for use in marketing, has moved away from demographic groupings over the last few years to a consideration of *lifestyles* (sometimes called activities, interests and opinions or AIO) and *motives*. The resulting segments are known as psychographic, as people differ in measurement of what are basically psychological variables. Researchers in consumer behaviour link AIO with motivations towards purchasing specific goods and services (Schiffman and Kanuk 1987), and in particular have found product-specific links; that is, AIO and personality differences tend to be linked with the selection behaviour for certain products, amongst which are travel and tourism. In addition, some psychographic dimensions or traits are much more relevant than others in tourist behaviour.

If it is possible to identify certain traits in behaviour, and then to categorise types of tourist by those traits which seem important, then there is a basis for segmentation, both for marketing and for economic analysis. Researchers (for example Schewe and Calantone 1978, Plog 1987) have identified a limited number of traits which seem to be especially important in tourists:

- *Venturesomeness*—the degree of 'risk' tourists want
- *Hedonism*—the degree of comfort required on a trip
- *Changeability*—the extent to which tourists are impulsive or seeking something new
- *Dogmatism*—the extent to which a tourist cannot be persuaded to change ideas
- *Intellectualism*—the degree of 'culture' tourists want.

Psychographic research would attempt to provide measures of these traits in order to split tourists into meaningful types. Each trait can be considered as a continuous scale on which tourists are 'scored' to try to identify groups with common scores or profiles. Behavioural economics then examines the economic activity associated with each profiled group. An example of this modelling is given in chapter appendix A.

Traits are then seen to influence tourist activity or the *purchasing characteristics* of tourists, which enables tourism organisations to target profiled groups with specific tourism products at varying prices. For example Plog (1972) developed a well-respected model which can be used to divide tourism markets basically by their degree of venturesomeness. This cognitive-normative model identified tourists as being on a continuum from:

A *allocentric*—highly venturesome, through
B *mid-centric*—like to explore, but with home comforts, to
C *psychocentric*—disliking the unfamiliar or risky.

The purchasing characteristics associated with each type might be:

A   make own travel arrangements, visit remote destinations, board with local residents, learn local culture or study flora and fauna, rarely repeat visit

B   use travel distributors but make own 'package', travel reasonably afar but to recognised tourism destinations, balance novelty with home comforts

C   use organised inclusive tours, travel often *en masse,* seek destinations culturally similar to home, board in mass accommodation or self-catering, often repeat visit.

It is evident that tourist types A, B and C will not only demand different tourism products, but that they will also experience different demand conditions, respond in different ways to changes in economic variables, and make widely differing contributions to, and calls upon, the economies of destinations.

■ Interactional segmentation

Whilst an examination of AIO factors and personality traits is important to understand the background to tourist behavioural types, it may often be sufficient for economic analysis to classify or segment tourists by the *effect* of their behaviour. With respect to the effect on a tourism destination this can be called *interactional segmentation.* Grouping in this way may subsume demographic or psychographic types.

Table 2.2 is a synthesis of segments identified by various researchers.

Table 2.2   Types of tourist by interaction with destinations

Type	Effect on destinations and travel industry
Explorer	Small in numbers, virtually no consumption of 'tourism products', negligible economic impact
Elite	Relatively small in number, price-inelastic demand for very high quality travel and tourism products, may cause investment to follow into destinations
Hosted or *'second homers'*	Constant travel demand, but boarded by hosts or in own accommodation, hence low consumption of destination tourism products, but cause increase in general local expenditure
Individual or *incipient mass*	Numerous, wide ranging travel; demand may be rather price-elastic, significant demand for tourism products produced/owned by the destination
Mass or *charter*	Very numerous between specific generators and destinations; sectors of the travel industry wholly dependent on them (e.g. charter airlines); major impact and costs at destination, may cause significant investment in destination by generator-owned businesses.

(Sources: Cohen 1972, Smith 1977 *et al.*)

It is quite possible for a single destination area to be attractive to all the above types, although from the point of view of economic policy a government may only actively seek one group. Unfortunately, interactional segmentation is not on the whole a good basis for marketing activity. Whilst groups differ markedly in their interaction with destinations, they are not easily targeted in marketing programmes, as they are not discrete sectors in any main area of marketing activity.

In reviewing segmentation in tourism, each of the above methods has been used as an illustration in assessing the role of disaggregating 'tourists' in terms of tourism economics. For practical use in travel and tourism marketing, there are several other segmentation methods of value; see for example Middleton 1988.

◼ Changes in tourist types over time

The significance of motivations for travel, and hence the significance of different types of tourists, has changed over time. Prior to the eighteenth century, very few people travelled for pleasure purposes, with the majority of tourism being for trade, pilgrimages or other religious purposes, or education. Demand was largely derived from other areas in the economies prevailing at the time, or was an obligation, and therefore mainly institutionalised. Recreational travel in Roman times, the Ancient East and medieval Europe was confined mostly to day excursions—obviously over short distances—to activities such as fairs, festivals and travelling sport or entertainments. There was therefore little continuous demand for accommodation or passenger transport, which in any event was often primitive and unreliable.

Even in the eighteenth century, when the European 'Grand Tour' became fashionable as an educational but also recreational period for many upper-class young people, the majority of 'tourism' was for trade or commerce, including trips of exploration throughout Africa, the Americas and Australasia. These were normally paid for by governments or merchant companies in attempts to establish commercial trading ventures.

Spending discretionary income on 'final demand' tourism—that is, tourism purchased to satisfy personal motivations—really only became important in the eighteenth and nineteenth centuries. Travel for medical reasons had long been undertaken—visits from London to Epsom in England are mentioned by Samuel Pepys for example in the 1660s, to take the medicinal spa water—but only became fashionable amongst European royalty in the eighteenth century. The fashion spread, as did the later variant of sea bathing, again largely for medical reasons.

It was, however, only possible for mass tourism, and a mass tourism industry, to develop when the conditions of both supply and demand were met by economic development from industrial revolutions. In particular this meant the supply of transport, in the form of steam railroads and steamships, became much greater and cheaper, and the demand for recreational travel was boosted: people had higher incomes from industrial jobs, were no longer tied to the land, acquired statutory holiday rights, and sought escape from often terrible urban surroundings.

Another touristic consequence of industrial economic development was the motivational need for VFR tourism. As workers and their immediate families moved to industrial jobs in cities, and increased labour mobility meant further geographical break-up of families, so family reunions, for whatever purpose, meant a travel need. On a wider scale, colonisation and emigration to New World lands produced a need for long-distance VFR which flourishes to this day as a major segment of international tourism for many destination countries.

In the twentieth century, mass recreational tourism has become the largest segment of total global tourism, with the aircraft taking over from the steam train or steamship as the prime mode of transportation for large groups of travellers, and private road vehicles for small groups. Interestingly, the older forms of transport have undergone product modification to become, where they still exist, tourist attractions in their own right. For example, ships carrying only passengers are now largely cruise vessels rather than liners, and steam railroads (and often non-steam railroads) are frequently marketed as historic or picturesque tourist attractions.

In the latter half of the twentieth century, a couple of changes in importance of types of tourist are of note. First, corporate expansion and geographical diversification together with an explosive growth in the number of domestic and international associations have meant that convention demand has been one of the fastest growing areas of tourism demand for thirty years. Secondly, the increasing commercial ability of tourism industry suppliers has induced 'supply-led' tourism, where a market may be generated by the introduction and marketing of a specific tourism product. This will be discussed further in a later chapter.

■ Types of tourists today: a summary

It is not the intention of this section to provide a full statistical summary of global tourism today. This can be found through World Tourism Organisation statistics or many introductory texts. However, it is important to summarise the types of tourist purchasing today within domestic and international markets in order to examine overall patterns of demand, products required, and economic impacts upon destinations.

In North America and Europe, 85-90% of tourist nights are spent by domestic tourists; elsewhere it is less, ranging down to 7% in Pacific islands.

Globally:

- 40-45% of tourists are holidaymakers/vacationers (the percentage is lowest in North America)

- 40% or so are travelling on business, including conventions (this is even higher in the Americas)
- 8% are *purely* VFR travellers; most VFR travellers also take a vacation or are on business
- 5% or so are on government business

Source: WTO statistics

Total world tourism (by numbers) is growing through the 1980s and 1990s at around 4% per annum, but the relative importance of segments is changing. For example, newly industrialized countries are developing middle-class populations with new leisure demands, and the need for business tourism is being reduced by communications technology.

■ The needs and impacts of different types of tourists

Figure 2.2 shows a form of perceptual diagram for types of tourist by motivation and purpose of travel:

Figure 2.2   A Tourism Segmentation Space

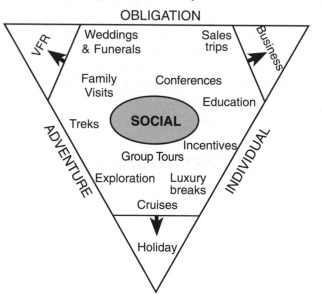

As noted in the example in Table 2.1, overall expenditure per capita is likely to vary widely between tourist types. In relation to Figure 2.2, the highest level of expenditure would be in the lower right area of the figure, and the lowest level in the upper left. The types of products purchased, and the distribution channels used for their purchase, will also vary between groups, with the lower central area of the diagram likely to indicate those groups making most use of formal mass-market distribution channels and inclusive tours.

Different types of tourist also make differing demands upon resources at, and on their way to, a destination. Table 2.3 demonstrates an example of segmentational differences:

Table 2.3 Resource Requirements of Tourists by Type

Typology	Resource Basis					
	Climate	Natural Resources	Amenities Facilities	Cultural & Customs	Culture	Access
Explorer	any	bush, desert, mountains, jungle	none	none	any	very remote
Wilderness lover/anth-ropologist	often extreme	"	none/ basic	only if approp-riate to culture	specific-ally different	remote
Experien-tial	any	any	good indivi-dual	museums, festivals, theatre, architec-ture	observe and interact	any
Individual Inclusive tourists	approp-riate season	usually 'pictur-esque'	"	sight-seeing	any	not too diffi-cult but off beaten track
Group tourist/ convent-ioneers	"	any approp-riate group accomm., attractions	confer-ence, centre	as a 'sideshow'	most home comforts	good & reliable
Mass/ charter	sun/ warmth	sea & sand	highly organized	none	as home	mass transit
Psycho-centric	as home	none local ent-ertainment	clubs,	local	"	local

Destinations and commercial suppliers must therefore be aware of resource need differences if they are attempting to provide tourism products for more than one segment.

In addition, economists analysing travel and tourism are likely to be interested in variations between types of tourist in:

- length of stay
- overall and seasonal demand stability
- repeat visitation and marketing costs.

Length of stay

Length of stay is of particular interest to tourism destination marketers and to accommodation suppliers. Not only is the overall length of a tourist trip important in generating expenditure, but also the allocation of stays to individual destinations. For example, VFR visitors tend both to have a long trip *and* to stay at a single destination. Trekking groups or culture-seeking 'wanderlust' tourists may make a long trip, but as linear rather than nodal tourists, they will stay over only a short time at each destination. A convention delegate may make only a three- or four-day trip, and may stay not only in the one destination but make most expenditure within the one hotel. Table 2.4 shows an example of differing lengths of stay on one destination:

Table 2.4   Estimated length of stay by tourists in Vienna, Austria 1992/3 (nights)

Business travelers	1.9
European vacationers	5.6
North American vacationers	2.5
Other vacationers	2.5
VFR (estimate)	14.0

Sources: OSZ/FW

Overall and seasonal demand stability

In addition to having differing types and levels of demand, different types of tourist vary in respect to the stability of that demand. Various pieces of research have indicated that VFR traffic and luxury recreational tourism are perhaps the least sensitive to demand variation (see, for example, Vlitos-Rowe 1993). Most recreational or holiday tourism is constrained by school vacations or place of work holiday entitlements, together with climatic conditions producing strong seasonal variations. Economic cycles in generating areas not only affect the long term stability of recreational demand, but also may influence patterns of business demand for tourism, through both the ability of businesses to meet travel costs and businesses' desire to maintain or restrict travel elements of their promotional or training budgets.

Repeat visiting and marketing costs

The stability of tourism markets is further influenced by the degree of repeat visiting, or repeat purchase, shown by tourist groups. The psychocentric type tourist mentioned above, or the owner of a second home or timeshare arrangement, is most likely to repeat a visit to a destination, perhaps several times and on a regular seasonal pattern. Cruise passengers exhibit exceptionally high repeat purchasing (brand loyalty); P&O Cruises have for example claimed over 90% repeat purchasing of their products at various times.

Repeat visiting has a significant effect on tourism marketing costs, that is the costs of developing, promoting and delivering tourism products. Suppliers in general attempt to maximise repeat visiting, as the costs of promoting and delivering tourism products to repeat visitors are far lower than when products have to be introduced to first-time buyers who cannot 'sample before they buy'. However, this preference must be tempered by the value of *marginal returns to promotion* achieved in new markets compared with those amongst repeat visitors.

■ Types of tourist and destinational economic policy

Studying segmentation in tourism economics assists in understanding the behavioural background to different types of tourist demand, and in comparing the economic interaction of each type of tourist in destinations and with other suppliers.

Assuming that commercial suppliers wish to maximise profits, and that destination governments wish, all being equal, to maximise the net value of tourism to their local economies, then it is sensible for a supplier or destination:

- to identify discrete tourist market segments
- to assess the stability and demand patterns of each segment
- to evaluate the returns, or profit contribution realised from each segment
- to allocate resources to attracting each segment in such a way that the marginal returns obtained from each segment are equal (assuming that the supplier can supply tourism products suited to identified market segments).

A more detailed and formal model of optimising the value of returns from each tourist segment is shown in chapter appendix A.

This chapter has not addressed inequalities in the economic benefits or costs, identifiable through social accounting, of various impacts on society and the environment which might be attributed to different types of tourism. However, many public resource suppliers (governments, National Park Authorities and the like) attempt to include such an assessment in calculating net benefits from different types of tourists.

Defining market segments and optimising their value

■ Segment definition

There have been several attempts to model the characteristics of market segments. The following is one example (based on Lessig and Tollefson 1972).

Let $\mathbf{B}^j_i$ be the ith 'buying characteristic' for consumer **j**, where **i = 1 to m**. The buying characteristics for a tourist might be the traits already identified such as hedonism or the degree of 'touristic culture' sought.

Let also $\mathbf{X}^j_1$, $\mathbf{X}^j_2$,....$\mathbf{X}^j_n$ be consumer j's personal characteristics, in terms of personality or character make-up. It is assumed that these characteristics are measurable and scalable in some way. Then:

$$\mathbf{B}^j_1 = \mathbf{f}^j_1 \ (\mathbf{X}^j_1, \mathbf{X}^j_2, \ .... \ \mathbf{X}^j_n, \mathbf{MS})$$
$$\mathbf{B}^j_2 = \mathbf{f}^j_2 \ (\mathbf{X}^j_1, \mathbf{X}^j_2, \ .... \ \mathbf{X}^j_n, \mathbf{MS})$$

$$\cdot \qquad \cdot \qquad \cdot \qquad \cdot \qquad \cdot$$

$$\cdot \qquad \cdot \qquad \cdot \qquad \cdot \qquad \cdot$$

$$\mathbf{B}^j_m = \mathbf{f}^j_m \ (\mathbf{X}^j_1, \mathbf{X}^j_2, \ .... \ \mathbf{X}^j_n, \mathbf{MS})$$

where **MS** = market stimuli. These may be divided too: for example into destination promotion, travel agents' recommendations, guide book information and so on.

Then, for tourists j and k, we could establish sets of buying behaviour characteristics:

$$\beta_j = (\mathbf{B}^j_1, \mathbf{B}^j_2, \ .... \ \mathbf{B}^j_m)$$
$$\beta_k = (\mathbf{B}^k_1, \mathbf{B}^k_2, \ .... \ \mathbf{B}^k_m)$$

A comparison for similarity of the sets:

$$\beta_j \ \mathbf{S} \ \beta_k$$

would then indicate whether tourists j and k are of the same market segment, assuming that buying response is linked rationally to behaviour characteristics. Cluster analysis may then be used to define segment boundaries.

■ Optimising segments' value

A destination or any tourism product supplier with a differentiated product should be able to use segmentation to maximise profit, by extending the methods of monopolistic price discrimination into all aspects of marketing. One such model (Frank, Massy and Wind 1972) examines the segmentation economics of promotional plans:

Let x_{mi} be the number of physical units of promotion type m directed at market segment i.

Let v_{mi} be the cost per unit of promotion type m for segment i,
where **m = 1 to m**

   i = 1 to n

and assuming costs per unit of media used are constant. Then the total cost of promotion type m to market segment i is:

$$g_{mi} = v_{mi}\, x_{mi}$$

A simple demand function for market segment i is:

$$q_i = f_i\,(p_i\,,\,x_i)$$

where q_i is the amount of tourism demand by this segment
p_i is the general price level, if such a thing can be calculated, for the tourism product offered to segment i
x_i is a vector of units of promotion types used for this segment $[x_{1i}\; x_{2i} \ldots.\; x_{mi}]$

Then promotional costs, and demand, across all markets are:

$$G = \sum_i g_i = \sum_i v_i\, x_i$$

$$Q = \sum_i q_i = \sum_i f_i\,(p_i\,,\,x_i)$$

and revenue:

$$PQ = \sum_i p_i q_i = \sum_i p_i\, f_i\,(p_i\,,\,x_i)$$

The relationship between revenue PQ and promotional costs G is then optimised when **incremental** returns per promotional dollar spent are equal for all promotional types and in all market segments. Optimising promotional efforts across market segments is particularly important to tourism destinations (National Tourist Offices and so on), the bulk of whose marketing activity is promotion.

Study questions

1 For what reasons might economists be interested in segmentation in tourism?
2 Investigate whether incentive travellers are likely to require any out-of-the-ordinary resources in tourism.
3 Categorize the five traits which researchers have found important in tourism purchasing behavior, then identify any special economic activity that 'extremes' in these traits might cause.
4 Find some examples of tourism destinations which might appeal to each segment in Table 2.2. Explain your choice.
5 What economic conditions made the growth of tourism possible in the nineteenth century?
6 Taking any current tourism statistics and forecasts, show how market segments are changing in importance.
7 Show how length of stay and seasonal demand stability might be important to a recreational tourism destination.

The economics of tourism demand

■ The nature of demand

Microeconomics focuses on demand as one half of the marketplace in which goods and services are to be exchanged. Demand is normally regarded as the driving force of *need* in the economy, which stimulates entrepreneurial activity in producing the goods and services required to satisfy that need, in exchange for the appropriate reward.

At an individual level, most economic analysis treats those initiating demand as examples of 'Marshallian man' (Kotler 1965); that is, they are concerned mainly with economic cues to their behaviour, and before considering each purchase they make a calculation of the amount of benefit, or *utility*, they will obtain from the purchase towards satisfying their needs. Consumer behaviour theory examines this activity far more closely, and behavioural economics as a branch of microeconomics attempts to integrate the Marshallian approach with the psychological and sociological influences in consumer behaviour.

A behavioural approach to demand analysis is important in travel and tourism since the products are complex, and as we have seen in the previous chapter, the needs, and levels of product knowledge, of intending tourists are many and varied (Goodall 1988). Thus it is vital to appreciate the motivations and characteristics of different types of tourist in making up a description of individual, and segment group, utility.

This said, economists are mostly interested in *aggregate* demand, which can be defined as the quantities of a product that buyers collectively are willing and able to buy at any potential price over some specified period of time. (For further exposition see, for example, Samuelson 1989.) This is specifically a definition of *effective* demand. That is, buyers must possess the wherewithal to buy as well as the willingness. There is no doubt a very large *latent* demand for luxury yacht cruises or for supersonic air travel, but few buyers have the ability to pay for them.

■ Products and buyer objectives in tourism

Travel and tourism products

In the first chapter, note was made of the problem in identifying exactly what is a travel and tourism product. It is evident from some of the motivational segments already examined that frequently tourists want products which are normally non-tradeable; for example a 'culture vulture' may wish to 'consume' views of historic buildings or the experiences of street life in a different society. Nonetheless, most buyers would accept that tradeable products such as the travel services needed to reach the required location and accommodation at that location during the visit are a necessary part of the whole bundle of products making up the tourism experience.

This means that in examining trading in tourism 'products' it is possible to view these products in two ways:

- as a total package, or set of complementary products which the buyer views as a single purchase, considered for example as the 'dream' experience. The tourist would tend to think in terms of a global price for the whole tourist trip, and the effect of a change in price of any one element, say accommodation, would depend on the relative importance of that element in the total package cost. Also, in one sense, each element of the package may be a substitute for another, in that each competes with others for a share of the tourist's total package budget.
- as individual products, which are complements certainly, but are considered separately by tourists in making their purchase decisions.

In general, the first approach is one which more accurately reflects tourist purchasing behaviour in the *pre-purchase stage* of extended problem-solving (Middleton 1988), whereas the second approach reflects routinized buying of, for example, car rental services and meals by a business person in the course of a trip.

Since, in global terms, the majority of tourism expenditure results from decisions made well before trips are undertaken, as the result of extended problem-solving about products where buyers often have little or no concrete product knowledge, the first approach will be concentrated upon here. The implication is that tourists view each trip as a product, with every element contributing some characteristic to that product. In turn this means that a Lancasterian approach to demand (Lancaster 1966), or one of its derivatives, is a more sensible theoretical model than straight classical demand theory.

The Lancasterian model sets up a programming approach to demand where a buyer seeks to maximise utility through an objective function; utility is a function of a set of characteristics, which may be possessed in varying quantities by products available in the marketplace. Demand exists under constraints such as price levels and available income. The model will be explored more fully later, but we must first address what constitutes utility, characteristics and constraints.

Buyer objectives

The main reason for marketers to segment tourist markets is to enable the formulation and promotion of products to homogeneous groups of buyers; so if segments have been chosen carefully, all buyers in segment i should possess similar motivations to purchase tourism products, all buyers in segment j similar motivations, but different from segment i, and so on. The objective of any one segment is then to satisfy its motivations as fully as possible.

Thus maximum utility for a particular tourist segment might mean such things as:

- developing maximum competence at snow skiing
- retracing as fully as possible the career of an author
- successfully completing a pilgrimage to Mecca
- completely forgetting workplace cares and acquiring the deepest possible suntan
- securing maximum prestige in a conference debate.

Naturally, utility may come from more complex sets of need satisfaction, where internal trade-offs occur. For example a family might wish to visit relations, whilst at the same time teenage family members wish to maximise social contact with the opposite sex, younger children to maximise playtime on the beach, and father to maximise fishing time. Nevertheless, once *internal* trade-offs are made, the family as a purchasing unit may have an identifiable average aggregate objective.

One major distinction between types of objective is important. The majority of tourists undertaking holiday or VFR trips are satisfying personal needs: that is, tourism is largely undertaken as an end in itself. These tourists can be identified as *consumers with final demand*. Most business tourists on the other hand are concerned in some way with the need to contribute to economic activity. Their tourism purchases are therefore analogous to any other inputs required by producers in the course of production, and their derived demand is dependent, through the business's production function, on demand for the business's own output. There are of course grey areas where tourist trips may be a mixture of both final and derived demand, such as incentive travel or educational visits.

The overall objective of tourist **i** (or by implication market segment i) may be expressed as a functional relationship:

- **maximise** $U_i = U_i (z_j)$

where U represents utility and z represents a vector ($j = 1$ to m) of quantities of characteristics, of a tourist trip, desirable to the buyer. Thus the characteristics which might be important to a 'sunlust' vacation consumer might be such things as:

* daily sunshine hours at the destination
* per capita beach space at the destination
* cleanliness of ocean at the destination
* similarity of accommodations to known standards
* suitable distance (expressed in travel time) to the destination (see chapter appendix A)
* reliability of carriage.

Assuming such characteristics are quantifiable, high z scores would be needed to maximise utility.

To the hedonist, important characteristics might be:

* luxurious accommodations
* gastronomic range and quality of meal experiences
* quality and amount of personal service throughout trips
* reliability of carriage
* prestige name suppliers of tourism services.

In this example, only one characteristic from the previous list is important, and perhaps other z values from that list are irrelevant to the hedonist.

A destination or overall tourism product may possess or *generate* quantities of characteristics. Or, it may be that a tourist has to combine elements (or complementary products) such as two or three travel modes and three or four destinations in the one trip to generate a particular bundle of characteristics. This is expressed, in Lancasterian terms, as a 'consumption technology' constraint:

$$z = g(x_k)$$

where x represents a vector ($k = 1$ to n) of elements from which characteristics z are derived. This now relates the objective of maximising tourist utility, through characteristics, to tourism products themselves.

■ Types of variables influencing and constraining tourism demand

As has been noted, tourism is a very unusual product in that consumers must physically go to the place of production—the 'tourism factory'—to acquire the product, and the travel element is part of the product itself. Frequently, the economic conditions prevailing in the destination are quite different from those in the generating area, particularly in international tourism and on long-haul visits. Thus it is not just economic variables affecting tourists in their home areas which will have an effect on demand. Table 3.1 provides a form of classification of the economic variables likely to affect tourism demand:

Table 3.1   Sources of economic influence on tourism demand

GENERATING AREA ECONOMIC VARIABLES (Group A)	DESTINATION ECONOMIC VARIABLES (Group B)	LINK VARIABLES (Group C)
Personal disposable income levels	General price level	Comparative prices between generator and destination
Distribution of incomes	Degree of supply competition	Promotional effort by destination in the generating area
Holiday entitlements	Quality of tourism products	
Value of currency	Economic regulation of tourists	Exchange rates
Tax policy and controls on tourist spending		Time/cost of travel

The group A variables are those which act specifically on demand by all intending travel and tourism consumers in a generating area, regardless of their destination. They are largely concerned with overall constraints on the ability of buyers to enter tourism markets at all—constraints such as income and time at their disposal, and the degree of government permission for them to be tourists.

Group B variables define the economic attractiveness, all else being equal, of a tourism destination to consumers, wherever they may come from. These variables may be product-related or supply-related. Since there is competition between, as well as within, destination areas, conditions in a number of competing destinations will functionally act together, through substitution effects, to influence tourism demand.

Group C variables are in many ways the most interesting, emanating from the specific link between one generating area and one destination. That is, they will act only on demand for that destination from the one generating market. Once again, a link cannot be considered in isolation, but consumers are likely to take into account the link variables of several links, to competing destinations, in making purchasing choices. Within this group of variables one would include frontier crossing (perhaps measured by a quantified dummy variable) as a tourism demand constraint.

The next step is to examine the forms of effect that these variables are likely to have on overall demand and tourist choice.

■ Levels of choice in travel and tourism demand

In considering the demand for a simple good, economists frequently assume that individual consumers have to make only two decisions:

- whether or not to purchase that generic type of good
- which particular good to choose from the range (of substitutes) available.

(One could argue that fixing on the *quantity* of a chosen good to buy is a third decision, but in a sense this is a repetitive consideration of the first two decisions.)

Individual demand for tourism products involves generally more complicated decision-making. There are several levels of choice for consumers, not necessarily made sequentially. Only when the outcomes of these individual demand decisions are known is it possible to examine properly the aggregate demand for any tourism product. The main choices, which will be examined here, are:

- the overall type of tourism required
- destination
- travel mode
- accommodation and attraction visiting
- purchasing method or distribution channel.

Type of tourism required

The first, and probably simplest, choice is of the type of tourist trip to be made (other than whether or not to buy at all). For many cases, this is a no-choice situation, as for example a business sales trip, pilgrimage, sports event attendance or invitation to a family wedding. The degree of *obligation*, discussed in Chapter 2, fixes the decision. In other cases there may be choices such as a beach or touring vacation, winter cruise or winter skiing, taking a post-convention tour or visiting with friends.

Destination

Secondly, there is choice between destinations. A destination may be a single location, a set of locations as part of a tour, or even a 'moving' destination such as a cruise vessel (Holloway 1989). Individual demand depends on the group B and C variables referred to above, and the consumption technology of the destination—how well it will supply the characteristics needed by the tourist to maximise utility. The degree of substitution between destinations will depend on the similarity of the characteristics set. Evidently, if a tourist requires a high score in 'possession of original Taj Mahal' as a characteristic, and regards nothing else as important, then no substitute for Agra, India as a destination is possible. 'A sandy beach' and 'average air temperature by day of 25°C' as the only required characteristics leaves the consumer with many substitutes.

However, choice is frequently restricted by imperfections in consumer knowledge about, and perceptions of destinations. Very few tourists know accurately about all destinations which might suit their needs, and therefore market equilibria are likely to be highly imperfect.

The most significant variable by far in destination choice appears to be relative prices. Research suggests that this explains at least 40% of variation in travel shares of destinations, and as much as 60% where those destinations are close substitutes (Edwards 1987). This can be incorporated into the formal model of tourism demand in chapter appendix B. As will be seen later, exchange rate variations are of major importance here for international tourism, and of minor importance for domestic tourism.

Travel mode

Thirdly, tourists must choose their mode of travel. Frequently, type of trip and destination dictate a particular travel mode, or make one mode the only practicable alternative. However, there may be desired levels of speed, convenience, comfort, safety and so on where the principal constraint on their attainment is the price of the 'optimum' travel mode, or the length of time available to the tourist in which to undertake journeys. For some market segments, travel itself may have a high positive utility: enjoyment of the point-to-point trip (not a 'day trip' excursion, which is more properly a form of attraction than transport). For others, all time and money spent on travel is a cost, to be minimised if possible.

The travel mode may include more than one type of carriage—as for example the only practicable way for an individual tourist to reach a destination hotel from an airport, whilst hauling luggage, might be a taxi; the same person might have driven a private car at home and parked it at the home airport. Travel therefore also incorporates demand for use of terminals, interchanges and parking areas, whose characteristics and price must be taken into account.

Where it is easy to substitute between competing carriage products, then the price or fare is likely to be the main variable influencing demand, as has been evidenced in deregulated US and European air travel. If fares are almost identical, as may be the case in near-perfect competition or where a cartel such as the International Air Transport Association exists, then specific characteristics such as convenient scheduling are important in influencing demand (Narodick 1972).

Choice of accommodations and attractions

As with travel, the choice of accommodations may become fixed in the light of other tourism decisions. A wilderness experience visit may imply bush camping, business travellers may have to stay in hotels of a chain with which their company has an account, and there may be lodging obligations as part of a VFR trip. For many people, the acquisition of a second home, unit, condominium or timeshare (or even a caravan or recreational motorvan) constrains them to use it at every vacational opportunity, even if secretly some might get higher utility from staying elsewhere on occasion.

The lodging product includes a large bundle of tangible and service characteristics, which often, even more than in transport, can be adjusted to meet the needs of specific consumers. Such elements as meal arrangements, views from lounging areas, and the number of people sharing may be flexible in negotiating with suppliers. In this case the remaining 'fixed' characteristics (such as location) and price become the major variables affecting demand.

Since accommodation costs are likely to be the largest element of total destination (group B variable) costs, it follows that the relative price of lodging can often influence destination perceptions, and hence destination demand. Switzerland has long been perceived as an expensive destination although its domestic transport and many other items are relatively cheap, because of high hotel prices in some areas and some seasons. Price may also be an important 'scare' factor, as unlike the situation with most products buyers are rarely certain what the total cost of their stay will be when they first check in—a little like automobile servicing, but unlike most products consumers buy.

Within any one type of lodging, such as hotels, consumers depend heavily on marketer communication on which to base product judgment. This has meant heavy reliance on establishments with 'known' characteristics such as members of standardised chains, especially by non-adventurous segment tourists. In this case price may be less significant, and chain hotels can frequently generate, at a premium price, equal demand to that for a lower-priced hotel in the same destination offering similar, but less well-known characteristics.

The demand for tourism activities, attractions and items such as souvenirs is probably the simplest within tourism. In most cases the product is either an intrinsic part of the tourist trip, a major motivator in its own right, or is an optional discretionary extra.

In the first case, demand has been established before trip purchase commences, and therefore consumers are willing to pay whatever price is necessary, within reason, to take part in a specified activity or enter the desired attraction. Demand is not highly price sensitive (Diamond 1969, Aislabie 1988).

Many major attractions are non-tradeable public products, or free resource-based attractions (see Chapter 1). Suppliers such as communities and governments may at some stage need to decide whether to initiate user-pays charges, as part of resource management plans (Gunn 1989). Establishing a suitable price level often requires some sophisticated market research. By 'suitable' is meant a price which may either cover costs of providing visitor services and environmental protection, or may restrict demand for the attraction to some environmentally or socially desired level. Such investigation is difficult and must be well-defined (Holloway and Plant 1992), as it is attempting to measure not just a 'what-if?' demand function for the attraction, but perhaps for an entire tourist trip.

Where products form an optional or discretionary extra purchase as part of a total tourism package, the purchasing decision is likely to be a low-involvement one (Engel *et al.* 1987). Simple classical demand theory would explain satisfactorily the nature of demand for most such products. The major variable influencing the level of demand is either the absolute (in-destination) price, or the price of the product relative to that in generating areas. This has been proven to be the case for Japanese tourists purchasing souvenirs and other discretionary items in Hawaii (Keown 1989).

Purchasing method

A final major choice faces consumers of tourism: the purchasing method. This is not simply the question of what type of retail outlet to use, but involves choices such as:

• whether to buy an inclusive package (IT) or separate services
• whether to buy direct from suppliers, such as airlines or hotels, or use an agent
• which tour wholesaler or operator, or which agent to use.

The acceptability of ITs in the tourism marketplace has grown since the 1950s, primarily as the result of the *convenience* of purchasing the product as a package (a product characteristic), and often as the result of a cheap total price compared with purchasing individual elements separately (Holloway 1989). The reasons for competitive pricing are discussed in a later chapter, but there is little doubt that convenience is a major characteristic contributing to high utility for those groups of buyers who are not very knowledgeable about markets for individual product elements, or not venturesome in making their own arrangements.

The choice to purchase direct rather than through an agent is more a function of habit and availability. It is traditional for most domestic tourists to make direct purchases, and frequently travel agents do not represent a variety of domestic suppliers, partly because they do not expect the custom, and partly because they feel that lower earnings per labour hour spent in processing bookings do not justify effort in the same way as handling air travel and international tourism. From time to time, principals selling travel and tourism products 'direct sell' aggressively, such as the tour operator Tjaereborg in Europe, but there is rarely a significant price advantage to the purchaser.

Price is also a less important variable in selection between agents. In those countries with fixed commission rates and some form of travel price control, demand for the services of any one agent at the expense of another can only be because of better characteristics, such as convenient location or customer service. Where discounting and price competition are permitted, prices between agents can only vary up to the level of their discounts as a percentage of total product price. Some market segments, such as 'cut-price student travellers', may then look around the market of travel agents to find the cheapest deal.

■ Constraints on tourism demand

To purchase any product, a consumer must give up scarce resources. In a market economy, this resource is normally money. The possession of sufficient money to allocate amongst goods and services whose bundle, or vector, of characteristics will maximise the consumer's utility is the main constraint on overall demand by that consumer. That money must come from *disposable income, business cash flow, or stock of liquid assets, such as savings.*

Virtually all tourism demand is similarly constrained by money. Possibly the only case where this is not so is for an 'adventurer' who backpacks, and walks or hitches free transport. By staying with friends or sleeping rough, and experiencing only free or public-good attractions, these tourists minimize their expenses. Tourism then takes place in the absence of any economic market activity. However, for most, tourism is not only a purchase but a major purchase from a budget. Money is a big constraint.

Two other constraints on tourism deserve special mention: political controls, and time. The markets for many products are under various levels of political control in different countries. Controls include those on drugs, firearms, alcohol, entertainment, housing and so on. Control on tourism may be less overt, but may still be there. Many countries of course restrict or prohibit the international tourist movement of their nationals, and elsewhere there may be selective control through passport and visa systems, sometimes even for domestic tourism. This is in addition to government intervention in the economic marketplace through price or fare regulation and travel and tourism taxes. These direct controls may constrain tourism from the generator, at the destination, or through the link.

The other major constraint is time. Few products demand the expenditure of scarce time as well as scarce cash, and of these tourism may demand the most. Whilst time is not an economically tradeable commodity—tourism suppliers do not 'receive' time from tourists in exchange for their products—the possession of a stock of disposable time, and the allocation of that stock to different tourism and non-tourism activities, constrains the ability of the tourist to do all the things desired, even if money is available.

The limits of disposable time may be set by such things as work and public holiday allowances, school and college vacation periods, or time limits on conducting business trips. Like money incomes, such things vary between countries and between market segments. It may be that tourist i has plenty of time for a proposed trip but is limited by money, whereas tourist j has no money shortage but severely limited time. In that case the lower constraint is the *effective* constraint, whilst the higher one is said to be *redundant*.

In a Lancasterian model, constraints such as time and money can be represented, for individual tourists:

$$Y > = p_k \, x_k$$

$$V > = t_k \, x_k$$

where Y = disposable income allocated to tourism and similar activities,
V = free time similarly allocated
p_k is a column vector of prices of x elements, as previously defined
t_k is a column vector of the time involvement necessary for each of those elements.

We assume here that some specific amount of a consumer's time is allotted to leisure activity, either as a primary objective or as whatever remains from a given time period after all other activity. This period we call V; it clearly falls, in the short term, within relatively narrow bounds, given that time is the same for everyone and that biological activity accounts for much of it.

Although Y was defined as disposable income allocated to tourism, it could be any form of money so allocated. Research suggests that many recreational tourism consumers allocate a 'slice' of money available per year or other time period specifically for tourism, which will be discussed in terms of income elasticity. Businesses of course would normally include a specific travel budget in their annual planning.

Any model such as this could be expanded to allow for other non-economic constraints such as restricted personal mobility or simple lack of travel opportunity. The formal model is presented in more detail in chapter appendix B. However, our next concern is to examine more closely the effects on tourism demand of *changes* in the primary variables such as product characteristics, incomes, prices and available time.

■ Income and price effects

As with the examination of changes in demand for any goods or services, analysis of tourism demand is hindered by the fact that in practice we normally only see, via empirical data, a Walrasian equilibrium of supply and demand in tourism markets, and that change represents a shift from one equilibrium position to another. Thus we are properly examining tourism *consumption* rather than tourism demand. Nevertheless, sufficient market research (describing 'what if?' rather than 'what is?') and time series or comparative studies exist to build reasonably accurate analyses of the effects on tourism demand of independent variables.

Income effects

The income, or stock of monetary assets, available to the tourism buyer is a 'group A' variable—it relates to all potential buyers of a generating area regardless of their preferred tourism destination. A great deal of research has been carried out to measure the effect of income changes on total tourism demand from a generator.

The strength of the effect of income change on demand can be measured by *income elasticity of demand*, defined as the ratio:

$$E_y = \frac{\% \text{ change in tourism demand}}{\% \text{ change in disposable income}}$$

between two time periods or two groups of buyers. It is normal to expect income elasticity of demand to be positive for most goods and services; the demand for basic goods and services should be income-inelastic ($E_y < 1$), whilst that for discretionary or luxury items would be elastic ($E_y > 1$).

Many empirical studies have been done on income elasticity of demand for tourism (for example, Summary 1987). In general, demand is relatively income-elastic if measured by tourism expenditure, but less elastic if the measure is total tourist nights or numbers. The reason may easily be seen: consumers whose incomes rise may still be constrained by time to the same length of tourist trip, but may substitute a higher priced one. Similarly, once a tourist trip, particularly a vacation, becomes an established part of a household's expenditure, a fall in income may mean cheaper vacations rather than fewer vacations.

Thus the income elasticity of demand for specific destinations may be much higher than expected if demand for those destinations emanates mainly from one generator. For example, when times are hard, New Yorkers may vacation in Atlantic City NJ, but with increases in incomes they may take the same length of vacation in Florida or elsewhere. This may actually give Atlantic City a *negative* income elasticity of demand (see p. 37) amongst some market segments, although other segments may replace those lost—perhaps people who could not previously have afforded a vacation at all.

Different forms of tourism also display different levels of income elasticity of demand. Business travel and luxury travel demand are relatively income-inelastic, reflecting the nature of assets out of which they are purchased. VFR travel demand is also less income-elastic than general vacation demand, reflecting, like business tourism, a degree of obligation rather than choice.

Figure 3.1 demonstrates the effect on tourism demand of different income elasticities. If income in a generator rises from Y_0 to Y_1, expenditure on tourism changes from Q_0 to each of the different levels Q_1 to Q_5 (assuming Q_0 to be merely a starting index for each type of tourism rather than an identical expenditure in each case).

Figure 3.1   Income elasticity of demand for different types of tourism.

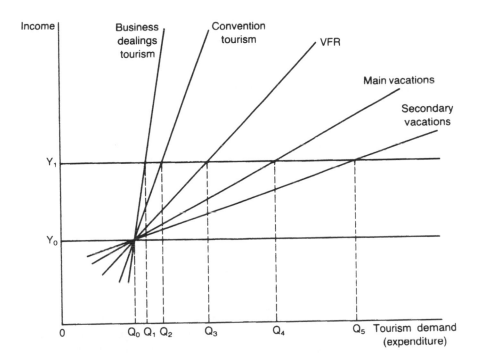

The example of a tourism destination whose income elasticity of demand is negative argues that within some markets certain tourism products may be regarded as *inferior* products. This is difficult to prove empirically without research to isolate changes in demand for a destination from one particular generator or a particular market segment, and to monitor those changes with respect to that segment's income. Overall tourism demand at that destination may meanwhile be increasing, as other market segments expand. Californians or overseas tourists might visit the casinos of Atlantic City more frequently as their incomes increase, and would certainly not regard it as an 'inferior' destination product.

There are however other examples of tourism product elements being considered inferior. Lodging houses, British holiday camps and long-distance bus travel have all been documented as losing demand amongst tourism market segments when the level of income increases in those segments.

Price effects

The effects of price changes are far more complex in tourism than are the effects of changes in income. Two particular price conditions are of note:

- although the product elements of a tourism package are complementary in terms of characteristics offered, they may well be *substitutes* in terms of price effects if they are competing for the same slice of tourist spending
- relative prices are important, between destinations and between destinations and generating areas, not just prices at destinations. A consumer is not simply faced with the set of prices in one geographical market, but with the relative prices in two or more markets.

In international tourism, *exchange rate variations* are usually the major contributor to relative price differences. Over recent years, for example, exchange rate variations have made Switzerland and Japan expensive destinations, but made Israel and Spain cheap. High inflation can wipe out these price advantages, but is often accompanied by readjustment of tourist exchange rates.

As with income changes, the effects of price changes on demand can be measured with elasticities—in this case, price elasticity of demand—through the formula:

$$E_p = \frac{\%\ \text{change in quantity of tourism product demanded}}{\%\ \text{change in tourism product price}}$$

The standard Law of Demand in economics holds that for most products E_p will be negative—that is, there is an inverse relationship between a product's price and the demand for that product. An E_p figure numerically greater than −1 indicates elastic demand (sensitivity of demand response exceeding the percentage of any price change) and an E_p figure numerically less than −1 indicates price inelasticity, or relatively unresponsive demand. Price elasticities are also unlikely to remain constant for any one product, varying between short term and long term, and according to the size of price changes.

The demand for tourism products runs the whole range of possible price elasticities. In general, the greater the degree of competition, and hence substitutability, amongst products, the higher the price elasticity of demand is likely to be, as price-conscious tourists search for cheaper alternatives. Once again, price elasticities have been found to be higher for recreational tourism than for business or VFR tourism, reflecting the discretionary nature of the one against the obligations of the other.

The choice of competitive destinations for vacation tourism appears especially responsive to price change. Long-term (6 year) price elasticity of demand for important destinations from major generating countries has been shown to vary from around –4 for a small cost change (2.5%), to around –1.5 for a large cost change (40%) (Edwards 1987: data for the United States and Western Europe). The resulting 'demand schedule' for average destination country x is portrayed in Figure 3.2:

Figure 3.2   Estimated demand responses to holiday price changes to destinations

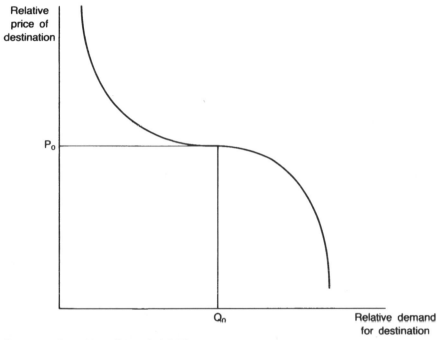

Source: adapted from Edwards (1987)

At a current relative price of P_0, the demand for tourism in the destination is quantity Q_0. The shape of the demand schedule represents demand response to varying degrees of relative price shift, and suggests a logarithmic, rather than straight-line, relationship between price and demand. The same piece of research found a similar set of price elasticities of demand for ITs to competitive destinations.

Two cautions are necessary in interpreting this data. First, tourism demand is here expressed in *relative* rather than absolute amounts, which may alter values from those found by a 'normal' elasticity measure. Secondly, aggregate data may hide the fact that for an individual consumer a small price change may trigger no change at all in demand, if that change is considered insignificant or below the perceptual price-change threshold of the consumer. This phenomenon is considered further in the Lancasterian model in chapter appendix B. An aggregate analysis also hides the extent to which the prices of individual elements of the tourism product influence overall demand; there is little doubt that the cost of carriage is one major variable, and that the overall cost of destination items, especially accommodation, is another, but the cost *and value* to a consumer of particular elements of the tourism experience is not always well identified. Current research on hedonic pricing—of the implicit prices possessed by characteristics of non-tradeable tourism products —is advancing knowledge in this area (see, for example, Sinclair *et al.* 1990).

For specific individual products within tourism the picture is clearer. Demand for budget accommodation and competitive passenger carriage services, for example, has been found to be highly price-elastic, and cross-price elastic. If cross-price elasticity is defined as:

$$E_{cp} = \frac{\% \text{ change in demand for product A}}{\% \text{ change in price of product B}}$$

then where A and B are close substitutes we might expect E_{cp} to be positive and maybe >1. This is frequently found in, for example:

- budget motel or hotel choice in major destinations
- selection of operator for local day excursion
- souvenir purchasing and duty-free shopping
- bus line or airline choice where these compete over the same routes.

In these cases the products may be viewed as nearly or completely identical, and E_{cp} values are high. Some tourists find utility from the act of 'shopping around' for best buys as part of their tourism experience (Keown 1989), or haggling in bazaars for a souvenir purchase—perhaps the closest a tourist can get to the overt display of an equilibrium market!

Complementary cross-price effects are also often seen in tourism. During the early 1980s when transatlantic airfares were driven down by competition initiated by Laker Airways, the demand for accommodation and other tourism services in New York, Miami, London and Paris increased markedly from the opposite side of the Atlantic. Similarly, car-rental companies generate increased demand by tying in (via referral trade agreements) to airlines which reduce their fares.

There may be cases in tourism of products exhibiting the *Veblen effect*. This is an abnormal price elasticity of demand where the E_p value may be positive over a certain range of prices for a product (McIntosh and Goeldner 1990). That is, demand may actually increase at a higher price. This effect is often associated with *ostentatious* products—perceived to be of high value in a discerning market with little in the way of a budget constraint. It is argued that wealthy art collectors would not demand a 'cheap' masterpiece, because it may not be a masterpiece at all, and because only an expensive work of art may provide the prestige cachet which is part of the utility in such a purchase. In the same way, some consumers may need to demonstrate wealth and prestige through a demand for luxury tourism products such as the highest priced staterooms on expensive cruise ships, or the most expensive restaurant in which to entertain clients on sales trips.

Exchange-rate variations also cause cross-price effects in tourism demand. Evidently, an increase in the exchange value of a destination (country B) country's currency will, if all else stays equal, make that country more expensive to all international tourists and is therefore likely to reduce international demand. However, many researchers have run into problems in isolating the exact effects of exchange rates (Summary 1987). A fall in the exchange value of a generating country's currency (country A) effectively reduces the international tourism demand from that country by acting through an income effect. But either of these events might also cause an increase in demand for domestic tourism in country A by its own residents, as they seek to substitute a cheaper product. This is analogous to *import substitution* in goods markets. All of the above exchange rate effects can also be expected to work equally in reverse—stimulating international tourism demand at the expense of domestic demand.

■ Other special variables in tourism demand

There are a number of economic and socioeconomic variables, other than prices and incomes, which have been noted to have a special influence on the demand for tourism. Some of the major ones will be discussed here.

Fashion

Tourism products, especially destinations, are often subject to fashion life-cycles. Whilst most products exhibit demand life cycles, in which the opinion leadership of those who first buy them (early adopters) forms fashion-stimulating demand, in tourism it is usually possible to identify exactly the market segments through which trends in demand are passing. This is because frequently tourists are named, rather than nameless, purchasers.

From the time of the eighteenth century when European royalty set fashions for spa visits, and later sea-bathing, destinations have been in demand with specific segments through fashion cycles. St Tropez, Bali and Montserrat all experienced Veblen-effect demand when they became fashionable through the leadership of one or more high-profile celebrities; when 'fashionable' demand moved elsewhere they faced demand in the markets of more ordinary vacationers, subject to tighter money and time constraints.

Taxation of business expenses

Corporations meet the cost of business tourism as an expense against corporate income. Government policy on the extent to which these expenses may be allowed against tax may alter the effective prices of tourism products, and hence demand. For example, suppose that the marginal corporate tax rate is 50%, and government introduces full tax-deductibility for tourism expenses. Figure 3.3 shows the effect on demand.

Figure 3.3   Change in tax deductibility of business tourism expenses

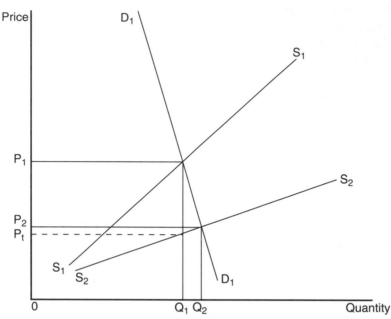

With an initial equilibrium market price of $0P_1$, businesses are purchasing quantity $0Q_1$ of business tourism. Introduction of full tax deductibility reduces effective prices by the marginal tax rate of 50%, thus effectively shifting supply from S_1S_1 to S_2S_2. The 'tax deductible' price of business travel falls immediately to P_1, and market movements may produce a new equilibrium at price $0P_2$ and tourism demand $0Q_2$. The increase $0Q_1 - 0Q_2$ is possibly rather small because of the inelastic nature of business travel demand.

In practice governments use tax deductibility far more selectively. The United States government for example varies the dollar limit of tax-deductible travel expenditures per person per day, and can allow greater deductibility for, say, domestic tourism than international tourism spending (and the daily allowances vary considerably between overseas countries visited). This changes relative effective prices, and can be used as a balance of payments policy weapon.

Negative characteristics of tourism products

In studies of motivation in the workplace (Herzberg 1966), it has been found that whilst some variables positively motivate employees to work harder, others may be merely grievance avoidance, or 'hygiene' factors. (A pleasant working environment for example may not make people work harder, but its absence may cause grievances). Various studies have suggested that a similar situation may exist in tourism demand: some characteristics of tourism products may be positive motivators to their purchase, whilst the *absence* of others may discourage demand.

The existence of a sewage treatment works or adequate parking facilities at a destination is unlikely in itself to create demand motivation, but if these 'hygiene' factors or *negative characteristics* are lacking, then consumers may soon withdraw demand. A prime example of negative characteristics is an airline's safety record; few tourists admit to selecting an airline specifically on its safety record characteristic (Narodick 1972), but demand for an airline often falls in the wake of demonstrated poor safety. Characteristics such as incidence of terrorism, political stability and reliability of essential services have a profound effect on tourism today.

Also, while many people enjoy the act of travel itself, to others the consumption of a journey may not provide any utility at all (especially to frequent travellers who may once have enjoyed a trip, but for whom the marginal utility has, with repetition, declined to nothing). To such consumers, negative characteristics may outweigh positive ones to such an extent that the journey is viewed as a *cost*, to be minimised or avoided, rather than a desirable product.

Time entitlements

In the same way that it is possible to calculate the income elasticity of demand for tourism, we can examine the effect of changes in time entitlements, such as the number of public holidays, vacation leave and business trip constraints. Generally, such entitlements are increasing worldwide as part of industrial-isation and automation's replacement of labour with capital, and with social pushes for more formal leisure time. However, as with income, there are global variations. In some European countries (for example, West Germany and Italy) standard vacation leave may exceed 28 days a year, in addition to twelve or fourteen public holidays, but in Japan 10 days' leave a year is normal.

Where time, and not money, is the effective constraint on tourism demand, any increase in entitlements has a very high positive 'time elasticity of demand'. Two particular cases are notable:

- extra time allows trips to temporally more remote destinations (see chapter appendix A), and tourists are therefore likely to substitute remote destin-ations for closer ones
- extra time often encourages longer stays in destinations, thus increasing spending at the destination.

As an example of the latter case, a tourist might be considering foreign travel from a country with a high propensity to use ITs, such as the United Kingdom or Japan. ITs may be available only as one or two-week packages. If the tourist is accustomed to taking one main vacation plus a small number of days off each year, a shift in vacation leave from say 13 to 16 days annually may encourage a change in demand from the one-week to the two-week product. Time elasticity of *spending in the destination* is very high.

Seasonality

Tourism has one of the most highly seasonal patterns of demand for any product, with less variation than demand for Christmas cards or air conditioners, but more than nearly all high-value individual purchases. Several factors contribute to seasonality (BarOn 1975)—principally climate, festivals and school vacations, which all primarily affect recreational tourism. The outcome is that in reality tourists and suppliers alike face more than one equilibrium position each year. Given that seasonality is largely institutionalised or directly affects major characteristics of the product (to do with climate), many bounds on demand are not variable by price or marketing inducements.

The results of seasonality are different market conditions of price and quantity of 'tourism products traded' at different times of year. A beach resort may have 'high season' and 'low season' with two different price levels, and lower supply—with a certain amount of accommodation closed down—in low season. Table 3.2 shows the four different seasonal markets for air travel between London UK and Sydney Australia:

Table 3.2   Seasonal economy class excursion air fares London–Sydney 1994/95

Season	Period of application	Fare(UK£)	Index
Basic	16 Apr – 15 Jun	860	100
Off-Peak	01 Feb – 15 Apr		
	16 Jun – 31 Jul	1045	122
Shoulder	01 Aug – 09 Dec		
	25 Dec – 31 Jan	1245	145
Peak	09 – 24 Dec	1400	163

Source: IATA 1994 Air Tariffs / Galileo CRS

Here, four seasonal markets have developed over a number of years, with ruling prices (which may or may not be equilibrium prices) varying up to 63%. The *need* for such a system stems from the inelasticity and 'lumpiness' of supply, which will be examined in a later chapter.

■ Summary

Demand for tourism is highly complex, especially in comparison with demand for single goods selling perhaps just to consumers as final demand with end benefits. This chapter has intentionally switched focus between individual demand, where a behavioural approach is important to establish individuals' objectives or utility, and aggregate demand, where we can view the overall marketplace for tourism products. It is thus possible to examine aggregate purchasing choices and the constraints on those choices.

The distance decay function

In passenger carriage, consumers are required to spend time as well as money, and the use of these resources is often more important as a constraint on tourism demand than physical distance of travel. Whilst for many people the act of travel is in itself a pleasurable experience, and they may not perceive a 'time-cost' in travelling, there is however an *opportunity cost* of time, as well as money, involved. The traveller must forego the opportunity of spending time doing something else in order to consume travel, although many travellers successfully do other things whilst on the move.

It follows that in measuring distance, a composite time + money-cost variable is a better measure for passenger carriage than physical distance. We might then expect that demand for passenger travel—where there is a choice of destination, as in recreational tourism—would vary inversely with this variable.

Empirical research has found (for example, Greer & Wall 1979, Holloway 1989) that in fact such a relationship does exist, but with some modifications. Figure 3.4 shows the relationship between time/cost and travel demand, which is known as the *distance decay function*.

Figure 3.4   Distance decay functions for tourist travel

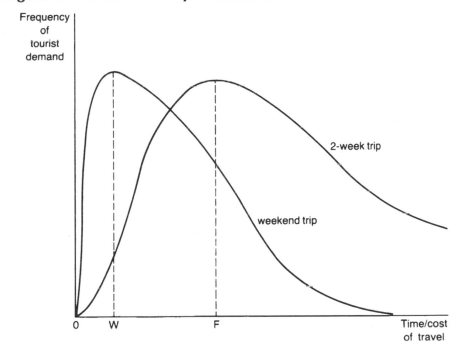

First, the relationship between time/cost and travel demand is not wholly an inverse function, but has a peak demand where time/cost is low but positive. (In statistical terms the relationship can be represented by a lognormal, rather than a negative exponential, distribution.) So if the time/cost of travel is very high, demand is small; if time/ cost is lower, travel demand is greater; but there is a level of time/ cost below which demand falls again. This can be explained by tourists perceiving that if, say, they only make a 20 or 30 minute trip away from home costing very little, that is insufficient to be worth making the basis of a tourist visit. There is a *preferred distance (in time/cost) to travel* where demand is highest.

Secondly, the preferred distance to travel varies with the total length of stay away from home—and presumably total expenditure. In Figure 3.4 the distance 0W would be that preferred for a weekend trip (which in Europe has been found to average about 90–120 minutes door-to-door), whereas tourists are prepared, and wish, to travel further for a two-week vacation, such as distance 0F. Not only is the preferred distance greater, but the whole function has shifted to the right.

Similar concepts of a time/ cost composite variable have been used as a proxy for distance in gravity, intervening opportunities and systems models for recreation and tourism trips. Such models, while not generally founded in economic theory, appreciate that mere physical and geographic distance measures of demand constraint are insufficient to explain the allocation of travel demand. This is evidenced by governments and other suppliers of tourism products who cannot physically move location, but can stimulate demand by providing faster or cheaper transport links from generator to destination.

The Lancasterian demand model applied to tourism

Classical demand theory is adequate to examine demand for single products or commodities. However, the straightforward concept for an individual of maximising utility from tradeoffs between products—to a point where indifference curve slopes match budget lines (see for example Samuelson 1989 or Sinden 1977)—is rather deficient as a tool of analysis for multiple-commodity or composite products such as tourism. A behavioural context is needed, particularly in pre-trip demand decisions with extended problem-solving on the part of the consumer. Most tourism expenditure is committed at this stage.

The following model is adapted from Lancaster 1966, Rugg 1971 and the author's own research. Further developments in, for example, hedonic pricing, and empirical measurement problems are discussed by Stabler (1988). The most common measurement technique is by conjoint analysis.

For an individual tourist (consumer) **i**, or an identifiable market segment **i**, assumed to be rational decision makers:

Objective function, to maximise 'utility':

$$\textbf{maximise } U_i = U_i \, (z)$$

subject to constraints:

$$z = g(x) \qquad \text{'consumption technology'}$$
$$Y >= px \qquad \text{income/money constraint}$$
$$V >= tx \qquad \text{time constraint}$$

and non negativity constraints:

$$x >= 0$$
$$z >= 0$$

where   **z** is a vector of characteristics of tourism products

x is a vector of the quantities of the elements of the overall tourism product (accommodation, transport and so on)

p is a column vector of unit prices of the x elements
t is a column vector of unit time involvement for each x element
Y = disposable income or budgeted funds for tourism
V = disposable or budgeted free time for tourism.

The consumption technology constraint is a simplification of the more correct original Lancasterian model in which elements or products *in combination* generate 'activities' from which characteristics are then derived. With or without the simplification, the result is a nonlinear programming model, albeit with some difficulties of specification and empirical examination.

An example

To illustrate the model we can propose a very simple example. Suppose two characteristics can determine utility for tourist i, namely:

the amount of night life   — z_1
water sports activities   — z_2

Three island resorts form the evoked set of products available to the tourist:

resort 1, very beach and water sports oriented   — x_1
resort 2, a mixed activities resort   — x_2
resort 3, a night owl's paradise   — x_3.

Figure 3.5 is a graph of the model:

Figure 3.5   Graph of simple Lancasterian model

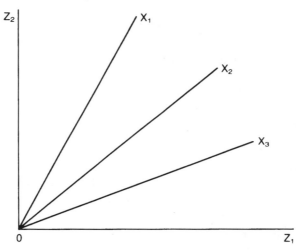

The consumption technology constraints are represented by rays $0X_1$, $0X_2$ and $0X_3$. The axes show quantities of characteristics z_1 and z_2.

Given a market price $\mathbf{p_k}$ per unit of each resort $\mathbf{x_k}$ (k = 1 to 3) where this price may be the full-board or American Plan daily accommodation rate, the maximum quantity, or number of days' stay, attainable is $\mathbf{M_k}$ where:

$$\mathbf{M_k} = \frac{Y}{\mathbf{P_k}}$$

Similarly, the maximum length of stay may be constrained by time available, V. The 'time cost' $\mathbf{t_k}$ of each resort may be adjusted for the length of trip to reach each resort destination, so a remote resort 'costs' more than a nearby one. The maximum stay attainable is then $\mathbf{S_k}$ where:

$$\mathbf{S_k} = \frac{V}{\mathbf{t_k}}$$

Figure 3.6   Graph of Lancasterian model of time/cost constraints affecting length of stay

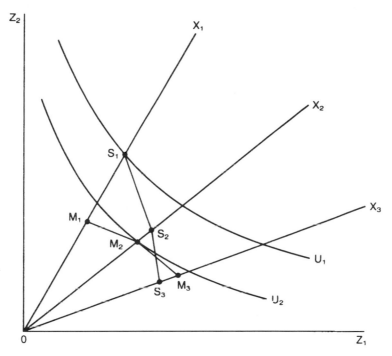

When graphed as in figure 3.6 the lines M_1—M_2—M_3 represent the budget constraint and those S_1—S_2—S_3 the time constraint. The lowest constraint is the *effective* one, so that M_1—M_2—S_3 represents the effective maximum attainable, or the *efficiency frontier*. S_1—S_2 for example is a redundant constraint, as the tourist is limited by money and higher prices in resorts 1 and 2 rather than time.

Given tourist segment i's current choice of characteristics to maximise utility, a slope U results, which reflects desired tradeoff between characteristics. This is similar to indifference curves, with commodities rather than characteristics, in classical demand theory. Maximising utility means reaching the highest possible U slope. Here, U_1 is unattainable, and U_2 is the constrained maximum, tangential to the efficiency frontier at M_2. In this case, tourists would demand OM_2 units of resort 2.

It is possible for tourists to have a straight-line indifference or U slope, but this is unlikely because of the effects of diminishing marginal utility when the tourist acquires ever-higher levels of either one or the other characteristic. It is also possible that a U slope of slightly different shape would not be tangential to the efficiency frontier exactly at M_2 or any other corner point. If the result were, say, at a point between M_1 and M_2, this would imply the tourist's spending some time at resort 1 and some at resort 2. If this incurred extra transport costs, it would mean the line M_1—M_2 would not be straight, but convex with respect to the origin, thus making a split stay less likely.

This model easily accommodates the effects of shifts in variables. First, if incomes or time allowances increase, M or S points on rays X_1, X_2 and X_3 may shift outwards from the origin, by an amount depending on the number of extra units or days' stay which can now be afforded. If each amount is constant, we may expect tourist i to purchase more of resort 2—a straight income effect. If amounts vary sufficiently, another resort may now become the optimum choice if a greater quantity of 'tourism' there can be bought—an income and substitution effect.

Secondly, if the price (or time-cost) of a resort changes, similar shifts of M or S points occur. A very small price increase in X_2 may reduce the maximum to M'_2, which is still an optimum buy, but a larger increase may cause a shift to M''_2 (see Figure 3.7), and to maximise utility the tourist may substitute, to $0M_1$ units of X_1. This is a very realistic situation, where tourists may absorb a small price increase but not a large one.

Figure 3.7 Graph of Lancasterian model showing change in product price

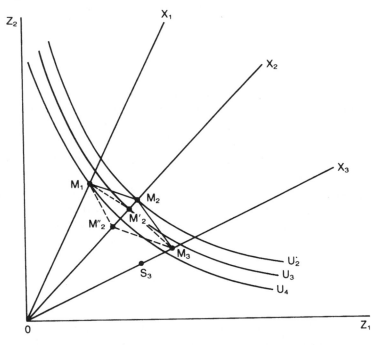

Finally, if a new resort is developed, or tourists are made aware of one which was not previously in their evoked set, we can introduce a new ray. If the resort is very expensive, or very remote, or its characteristics are extremely different from tourist preferences, there will be no effect on demand. On the other hand its ray may be X_4 (see Figure 3.8), the effective constraint M_4, and tourist i may increase utility by changing holiday plans!

Figure 3.8   Graph of Lancasterian model showing effect of new product on market

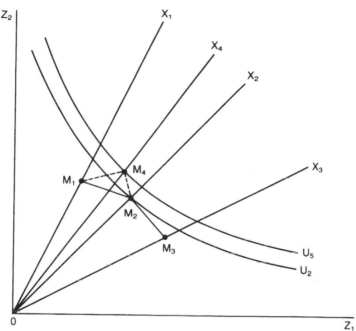

If there are n tourist segments (or tourists), we may sum the demand from them for each resort X_1 X_2 and X_3 to find aggregate demand, complete with predictions of shifts in demand given changes in relative and absolute prices, incomes, travel times and other predictor variables.

Study questions

1 Identify the peculiarities of tourism as a product compared with every-day goods and services which consumers may demand.
2 Why is prepurchase consumer decisionmaking particularly important in travel and tourism demand?
3 Find ten people and ask each one the *real* motivation for their last tourist trip. Are there any noticeable market segments?
4 Construct a flowchart of the likely choice sequence in elements of a tourist trip for:
   a   a business delegate to an international convention
   b   a family seeking a short recreational break.
5 Identify the major constraints on tourism demand amongst different groups (for example, students, businesspeople, retirees) in your locality.

6 Why is income-elasticity of tourism demand based on expenditure different
   from that based on tourist nights?
7 From published statistics, compare the exchange rates and rates of inflation
   of any two destination countries now and five years ago against the US
   dollar or Japanese yen. To what extent do you think intervening change
   may have affected tourism from the US or Japan?
8 Describe four major factors, other than price, likely to influence demand
   for a resort hotel in Acapulco or Tenerife.

CHAPTER

4

Tourism enterprises

■ Introduction

Within travel and tourism there is not only a wide variety of economic activities taking place, but the supply of travel and tourism products comes from a whole range of different types of enterprise. It is inevitable that an industry with such a diverse range of products will support forms of ownership from small sole proprietorships to multinational corporations and state-owned semi-commercial organisations.

It is equally inevitable that suppliers will not all operate with the same commercial objectives. As noted in chapter 1, the industry is often attractive to many suppliers with non-pecuniary objectives in mind. There are also many government departments and government-owned enterprises which have a supply role, frequently with conflicting objectives which threaten management difficulties. In between, almost every type of legal enterprise may supply travel and tourism products; most claim to operate with the classical long-run objective of profit maximisation, but for various reasons this objective may be subordinated to other short-term or recurrent needs.

Finally the dynamic and increasingly international nature of the travel and tourism industry produces change in its structure, as suppliers move in and out of different sectors or adjust to conditions in new markets. To understand the nature of supply in tourism it is therefore valuable to examine the possible objectives, organisational structures and dynamics of supplier enterprises. It is also necessary to make international comparisons where valid, and in particular to look at drives towards integration between enterprises.

■ Objectives of tourism enterprises

Studies in the theory of the firm provide a number of alternative objectives for enterprises. Table 4.1 summarises some of the most frequently studied types of objective.

Table 4.1 Alternative Business Objectives

Objective	Conditions	Likely type of enterprise
Profit maximisation	-	Competitive or monopolistic owner-driven business
Sales revenue maximisation	May be short term only Minimum acceptable profit con-straint (MAPC)	Aggressive growth seeker Board heavily influenced by marketers
'Empire building' or prestige	Sufficient cash flow	Managers separated from owners/public 'Prestige' organisation
Output maximisation	-	Public enterprise in a collectivist economy
'Satisficing'	MAPC	Large public or private enterprise in market economy Board heavily influenced by accountants
A quiet life (Profit minimisation)	MAPC	Sole proprietorship, owner seeking simple living with minimum problems/effort

The classical objective of profit maximisation requires a firm to maximise the difference between long-run total revenue and total cost, which further requires the ability to identify marginal revenues and costs. This may be relatively straightforward in the very short-run for such businesses as airlines or restaurants (especially where the majority of costs are fixed and profit-maximising tactics are concerned with filling unused capacity), but it is very difficult in the long-run with most service enterprises. Consequently many tourism enterprises work with series of short-run goals rather than a single long-term strategy.

One major example of profit maximisation through increasing revenue occurs frequently in travel and tourism through discriminatory pricing. This will be further investigated in the next chapter, as it is of great importance to carriers, hotels and many other sectors of the industry which have a largely fixed supply of their product. To increase profits in these circumstances implies adjusting total and marginal revenues through pricing (and promotion), to equate best-price demand with capacity. Price discrimination normally implies a degree of monopoly, and hence the chance to make 'supernormal' profits, but in travel and tourism it is more a function of non-resaleable services and the ability to segment markets.

Sales revenue maximisation may often replace profit maximisation by default (Baumol 1977). In travel and tourism enterprises this normally occurs, whether explicitly or implicitly, for one of three main reasons:

- A business with relatively fixed capacity, as above, concentrates on revenue far more than on costs. Thus competitive airlines seek to maximise 'yields' within given markets—that is, to earn the highest possible revenues from the optimum mix of fare-paying passengers on a given flight.
- In many areas of travel and tourism, enterprises are relatively new and growing. In year A managers perceive the need to establish a market base for future growth and long-term profits. However this may still be needed in year B, and again in year C. Long-term profit maximisation disappears behind a series of short-run growth decisions. Heavy promotional costs are common here, particularly in, for example, some 'new' destinations and travel insurance businesses.
- Since product communication and promotion are so important in travel and tourism where consumers cannot sample the product before purchase, many enterprises are controlled or heavily influenced by marketing-oriented people. Such managers frequently measure success by sales revenue and market share (The Austrian National Tourist Office, like many others, incorporates these measures in written plans). Again, heavy promotion costs are likely.

Growth and revenue maximisation can only continue subject to a *minimum profit constraint*. This is the level of profit required to maintain the viability of the enterprise. In a company listed on the stock exchange the level will be the *opportunity profit* level obtainable within the market for stock in that type of business, below which stockholders would sell out and invest elsewhere.

As enterprises grow and change shape, so there is likely to be a separation of ownership from control, with objectives being set by a 'techno-structure' of professional managers (Galbraith 1967). In these circumstances the personal objectives of managers, such as **empire-building** or **prestige**, may become paramount. There is a tradeoff between the utility of profits and that of non-pecuniary interests (Hawkins 1973).

Travel and tourism provide significant opportunities for such objectives. Ostensibly because of the need for a quality image, many National Tourist Offices (NTOs) and airlines maintain corporate offices, staffing and executive hospitality which may make only a dubious contribution to commercial utility. Even where ownership and control are not separated, entrepreneurs frequently seek prestige tourism developments which potentially or actually could be less profitable than more everyday areas of business. Resort developments and operations are notable examples, such as the Aga Khan's Costa Smeralda in Sardinia, or Hayman Island in Australia.

Output maximisation is more extreme than sales revenue maximisation, implying that revenue is secondary to volume of goods and services produced. The enterprise supplying in this fashion is product-oriented rather than market-oriented, and may be forced to reduce price to clear supply, perhaps even by giving the product away. Enterprises in the former Soviet Union and other collectivist economies were often output maximisers by central direction in national economic plans. During the 1950s and 1960s the success of Intourist, the Soviet Union's umbrella tourism organisation, was measured in this way by the number of tourists handled. The privatisation and commercialisation of tourist offices in many countries during the 1980s and 1990s have reduced the number of organisations operating with an output maximisation objective.

Nevertheless, some NTOs still partly work with this objective, in terms of the number of tourists they attract from other countries. Protecting and enhancing market share in a sector with intense competition also leads in the same direction. In the United States during the period shortly after airline deregulation, airlines scrambled to offer more seats on more routes, although at depressed market fares. In the United Kingdom during the early 1970s, ruthless competition between tour operators to obtain higher market shares drove holiday prices down. Inevitably a minimum acceptable profit constraint exists here too, and when breached leads to business failure. This happened to a number of American airlines in the late 1980s, and to the United Kingdom tour operations of Court Line in 1974. The collapses of Laker Airways and Braniff in 1982 were also partly due to overactive growth in output.

Herbert Simon originally developed the notion of '**satisficing**' to explain an enterprise's behaviour (Simon 1959). This is basically a behavioural objective which argues that the business knowledge and abilities required to maximise *anything* are beyond most managers, who therefore are content with a goal that is merely satisfactory—hence 'satisficing'. The theory has been refined by many other researchers, but basically implies the setting of a satisfactory or target rate of profit.

Good examples of satisficing may be found in the records of a number of large enterprises in travel and tourism, especially where those enterprises are:

- multinational, or so large and diverse (but centrally administered) that sufficient maximising knowledge is difficult for central management
- publicly-owned, where a target in terms of the rate of return on assets or something similar is set from outside, and managers' salaries are not profit-linked
- non commercial operations such as National Parks Authorities or heritage conservation foundations, which are mandated to provide particular services within a target budget.

State tourism enterprises, large national airlines and international hotel chains have all been satisficers at some stage, with for example a target of 10% rate of return on assets or 5% on sales, rather than maximum anything. It is interesting to note, however, that commercial realities of the 1980s have forced many traditional satisficers to reappraise their objectives. British Rail for example, often quoted as 'happy to return 1%', now work with a strategy statement: 'To operate the best (in terms of customer estimates of product quality) and most profitable transport and travel company in Europe'(Percival 1987); clearly a potential profit maximiser.

Some industries attract producers who wish to use their entrepreneurial skills not to maximise profits but to have a **quiet life**—that is, to engage in production with the minimum amount of effort commensurate with a sufficient level of profit to provide a living, but to obtain intrinsic satisfaction from some other aspect of the business. It is obvious that a minimum return is required to stay in existence, but such enterprises will tend not to expand, diversify, nor engage in aggressive market activity. This type of objective is most often found with small, sole-proprietor type businesses, whose aims are the personal aims of the owners.

Many enterprises of this type are found in the travel and tourism industry. For example:

- husband and wife ('mom and pop') run a small hotel, motel or restaurant almost as a hobby, and because they 'like to meet people',
- an individual sets up as a travel agent, primarily to enjoy the benefits of agents' discount airfares and educational or familiarisation trips,
- owners of boats, stables or attractive rural properties may provide these as tourism facilities as well as personally enjoying their use.

The selection of an objective by an enterprise affects decisions on what to produce, how and how much to produce, and what price to try to sell at, so that frequently enterprises are found to be operating in areas and at points other than those that classical profit-maximising supply theory would suggest.

■ Market structures

Perfect and pure competition

The market structures within which tourism enterprises operate vary, between countries and between sectors—from virtually pure competition to outright monopoly. Perfect competition may be defined, from the seller's point of view, as the situation where that seller is faced with a market-set price level but can sell all their output at that price; that is, the seller faces a horizontal individual demand schedule as in Figure 4.1.

This enterprise, faced with demand AB, can sell any amount of output at market price P_1, but cannot attempt to sell at a higher price since buyers would immediately move to other, perfect, substitutes at the going price P_1.

This situation is rarely related to industries other than agriculture, where many small producers are all 'price takers but quantity makers'. The situation

Figure 4.1   Individual enterprise's demand in perfect competition

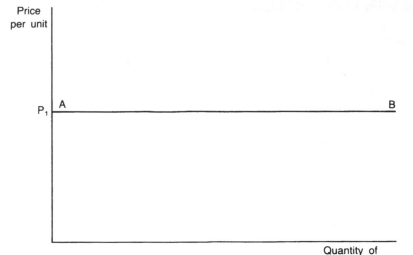

nearest to this in travel and tourism may be the example of taxi operators in major cities, or small motels or hotels in very large holiday destinations. However, these are not *perfectly* competitive. The motels, for example, may be able to vary their prices a little, and keep their customers, by trading on minor differences in location, service quality or decor (Bull 1994). They are thus making use of *comparative advantage* and *product differentiation*, which is not possible in perfect competition (Chamberlin 1956). Nonetheless, there may be an acceptable price band within which sellers will operate, as on their own they do not possess enough power in the market place, nor quite enough individuality to set prices at any level they wish. This is a form of imperfect competition, close to pure competition, which in the case of the individual small motel may yield a demand schedule something like that in Figure 4.2.

From Figure 4.2, P_m is the effective maximum price that the motel can charge, before finding that its product attributes can no longer outweigh the cheaper rates of its rivals. Q_F is full capacity—every unit occupied. The stepped demand schedule AB shows the range of price variation open to the motel (the stepped nature assuming 'sticky' demand in response to small price changes). The actual price set will depend on the motel's cost structure and business objectives.

The structure of imperfect competition is very common amongst travel and tourism markets, especially where there are many small enterprises. A key differentiator is the style and level of service. Service as an attribute—and product input—can be cheaply and easily varied so that the marginal revenue obtained from extra service (or a different style) will exceed the marginal cost of providing it. One important consequence of this concern with service,

Figure 4.2   Sample demand schedule for small motel in imperfect competition

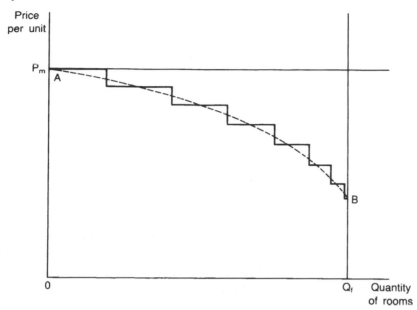

however, is that there may only be limited needs for expansion and amalgamations of businesses, since expansion in service is less likely to provide economies of scale than expansion in technical production of goods. Many travel and tourism businesses in monopolistic competition therefore remain small.

Whilst this structure serves to describe some relatively well-defined competitive sectors within destinations, such as taxi services, motels and souvenir outlets, market structures in travel and tourism generally are complicated by:

- the difficulty of defining products, and hence sectors
- the geographical bounds of markets and location of producers and consumers, especially where international tourism is involved.

Many enterprises transcend national frontiers, and may operate in different market structures within different countries; for example Olympic Holidays faces considerable competition as a tour operator selling ITs in Western European countries, whereas within its home country Greece it possesses considerable monopoly power. This variability is even more marked with government-owned inbound operators of many less-developed economies. It is therefore necessary to consider the effects of market structure on travel and tourism enterprises *within each consuming market,* and if possible for each variety or group of products as well.

Monopolies

For all the above reasons it is also sometimes difficult to identify true monopolies in travel and tourism, as there are many shades of substitutability. For example, a business tourist may require fast transport to a destination served by only one airline, and ground transport may be too slow. To many consumers this situation could amount to a monopoly, yet to others there may be a possibility of private air charter, or an increasing chance that modern telecommunications technology can provide a substitute such as teleconferencing. However, a monopoly can be said to exist when these substitutes are:

- not available at the time required, or
- not price-attainable by consumers, or
- sufficiently different in their attributes-set to be regarded as unsatisfactory in meeting consumer demand objectives.

A monopolist has the opportunity to set price or prices only with regard to its own enterprise's costs and objectives, and in the light of market demand. Lack of competition allows latitude in decision-making, and for this reason many enterprises seek monopolistic trading positions. It is often relatively easy to do this in travel and tourism where products can be differentiated:

- in *fact*, by service, locational or other characteristics,
- in consumers' *perceptions*, especially of untried travel and tourism services, by sophisticated product-positioning promotion.

Another major strategy open to a monopolist is *price discrimination*—the setting of different prices to different market segments. Classically, this is possible only where market segmentation can take place, and where products are buyer-specific (that is, buyers cannot resell products purchased at the lower price and undercut direct sales to the other segment at the higher price). Market segmentation implies differing demand conditions, and therefore a variable willingness to pay by consumers.

A standard, and simple, example of price discrimination is that of a carrier such as an airline which identifies business travellers and recreational tourists as its two main market segments on a particular route. The business travellers may *have* to make their trips, hence demand is rather inelastic, where recreational tourism may be more optional and hence price-elastic (Toh, Kelly and Hu 1986). Classical economic theory dictates that to obtain profit maximisation the airline should fix fares to equate the levels of marginal revenue in the two markets (Baumol 1977). The algebra of this is demonstrated in chapter appendix A, but the *effect* is shown in Figure 4.3. If demand in the two markets is aggregated in such a way that the line AB represents the demand schedule for business travel and the line CD the additional recreational travel demand, then P_1 represents the airfare for business travellers and P_2 the airfare for vacationers.

The corresponding quantities of seats Q_1 and Q_2 are sold to business travellers and vacationers. The airline's total revenue is $P_2Q_2 + (P_1 - P_2)Q_1$, whereas by

Figure 4.3   Fares set by price-discriminating airline

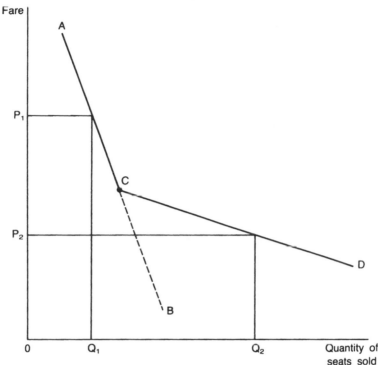

selling all at fare P_2 it would only make P_2Q_2, or by selling all at fare P_1 it would make P_1Q_1. The extra 'bite' of revenue cuts into *consumers' surplus*, the extra value of a product perceived by consumers over and above the price they otherwise have to pay.

Airlines, like many other travel and tourism enterprises, are able to enforce price or fare discrimination, since they are selling a buyer-specific service; they can also impose conditions of sale to forcibly distinguish market segments. For example, the lower fare P_2 may only be available on a round trip (return) basis, with a minimum destination stay and a requirement to purchase tickets X weeks in advance. None of these conditions may suit the business traveller, who is effectively debarred from using the fare. The question then arises of whether the airline is really selling two different products, as would be the case with different classes of travel; it can be argued that this is true if the conditions imposed *alter the costs to the airline of providing the product.*

Oligopoly and other imperfect competition

As in most other industries, enterprises in travel and tourism operate largely in imperfectly competitive markets, with elements of monopolistic activity (but only within certain limits at which they must take competitors into account). Tourism destinations attempt to differentiate their product characteristics as much as possible by promotion, but are aware that other destinations with similar characteristics are substitutes (albeit imperfect ones). Exactly the same may apply to convention centres, attractions, car rental businesses, and, within destinations, to a whole range of tourism enterprises and activities.

Oligopoly is a market structure where supply is completely or predominantly controlled by a small number of enterprises. These enterprises each have a substantial market share, will be sensitive to each others' supply decisions, and may or may not compete intensively. In such sectors there is said to be a high degree of *concentration* of enterprises. Profit or revenue maximisers often face a 'kinked' demand schedule (Baumol 1977) such as that in Figure 4.4, where an enterprise currently selling quantity of output Q_1 at price P_1 is faced with an inelastic demand should it lower its prices, but elastic demand if it increases them.

Figure 4.4 An oligopolist's 'kinked' demand schedule

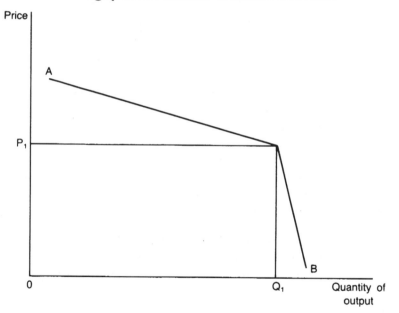

The reason is that competitors are expected to match swiftly any price reductions as their market shares would otherwise be eroded—so nobody gains significant demand through reduced prices. If the enterprise raises price above P_1, others will not follow, and it loses market share to its now cheaper competitors. This explanation has been advanced to explain the frequent 'stickiness' of prices in oligopolistic markets; however, imperfect consumer perceptions and differences in product characteristics as noted in Chapter 3 often allow some price variation without retaliation.

This situation is common in travel and tourism markets. For example, to Northern Europeans, there is a small number of competitive countries which may be regarded as sun, sea and sand destinations at inexpensive prices. These may include, typically, Spain, Italy, Greece and Tunisia as principal suppliers, with a number of 'smaller' producers. Each country keeps a close eye on the others' tourism products, marketing activity, prices and comparative exchange rates. To each of these destinations tourism is sufficiently important to warrant countervailing activity in these areas.

The worldwide international market for car rental is dominated by no more than half-a-dozen firms, including Avis, Budget, Europcar/National and Hertz. These firms have demonstrated extreme sensitivity to competitive activity from each other, and consequently end up with very similar product lines and tariff rates (see Table 4.2); this ensures market stability.

Table 4.2   Comparative car rental company rates
(California, one-day rate, group E, June 1994)

	$US
Able	24.90
Avis	26.95
Dollar	26.85
Enterprise	23.99
Hertz	24.99
National	29.99
Thrifty	23.79
Average	25.92
Range: from -8.2% to +15.7% of average	

Source: Galileo CRS

Any price reduction by one firm in a country in which the others compete tends to lead to competitive reductions and little net gain in demand to the price leader. Similarly, no firm is likely to increase its rates unilaterally, at least by very much, unless forced to do so by rising costs which are likely to influence its competitors equally—such as increased vehicle prices or wage claims. The car rental companies, like other oligopolists, indulge instead in non-price competition based on promotion, service quality or tactical short-term price reductions to particular target markets which do not give time for competitors' actions to be put into effect. This competitive activity is evidenced by 'No. 1' or 'We try harder' campaigns, frequent user schemes for business tourists (who, for companies other than Budget, account for around 70% of total revenue), or special semi-restrictive trade practices (for example, premium-level commissions to preferred agents).

To avoid a 'price war' oligopolists may overtly, or covertly, conclude an agreement not to compete on price, and possibly to restrict competition further with quota or market-sharing arrangements. Such an agreement, if overt, is a *cartel*, and is generally not permitted by national governments nowadays if it is considered to restrain free trade. However, collusive activity of this kind is still frequently found in travel and tourism.

The best known case of a cartel in the industry is probably the International Air Transport Association—IATA—in its original form. IATA (membership of the active tariff agreement) consists of about 82 major airlines, mostly international passenger carriers, who collectively represent the bulk of the international air passenger industry. It has many roles in interlining agreements, reservations and ticketing procedures, trade representation and so on (see for example Doganis 1985); in terms of market collusion it has been responsible for setting fixed airfares, although compliance has been purely voluntary since 1978. The original rationale for fixed airfares was to ensure simple international travel, with interchangeable tickets and simple inter-airline accounting. Unfortunately the result was frequently pressure from less competitive IATA members to sustain high fare levels to protect their business. This collusive activity has ultimately been found to be unsustainable, and for many airlines self-defeating, as the maintenance of fares well above competitive equilibrium levels on many routes meant insufficient demand, and hence revenue, to meet the largely fixed costs of operation (see Chapter 5).

IATA's fare-fixing cartel has virtually disappeared since 1978, owing to these major factors:

- prevailing free-market philosophies, and especially the deregulation of United States and European air services, providing a role model for other countries,
- the emergence of new, powerful and efficient airlines which have elected not to join IATA fare-fixing agreements; in Europe these have mostly developed from charter carriers, in the United States from deregulation shakeout of scheduled carriers,
- changing airline operational methods tending towards specific two- or three-carrier agreements to co-operate, and minimising interline carriage (Hanlon 1989).

Similar forces have reduced the number and strength of cartels in other areas of travel and tourism, from the government-supported fixed price-band system for hotels in Greece to the fixed commission rates paid to member agents of the Association of British Travel Agents. In general, although (restrictive) operational and distribution agreements may remain, overt price collusion is disappearing.

■ Carriers

Carriage for travel and tourism is dominated by two forms of transport: private vehicles—mostly cars—for short-distance (mostly domestic) travel, and air transport for international or long-distance travel.

Table 4.3   Examples of travel modes used by tourists (%)

Country	International departures			Domestic departures		
	air	private car	other	air	private car	other
USA	58	38	4	18	77	5
Japan	99	0	1	4	57	39
UK	51	26	23	2	80	18

Sources: individual country NTO statistics

Airlines supplying carriage to tourists have developed in different ways in different places. In the United States, major airlines are large, commercial corporations with profit and revenue maximisation objectives. Since deregulation, competition has produced a situation where:

- the product is made up almost entirely of scheduled services
- airlines concentrate on business tourists
- an oligopoly exists, with eight major carriers
- these eight carriers supply 95% of the US market
- price competition is obscured by product differences (schedule convenience, routes offered).

The major carriers such as Delta, United, American and Continental are the world's largest airlines, and are very significant suppliers internationally as well as inside the United States.

In Europe, most of the major airlines have been under partial or total government control, which has often meant that profit maximisation objectives were tempered by political considerations such as providing 'socially necessary' air services or 'flag-waving routes'. This, coupled with less strict regulation during the 1990s, allowed the emergence of charter airlines such as Sterling, Britannia and Aero Lloyd. Leaving scheduled operators to supply air travel on routes used mostly by business travellers, the charter airlines have concentrated on recreational tourists moving en masse to tourism destinations from the main generating areas in the population centres of northern Europe. These airlines:

- operate with very cheap fares and high load factors
- usually provide air travel as part of an IT
- are often owned by tour operating enterprises
- use capacity off-season to provide some scheduled services or lease to carriers elsewhere.

Further European deregulation will blur the scheduled/charter distinction.

In other parts of the world, many airlines important to travel and tourism are national flag carriers. If government owned, they may well be required to contribute to national diplomacy or trade development objectives rather than purely commercial ones. Many of these airlines are enthusiastic members of the tariff co-ordination side of IATA (Taneja 1988).

Increasingly, however, privatisation or competition against more efficient privately-run carriers has forced carriers to become more profit-oriented, which to suit the needs of the marketplace may mean flight-code sharing, joint operations or consolidation with other carriers. During the 1990s there has been significant activity of this type by carriers such as United Airlines, British Airways and KLM. It has been suggested that by the year 2000 the bulk of the world's passenger air carriage may be provided by no more than twenty 'megacarriers' (Waters 1989).

Both road/rail and sea carriage also pass through phases of government ownership → regulation → objectives reassessment → deregulation/ privatisation → competition. Sea transport for tourism, as distinct from cruising, is relatively unimportant except for ferry travel in such areas as the Mediterranean, the North and Baltic seas, and to island destinations off coastlines. Rail travel is important to European and domestic Japanese tourism, owing to population densities and route networks, but few rail enterprises distinguish tourist traffic from other demand in a meaningful way. Exceptions include:

- specific (charter) trains for ITs in Western Europe
- semi-differentiated products such as rail passes
- car carrying services.

Most rail enterprises are monopoly providers of *rail* services in their areas, but must compete with other forms of carriage.

Intercity bus enterprises have far more prominence for recreational travel and tourism, particularly where they supply inclusive bus tours as well as scheduled line services. This is partly due to cheaper fares attracting the more price-elastic demand of some recreational markets, and partly due to flexibility of operation allowing market specialization. During the 1970s and 1980s many countries deregulated bus services, usually resulting in a competitive shakeout. For example, on the main East Coast route of Australia, ten bus companies operated in 1987, and ten in 1989, but only five were the same. By 1994, only six were left. As with airlines, price competition has forced sellouts and consolidations, thus increasing concentration ratios. In the United States in 1989, the Greyhound/Trailways group accounted for 60% of total intercity bus revenue (Waters 1989).

■ Accommodation

The worldwide lodging industry is perhaps more fragmented and diverse than any other sector in travel and tourism. For a start, commercially provided accommodations must compete with hosting by friends or relatives, which usually accounts for 30-50% of tourist nights, even including business tourists. Secondly, the range of product types varies from unserviced rough bush campsites through to luxury hotels and cruise vessels. Starting with locational characteristics, it is possible to have almost infinite product differentiation. Thirdly, the supplying enterprises range from state-owned National Parks, who may provide a 'free' product for social rather than economic reasons, through individuals or families who may rent out apartments or houses just to cover variable costs of what is otherwise their own vacation property, to multinational corporations seeking profit maximisation.

In general, 'the accommodation product' can be divided into three main sub-products, as shown in Figure 4.5:

Figure 4.5   The components of accommodation

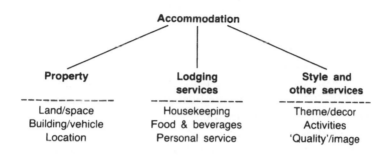

The way in which these sub-products are combined controls the market position of a specific lodging product, so that for example a luxury cruise vessel which is used primarily to offer passengers a variety of ports (rather than a specific shipboard atmosphere) may compete directly with a resort hotel, the property being the only major difference. Increasingly, lodging suppliers recognize that they are supplying separate sub-products. Hotel management companies such as Hilton or Hyatt supply lodging services and aspects of 'style' via name and marketing activity, but properties are often owned by different enterprises.

Competition in accommodation also depends on the geographical market coverage possible. Most accommodation is offered only in domestic, or sometimes just local, markets. In this case there is limited competition in property, lodging and other services depending on the size of that market, and prices reflect local conditions. Where accommodation suppliers serve international markets, they are competing with other countries (where different cost structures may exist), with other large and efficient suppliers, and for consumers with widely varying demand patterns. This structure is especially true for:

- multinational lodging chains (such as Holiday Corporation, Sheraton, Ramada or Club Mediterranee)
- multinational referral chains (such as Best Western)
- exclusive, high-quality suppliers whose prices and style restrict demand to a necessarily worldwide clientele (e.g. the Paris Ritz, Cunard cruises)
- international time sharing consortia.

There are very few examples of monopoly operation in lodging, since even in the remaining collectivist economies, governments see benefits for tourism in allowing competitive markets amongst lodging operators.

■ Attractions and support services

Like accommodation, the sector supplying tourism attractions and support services is highly fragmented and diverse. *Unlike* accommodation and transport, its products tend to be dedicated specifically to particular tourist markets, and suppliers admit to being within the travel and tourism industry.

Attractions can cover the following ranges:

- *resource-based — user-oriented*
  from those which are largely natural, such as mountains, safari parks or beaches, or those which are non-tourist manmade attractions such as historic monuments, to tourist-dedicated places and activities such as theme parks, conventions or carnivals
- *public goods — full-profit commercial*
  from attractions which have no resource-use requirement other than public agreement to allow tourist use (such as viewing Venice's canals) through attractions which are heavily subsidized by government or other activities (many cultural attractions) to attractions which must return commercial profits
- *publicly-owned — privately-owned*
  a complete mix is quite possible in, say, a marina development such as those in Languedoc-Roussillon, France or in California—individuals may own pleasure craft rented or chartered out by commercial agencies operating from a publicly-owned marina
- *'lifestyle' — events — fixed attractions*
  from one extreme at which tourists visit a destination to experience local colour or lifestyle, through the attraction of specific activities, such as sports events or festivals, to 'concrete' or permanent attractions.

In view of such diversity, it is hard to claim that there is a single tourism attractions sector. Definitional problems also impinge: whilst Walt Disney World/Epcot, Florida is the United States' biggest single *commercial* attraction (32 million visitors in 1993), how can this be compared with visiting the beach of Torremolinos, Spain or the central shopping area of Kowloon, Hong Kong? To a tourist, these may arguably be single attractions. This subject will be discussed in Chapter 9.

Support services tend to be far more closely defined, and to be related specifically to the needs of travel and tourism in either generating or destination areas, as in Figure 4.6:

Figure 4.6   Examples of travel and tourism support services

	Services to tourists	Services to suppliers
Generating area services	travel insurance travel finance visas & passports NTO information	trade press guides & timetables CRS and hotel reps brochure distribution
Destination area services	tour guiding banking medical local information	NTO/RTO support tourism training marketing support specialist financing

The nature of the market and degree of sophistication of these activities depends on the country or area in which they operate. Most National Tourist Office (NTO) and Regional or State Tourist Office (RTO) activity is a monopoly government function whose objective for tourism generally is likely to be maximisation of tourist numbers or revenue. The NTO itself is likely to be a satisficer: to accomplish its activity or supply its services within a given budget.

One interesting area of internationalized supply is in CRS (computerized reservation systems). Based on airline reservation systems, but incorporating single-terminal access to accommodations, car rental and so on, the major value to a buyer such as a travel agent is breadth of coverage. Consequently the CRS industry has become an international oligopoly of groupings dominated by a few systems with worldwide coverage, such as Sabre, Covia/Galileo and Gemini/Pars. Most of these systems are co-operatives and have as their objective the maximisation of market coverage for their owner enterprises.

■ Middlemen

The final group of travel and tourism enterprises consists of 'middlemen' who arrange and distribute travel and tourism products. These are mainly travel agents and tour operators. Travel agents, as selling agents for principals supplying transport, accommodation and so on, are supplying *the service of selling* to the principals who are the buyers of the service. However, agents are also held to be supplying *the service of selecting a principal* to intending tourists (Gregory 1985). In a sense therefore, they should be regarded as brokers rather than agents, as they are bringing two market sides together. Their income, however, is almost entirely derived from commissions paid by principals as the price of the service of selling.

In major generating countries, travel agents are operating in a situation of pure competition, as there are many of them (about 25000 in the United States, and about 5000 each in the United Kingdom and Germany), offering very similar services with basically only location or selling skills as differential advantages. Where standard rates of commission are negotiated by travel agents (usually through a trade association), this effectively constitutes a cartel, which is sometimes defended by both agents and principals in the interests of 'orderly distribution'. The cartel's dominance is broken, however, in three ways:

• Principals offer a system of *overriding commissions* to preferred agents or for special services; this provides differential payments to different agents. Travel agent X, by selling particularly well for one principal, will receive a higher commission price than travel agent Y for what is really a better selling service 'product'. For example, Australian and New Zealand agents could earn up to 26% commission, including overrides, by working hard to sell CTC cruises during 1988 after a highly-publicized sinking off the New Zealand coast.
• Agents use part of their commission to give discounts on principals' prices to tourists. In one sense this could be regarded as a marketing *cost* to travel agents, whose commission rate technically is fixed; but competition often makes discounting a normal activity—much to agents' chagrin, as this effectively changes net prices (commissions) received. Only where a government enforces resale price maintenance will this not happen.
• Distribution of travel and tourism services may omit the travel agent as middleman altogether. There are many alternative methods of distribution; eight major ways have been identified in the United States (Bitner and Booms 1982). Most domestic products are sold without the use of agents, and where marginal efficiency and returns of alternative distribution channels are higher, rational principals use them. Direct selling, for example, becomes more cost-efficient as communications and reservations technology improves; given that travel agents rely heavily on personal advice and selling, this is a classic example for principals of a capital/labour tradeoff.

Tour operators, or tour wholesalers, are really manufacturers of a specific tourism product. The product is an *inclusive tour* (IT) which may consist of one or more travel and tourism services 'packaged' for sale to tourists. Clearly tour operators are principals, and the buyers of their products are tourists. The common factor amongst tour operators is that they are supplying the quintessential travel and tourism product—if anyone can be said to supply 'tourism', tour operators do. There are many different kinds of operator, such as:

- generating area based enterprises supplying ITs by air—either charter or scheduled
- suppliers of extended bus tours or other land or sea-based ITs
- those who act really only as a wholesale outlet for groups of accommodations, vehicle renters and so on
- destination based excursion operators who frequently act as local ground handling agents for offshore enterprises.

Operators of the first type have developed strongly in the United Kingdom, Germany, other Northwest European countries and Japan. The industries in these countries support a range of competitive tour operators from small, highly product-differentiated specialists to major mass-market enterprises such as Jetour (Japan), TUI (Germany) or Thomson (UK). Conditions and market preferences in other countries have not, on the whole, favoured the development of this type of operator. Competitive enterprises of the third and fourth type exist almost everywhere except once again, until recently, in command economies where arrangements were almost entirely in the hands of state monopolies such as Orbis in Poland or Cedok in Czechoslovakia. These too, however, face competition in the free-market 1990s.

The role and objectives of tour operators also vary, from out-and-out profit maximisation to supporting functions for developing tourist numbers, in government-owned enterprises, or generating traffic (possibly as a loss-leader) for the owner of the tour operator, which may be a carrier for example. This will be investigated further in the next section.

■ Integration

Long-run decision-making by a producer, especially one which is a profit or growth maximiser, is likely to concentrate on three main areas:

- the opportunity for economies of production in large-scale operations
- the ability to control and develop inputs and markets more closely
- the chance to use existing differential advantages to operate profitably in related fields.

An enterprise may expand or develop on its own to make use of these opportunities, or it may seek to consolidate with other enterprises. The three areas are mirrored by three main types of integration, as depicted in Figure

4.7. This shows examples of, firstly, *horizontal integration*, where producers A and C (perhaps both hotel-owning enterprises) join, probably to obtain economies of scale.

Figure 4.7 Main types of integration in travel and tourism

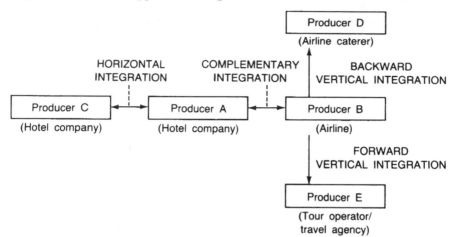

Secondly, producer B (an airline, say) may wish to secure its inputs such as catering or airport services. It therefore acquires producer D, in what is a process of *backward vertical integration*. To control its product distribution more closely, producer B may obtain *forward vertical integration* along the production chain with producer E, its distribution outlet. Finally, producers of complementary products such as A and B may merge to their mutual benefit.

As in other industries, forms of integration in travel and tourism vary from straight takeovers or buyouts, through corporate mergers, to minority and majority cross-stock holdings or merely joint management or consortium agreements. These last forms of looser, more flexible 'integration' have tended to predominate in travel and tourism. This reflects the types of business advantages available in travel and tourism, which are not generally single-plant 'manufacturing-type' economies of large-scale purchasing, production and distribution, but rather the advantages which accrue from operating *networks* of linked activities. Such advantages stem from the recognition that enterprises are increasingly market-oriented in management philosophy, and must serve consumer needs:

- across geographical divisions between generating areas and destinations
- in providing parts of a total travel and tourism product, as perceived by consumers, rather than concentrating on individual sectors.

The inherent spatial features of travel and tourism mean that networking businesses in different geographical areas is likely to provide operating economies. These will occur both in horizontal and vertical integration. For example, a high-fixed-cost reservations network needs wide use to be efficient, and since global telecommunications technology is constantly becoming cheaper in real terms, the marginal cost of extending the system to fresh locations is very low. If the marketing advantage of accessing multiple destinations from multiple generating areas is added, there is a powerful incentive for systems to merge.

Horizontal integration

Enterprises at the same stage in the same industry usually join forces to obtain external (multi-plant) economies of scale in production, power in purchasing or distribution, or to remove or countermand competition. With worldwide growth in demand for mass tourism, opportunities in each of these areas have led to significant horizontal integration. With passenger carriage and travel services for example, horizontal integration brings more efficient use of fleets, by sharing where fleets have different usage peaks or can be jointly maintained; it also allows greatly increased travel-route combinations to be offered to the market and the exploitation of large CRS in distribution.

Because the capital requirement is relatively small, integration amongst travel agents and tour operators frequently means full mergers and buyouts. The majority of the businesses thus formed are domestic, although a few large international chains such as Thomas Cook exist. (Thomas Cook itself is part of a 'complementary integration' in financial business, being a mostly-owned subsidiary of the Westdeutsche Landesbank of Germany.) By contrast, the capital costs of say airline acquisition are making working 'partnerships', code-sharing and co-operative promotion an easier form of integration. This is the case currently with, for example USAir and British Airways, United Airlines with Ansett, and Delta, Swissair and Singapore Airlines. The objectives of such joint working arrangements are clearly to secure demand in competitive markets rather than make production economies. The major economies in tour operating, for example, are in securing large volume discounts from suppliers (Sheldon 1986).

The same is mostly true in lodging and other sectors of travel and tourism, particularly where efficiency means controlling demand *to match a fixed supply*. Hotel and motel chains can obtain some economies in centralized management, finance acquisition and purchasing, but the major value of horizontal integration is in marketing, including distribution. Referral chains such as Best Western or Flag Inns have virtually the same advantages here as wholly owned-chains. 'Strategic alliances' are often cited as producing highly visible market coverage, and the globalization of resources (Dev and Klein 1993). The advantage of a strategic alliance, rather than complete integration of operation, is that each unit in the alliance can operate at its economically most efficient size (that is, where there are no further *internal* economies of scale to be gained by growth); the alliance economies are *external*.

Vertical integration and complementarity

Again, marketing and distribution advantages are the main reason in travel and tourism for vertical integration. An airline may set up its own tour operating subsidiary to act as a distributor for output which is difficult to sell directly; the tour operator will do this by constructing and selling ITs to a market segment which might not otherwise provide customers for the airline's product. The airline might not be concerned if the tour operator only breaks even, or even makes a small loss—provided that the increase in sales of aircraft seats brings the group a net marginal (increased) profit. The airline may also buy into travel agents to ensure that its products are distributed more strongly than those of its competitors.

Equivalent reasoning applies to integration between suppliers of complementary products, here referred to as *complementary integration*. An airline or tour operator may buy or become associated with hotels and motels in cities which it serves in order to ensure that customer tourists have accommodation available to reinforce their flight purchasing decision. (This is what PanAm did with Intercontinental Hotels between the 1950s and 1981—see, for example, Van Doren 1993). The group may acquire a bus company in order to control ground transfers and provide excursions, and develop tourism attractions to reinforce the tourists' need to travel. Any sector of the travel and tourism industry may initiate these moves: for example the Walt Disney Company operates hotels and ground transportation in Florida, Hapag Lloyd runs air services, cruising, travel agents and tour operation from Germany, and organisations such as Thomson (United Kingdom), Accor/Wagon-Lits/ PLM and Club Mediterranee (France), Canadian Pacific (Canada), All Nippon Airways (Japan) and Ansett (Australia) have highly integrated, almost 'total tourism' operations. Many domestic and international airlines in particular have hotel interests, with groups such as Golden Tulip, Penta and Nikko Hotels being mainly airline-owned.

Diversification

Finally, it is interesting to note the extent to which *diversification* into and out of tourism takes place. It is relatively rare for enterprises wholly or mostly within travel and tourism to diversify into other non-tourist industries. Possible reasons are that:

• few enterprises in travel and tourism are large, highly cashed-up, and have a large asset base
• struggling enterprises within travel and tourism are not in a financial position to diversify, and those that do well ascribe success to the above average growth obtainable in travel and tourism compared with many other industries; they would therefore tend to expand within the sector.

By contrast, we frequently find diversification into travel and tourism from all manner of industries and government activities, from steel companies to forestry departments. This is caused by the generally limited barriers to entry (including in many areas of travel and tourism a low capital requirement), perceptions of industry growth, a counterbalance of activity and seasonality to other sectors, perceptions (often misinformed) of the pleasures and ease of operating within travel and tourism, and opportunities for investment in alternative-use resources such as resort property. Many major travel and tourism enterprises, such as American Express, Ladbroke plc, Daikyo or Sheraton, developed from inward diversification.

■ Concentration

The result of individual enterprise growth and integration within travel and tourism is an increase in the *concentration* of that industry—that is, the degree to which output is produced by fewer and fewer enterprises. This can only be accounted for realistically within the context of an individual economy—although a later chapter will investigate the role of multinational enterprises in concentration of travel and tourism worldwide.

Levels of concentration in any part of travel and tourism in the future are likely to depend on two opposing factors. First, there is constant demand by many tourist market segments for new experiences and products, which encourages the development and survival of more and diverse enterprises, and therefore leads to the reduction of concentration. Secondly, technology (which in travel and tourism frequently calls for large capital outlays and requires mass markets for efficient use) promotes integration and large-scale enterprise, especially in air travel and non-personal services (marketing and information communication, travel insurance, tourism payment methods). In these areas, concentration will undoubtedly increase.

Concentration can be measured in a variety of ways. One simple, and relatively naive, measure is the percentage of a sector's activity which is accounted for by a small number of the largest enterprises. Table 4.4 shows, by this method, the comparative concentration in four sectors of travel and tourism across a sample of four countries.

The airline sector clearly has the highest level of concentration in all these countries. This is due to economies of scale in technical operation and capital requirements, together with the legacy of a monopoly flag carrier. In France, for example, the Air France group alone accounts for 81% of French air passenger carriage. Businesses in both the airline and tour operating sectors have national coverage in most countries, whereas hotels and travel agencies may not. As previously discussed, there are far fewer opportunities for economies of scale in businesses such as hotels. In addition, there is the historical development of individual hotels by individual hoteliers, together with relatively easy entry to and exit from the sector. Thus concentration levels are much lower, with the largest hotel chains (Choice in Canada, Prince in Japan, Forte in the United Kingdom, and Accor in France) each accounting for only 5–6% of their national market, expressed in room numbers.

Table 4.4   Percentage of each travel and tourism sector in the hands of the largest three, and largest five, businesses in a sample of countries

Country	Tour operators (% of pax)	Travel agents (% of outlets)	Hotels (% of rooms)	Airlines (% of pax)
Canada				
top 3 firms	54	fragmented	14	91
top 5 firms	76		21	99
Japan				
top 3 firms	32	10	12	84
top 5 firms	40	13	15	91
United Kingdom				
top 3 firms	55	18	13	69
top 5 firms	63	28	15	78
France				
top 3 firms	52	23	fragmented	91
top 5 firms	61	28		95

Source: Various sources, in *Travel and Tourism Analyst* 1993 and 1994.

Note: These are basically volume figures. Different statistics would be obtained through measuring by revenue earned, passenger-kilometres, or asset values.

Inevitably, data on tourist attractions and other sectors is less easy to find, but evidence suggests that concentration levels in most countries are also low, reflecting individuality and limited opportunities for economies of scale.

The discriminating monopolist and airfares

(adapted from Baumol 1977)

Assume that an airline has identified two discrete market segments **1** and **2**, for business travellers and holiday vacationers respectively. It has also identified the two demand functions:

$$P_1 = 400 - 3Q_1 \qquad P_2 = 240 - Q_2$$

The fixed cost of operating its aircraft is 18 000, and the variable cost is 40 pax (passenger), giving a total cost function of:

$$C = 18\,000 + 40\,(Q_1 + Q_2)$$

where P_1 and P_2 are airfares, and Q_1 and Q_2 are quantities of seats sold in each market by the (monopoly) airline.

Then total profit π will be:

$$\begin{aligned}\pi &= P_1\,Q_1 + P_2\,Q_2 - C = 400Q_1 - 3Q_1{}^2 + 240Q_2 - Q_2{}^2 \\ & \qquad\qquad\qquad\qquad - 40(Q_1 + Q_2) - 18\,000 \\ &= 360Q_1 - 3Q_1{}^2 + 200Q_2 - Q_2{}^2 - 18\,000\end{aligned}$$

Finding partial derivatives and setting them to zero:

$$\frac{d\pi}{dQ_1} = 360 - 6Q_1 = 0 \ \ \textbf{so } Q_1 = 60$$

$$\frac{d\pi}{dQ_2} = 200 - 2Q_2 - 0 \ \ \textbf{so } Q_2 = 100$$

Substituting these values into the demand and profit equations yields:

$$\pi = 2\,800 \qquad P_1 = 220 \qquad P_2 = 140$$

Business travellers will have to pay 220, and will take up 60 seats, whilst the vacation market will pay 140 and take up 100 seats. Marginal revenue in the two markets is equal:

market 1:

$$\frac{dP_1Q_1}{dQ_1} = 400 - 6Q_1 = 40$$

market 2:

$$\frac{dP_2Q_2}{dQ_2} = 240 - 2Q_2 = 40$$

The whole discriminatory position relies on the airline's ability to prevent market 1 consumers from buying the product at a market 2 price, although this is sometimes difficult (Toh, Kelly and Hu 1986 op. cit.).

Study questions

1 Obtain annual reports from at least four enterprises engaged in tourism activity. Try to find out from these reports what the enterprises' objectives are, in economic terms.

2 Is satisficing legitimate as a true objective?

3 If a tourism enterprise is a monopolist in one market but a competitor in another, examine how it may treat those markets differently.

4 Examine the theoretical effects of the reunification of East and West Germany in 1990 on the market structures of tourism enterprises. If information is available, compare these effects with what has actually happened.

5 What really constitutes a monopoly in tourism? Give some supporting examples.

6 Find local examples of businesses offering similar or identical travel and tourism products. Are they price-competitive?

7 Briefly analyse the differences in market structure between European and American air carriage.

8 Can the lodging industry be said to be supplying a discrete product?

9 Why is an association of travel agents with fixed commission rates not always effective as a cartel?

10 Identify the reasons why integration is especially important for many enterprises in travel and tourism.

11 Taking any sector of tourism in your locality, investigate its level of concentration (into few or many hands). Suggest reasons for your findings.

Supplying travel and tourism products

■ The decision to supply

The act of supply requires the willingness and ability of an enterprise to acquire resources, including goods and services produced by other enterprises, and to process those resources into output of products for sale (even at a zero price) to consumers. Most analysts would nowadays include the roles of marketing the products as part of supply.

Enterprises which make a decision to supply products in the travel and tourism sector base that decision on estimating their ability to attain objectives. This was discussed in Chapter 4. These enterprises must also consider what barriers to entry may exist, and whether they can be surmounted— they must consider how *contestable* markets are (Baumol *et al.* 1982). On the whole, barriers to entering travel and tourism are not overwhelming. The main barriers are likely to be:

- A significant capital requirement for some sectors, notably passenger carriage (certainly by air) and high quality accommodation (although leasing methods and management contracts or franchising often reduce this). Probably the most expensive sector in which to invest is ocean cruising, where a vessel alone may cost up to US$750 m.
- Government requirements for enterprises to hold licenses or bonds. This applies to travel agencies and to carriers in most countries, and although deregulation normally removes the need to obtain permission to supply *specific* products (for example, to serve a certain route), *general* requirements may still exist, such as those for qualified personnel or safety-tested vehicles.
- Competitive reaction from existing enterprises, particularly monopolies or cartels, who may block entry by a price war or similar tactics (it is generally accepted, for example, that the Laker Airways transatlantic Skytrain service failed partly for this reason).
- Planning or other restrictions on resource use for tourism by governments, especially for the development of resorts or tourism attractions in sensitive natural, heritage or cultural areas.

- The need for 'knowhow', which more often than not in travel and tourism does not involve technical qualifications, but entrepreneurial ability, political connections and trade contacts. This can often be overcome by hiring appropriate people. For example, the Walt Disney Company provides a comprehensive theme park development consultancy service commercially.

Once an enterprise has made the decision to enter an industry, it must more clearly address the questions:

- Exactly *what* product or products will it produce?
- *Where* will it produce?
- *When* will it produce?
- *How* will it produce? (That is, with what combination of resources and by what process method?)

These are not only economic questions, but they are at the core of strategic decision-making for the management of each enterprise. Economic analysts must also examine the effects of total or aggregate decision-making by all enterprises in a sector to understand aggregate industry supply.

   The analysis is complicated in travel and tourism by the fact that many entrepreneurs consider themselves not as producers of a 'tourism product' but as working within some different sector, such as catering, retailing or insurance. Unless perhaps all of their demand comes from people identifiable as tourists, their supply responses and production decision-making may be influenced more by factors other than 'tourism industry' ones. This means that the supply response within tourism as a whole is rarely homogeneous, except in relation to factors which influence an entire economy.

■ Time frames in tourism supply

In any industry it is important to look at the differences between short-run and long-run supply. The short-run can be roughly identified as a period within which the level or scale of use of most of an enterprise's resources, or factors of production, is fixed. Factors such as land, property and other fixed assets are those whose input level is least variable, but also it is important to consider an enterprise's planning horizon, management flexibility and ability to raise finance as delimiters.

   What is considered to be short-run varies between different types of enterprise in travel and tourism. An example is shown in Figure 5.1:

Figure 5.1   Samples of possible short-run time horizons

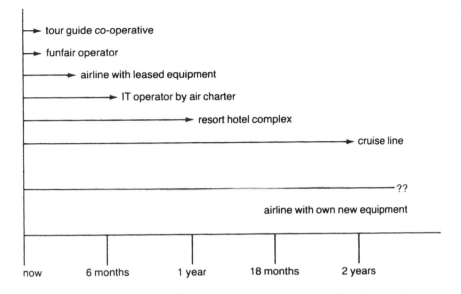

At one extreme the tour-guide co-operative can adjust the scale of production of its services very quickly, with little capital or land requirement. At the other extreme, an airport authority may have to wait years for an expansion, as an airline might wait for the delivery of new aircraft.

An alternative meaning for short-run is the period within which almost all costs are fixed (classically, when investigating diminishing marginal returns, all costs save one are fixed). To avoid confusion, this definition will not be employed here, as it is more useful when undertaking applied analysis (certainly within travel and tourism) to relate fixed, semi-fixed and variable costs *as they apply* to specific events (such as a 14-night IT, a bus excursion or a skiing season).

Most static supply analysis relates to short-run situations. In addition, although it is necessary to point out the effects on individual supply decisions that different enterprise objectives may have, for the most part analysis assumes the classical objective of profit maximisation. This must certainly be assumed for aggregate supply.

■ Production functions and inputs

Classical production theory suggests that an enterprise can produce a level of output **Q** from alternative combinations of inputs $x_1...x_n$ (see for example Henderson and Quandt 1971). The relationship of production is expressed as:

$$Q = f (x_1, x_2 \; .... \; x_n)$$

Productivity of input **i** is expressed as the derivative $\dfrac{dQ}{dx_i}$ where all inputs other than i are held constant. The best example of the ability to vary productivity in tourism is probably that of labour within a food and beverage operation. In a given restaurant with a certain number of covers (places), fixed space and equipment, more or less food service (and food production) staff may be used to serve the same number of diners, so restaurants may have different levels of productivity. In practice however, staffing levels in 'front of house' areas (those with public contact) throughout travel and tourism are used to *vary perceived service quality*. This changes the product's characteristics and therefore the product itself. Labour productivity and equipment and asset productivity are more easily identified in 'back of house' areas.

Secondly, a given amount of output Q may theoretically be produced from varying combinations of inputs. The alternative combinations, when graphed, are referred to as *isoquants*. The optimum combination at any particular time relates to the comparative costs of inputs $x_1 \dots x_n$ in such a way that the minimum total cost combination (*isocost*) should be obtained. There are severe difficulties in applying this analysis to individual enterprises in travel and tourism short-term. Principally this is because most tourism production involves fixed short-run relationships between inputs, unlike, say, horticulture, where it may be possible to substitute labour and greenhouse-intensive hydroponic growing methods in areas where land prices escalate. In tourism, for example, one tour bus requires one time slot and one driver. More would be redundant, fewer impossible. It is only in the long run that substitution of inputs becomes more important, as in the example of travel and tourism distribution by principals, where capital and technology in the form of electronic direct selling can be substituted for labour-intensive travel agents. Similarly, an NTO must make strategic decisions between spending on a personal sales force and media advertising when allocating its budget.

Programming approaches

More useful methods of examining production problems in travel and tourism are those of linear or nonlinear programming. These techniques allow for fixed relationships between inputs in the short run as well as for allocating inputs towards the production of more than one product. This is important to enterprises such as city hotels, which must allocate finance, manpower, space and equipment between staying-guest services, conventions, functions and so on, or a railway preservation project providing for education, preservation and recreational tourism (Bull 1985).

A programming approach further allows specifically for *fixed capacities* as system constraints. Fixed capacity is a hallmark of enterprises in carriage and accommodation, where short-run supply capacity is both 'lumpy' and limited.

A vehicle, for example, has X seats and can only be used in one way at one time. If no more vehicles are available, then capacity is X; if further vehicles are available, then marginal increases in output can only be in 'lumps' of X seats.

A simple linear program starts by specifying an objective function, such as profit maximisation, from one or more products. This may take the form:

Objective: Maximise $P = aX_1 + bX_2$

where **P** = profit

X₁ and **X₂** are products

a and **b** are profit contributions per unit of product.

The production relationships between inputs and outputs are then imposed in the form of constraints, which specify the amount of inputs required to produce certain outputs, and the capacity of those inputs available. These may take the form:

Subject to: $i_1 X_1 + i_2 X_2 + S_1 = C_1$

$j_1 X_1 + j_2 X_2 + S_2 = C_2$

where i_1 , i_2 , j_1 and j_2 are the amounts of inputs i and j required to produce one unit of products X_1 and X_2 respectively,

C_1 and C_2 are capacities of those inputs available,

S_1 and S_2 are any unused capacity left of these inputs (normally referred to as *slack variables*).

In addition, all variables must be positive or zero (the *non-negativity* constraint); the enterprise cannot supply negative amounts of product.

The methodology is more fully described in several texts—see for example Baumol 1977. A worked example relating to the configuration of an aircraft to supply different classes of travel is given in chapter appendix A.

This simple linear program form assumes constant returns to scale and fixed relationships between the use of inputs. Alternative relationships, and varying marginal returns, can be analysed by more complex nonlinear and point programming procedures. Similarly, the objective function here is to maximise profit contributions under fixed conditions (that is, fixed prices over the output range)—a situation only likely to occur where there is perfect competition. A more realistic picture, of imperfect competition in travel and tourism, and alternative objectives, requires nonlinear objective functions.

Long-run analysis of production is still more complex, as it means:

* the scale of production can change and capacities can be altered, by methods such as raising further finance, building hotel extensions, gazetting more land into a National Park or acquiring new vehicles
* production *methods* may alter to reflect changing relative input costs. In particular, capital may be substituted for labour in the total production system, rather than just at the margin

- products themselves may change characteristics. For example, a theme park may add a new attraction, or a restaurant may alter its style of cuisine—not to reflect actual demand, but as the result of management choice.

■ Costs and supply in tourism

Basic economic theory of costs and supply normally assumes that goods are being produced, and that there is a rough equivalence between fixed and variable costs over a given period. For the bulk of travel and tourism activity, neither of these assumptions is valid. Most products are services, and most of those services involve the consuming tourist physically going to the producer's 'plant'; that plant therefore has to exist and operate in many cases regardless of the number of tourists provided for, or 'product units supplied'. Consequently, a major feature of tourism supply activity is the heavy preponderance of fixed costs. For example, resort hotels such as the Hyatt Regency Resorts in Hawaii have a heavy property investment with fixed financing costs, and facilities such as golf courses, swimming pools, tennis courts, stables and health clubs which must be maintained regardless of user numbers, as well as ongoing marketing and administrative overheads.

A total cost function for enterprises such as motels, resorts, airlines, tourism attractions and bus operators is likely to resemble that in Figure 5.2.

Figure 5.2   Costs in travel and tourism

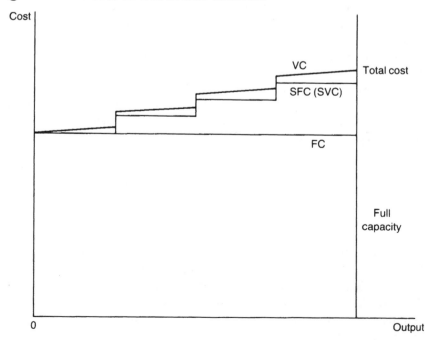

Fixed costs (FC) represent a high proportion of total costs. Semi variable costs (SVC) are those 'lumpy' costs which increase with production but not on a unit basis (such as a guaranteed shuttle air service using an aircraft with X seats in a situation where X+1 or X+2 passengers want to travel: a complete second aircraft is supplied). Variable costs (VC) are frequently very small.

If output can be sold at the same price throughout (or the same *average* price to a consistent split of segmented markets), then total revenue (TR) will increase as the line TR_1 in Figure 5.3, the maximum profit position will be the same as the maximum production and revenue positions, and the enterprise will seek always to supply to its full capacity.

Figure 5.3   Costs and revenue

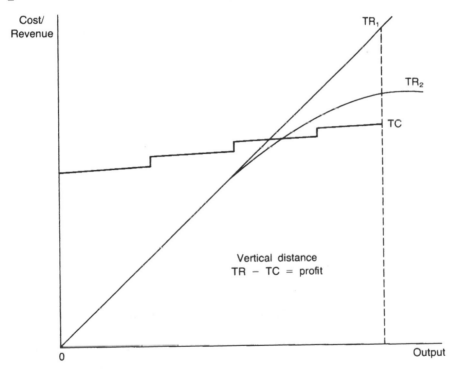

If the market price falls for all customers, the optimum supply position is still full capacity—albeit with reduced profits. This is the situation with seasonality, which is very frequent in travel and tourism. In some seasons tourism enterprises must either accept considerably reduced demand or reduce prices, and hence TR, to fill capacity. Either way, provided TR exceeds VC + SVC, a contribution is being made to fixed costs, and the enterprise will hope to recover the rest of its fixed costs, and make its profit, from peak season. Many enterprises will opt for full capacity utilization for two reasons:

- the contribution to FC is likely to be greater (if TR_1 in Figure 5.3 is considerably less steep but still straight, the maximum contribution is still likely to occur at full output)
- continuity of full operation helps to keep staff and maintain high productivity, as well as being a perceived benefit in marketing.

The situation depicted in Figure 5.3 by the line TR_2 is one where lower unit prices are required to get extra customers—that is, even in the short run the supplier faces a downward-sloping demand schedule of some sort. Even in this case, however, the maximum profit position is likely to be full capacity unless the marginal revenue obtained from an extra sale is very tiny—less than variable cost. This is because the total cost function is relatively not very steep—a result of the heavy fixed costs. Therefore, if a hotel manager or airline station manager has a good idea of variable costs, he or she should be able to bargain a low price with last minute 'walk-in' or 'standby' customers at a level sufficient to cover VC and still improve profitability. Such tactical marginal market pricing is common in many competitive travel and tourism enterprises. In classical marginal analysis terms, whilst marginal revenue (MR) still exceeds marginal cost (MC), it is profitable to produce more. Since MC is almost entirely extra variable cost which is tiny, it follows that in many circumstances the chargeable price or MR will exceed MC right up to full capacity supply.

Clearly, not all enterprises in travel and tourism face the above conditions. Travel agents or NTOs do not have specific capacity constraints, and their willingness to supply will depend more on costs of increased labour necessary to provide extra services. Their cost structure, like that of tourism *goods* suppliers (selling items such as souvenirs), will tend to produce a more 'normal' supply willingness.

■ Pricing

At this point, it may be helpful to examine briefly some of the ways in which enterprises in travel and tourism set their prices. Since perfect competition is almost non-existent, no suppliers are 'price takers' in the marketplace—that is, they do not accept and work with a price wholly set by market interactions. Most suppliers have a degree of discretion in price determination.

A standard method of price determination for many suppliers is *cost plus* pricing. This implies summing the costs of the operation, dividing the total by either the number of units of the product supplied or by the number the supplier expects to sell (see the next section), and adding a fixed percentage mark-up for profit. This corresponds to a satisficing objective for the business, where the mark-up indicates a satisfactory rate of return on sales, but not necessarily maximum returns or maximum profits. Because firms in travel and tourism operate mainly in monopolistic competition and offer highly-differentiated products, mark-ups—like retail margins—vary enormously (Van Dijk and Van der Stelt-Scheele 1993). If prices are set this way initially, they are unlikely to take account of price elasticity of demand. As a result, many tourism enterprises must then adjust their actual prices continually to respond to demand changes. So, for example, hoteliers may set their basic *rack rates* for their rooms, but may never actually charge those rates; they offer constantly varying levels of discount on those room rates in the face of different levels of demand for accommodation. Similarly, air, train and bus carriers may set cost plus fares, but discount them constantly at various levels.

At one extreme, this behaviour can turn into haggling, between buyer and seller, such as that for souvenirs in an Oriental bazaar. At the other extreme, variable pricing can be institutionalized—for example, into seasonal price differentials. This is important for any enterprise with fixed capacity constraints, as seen in the previous section; variable pricing is used to regulate demand.

Another special case in tourism deserves mention. Since tourists acquire physical products, services and the use of resources during their 'consumption' of tourism, and they often share these things with other tourists, the price that suppliers can set may need to take account of these issues. Valuing and pricing the use of environmental resources, for example by user pays systems, will be covered more extensively in Chapter 9. Pricing personal service is a topic which provokes much discussion. In many places, this takes place through *tips* or *gratuities,* so the consumer effectively sets the price for each service encounter. However, there are often expectations of what may constitute a 'normal' tip; anything less may provoke an aggressive encounter between tourist and service provider. Elsewhere, the tip becomes either a separately stated service charge, or is incorporated into normal prices, as labour costs in most industries normally are.

Very few suppliers take account of the influence of facility sharing, when setting prices. There is evidence, for example, that air passengers prefer a half-empty cabin to a full one on a long flight, and might pay more for the privilege, yet airlines do not price accordingly. The opposite situation can occur, where part of the tourist experience is the excitement of sharing it with others—especially if it is a fashionable experience. It has been shown (Becker 1991) that there are alternative possible prices in this situation, and that suppliers may not be aware of profit-maximising potential.

■ Elasticity of supply

The analysis of supply shows that for probably the bulk of travel and tourism enterprises (both privately and publicly-owned) there will be an aim of operating at full capacity. In the lodging sector, operators refer to their *occupancy rate*, expressed as a percentage of capacity taken up by the market, and evidence of their attitude towards maintaining demand and supply near full capacity is shown in the detailed attention paid to increasing occupancy rates (Greene 1983) by techniques such as yield management (Relihan 1989). In travel and transport, the same is true except that the measure is known as *load factor*. Many tourism attractions such as theme parks or golf courses measure their *usage rate*, which they compare with some theoretical optimal visitor capacity.

As a result, most short-run, individual-enterprise supply is extremely inelastic in travel and tourism. If market prices are high, supply will be at full capacity, and even if low, there may still be pressure to operate at full capacity. In turn this means that short-run industry supply is also very inelastic. Instead, suppliers will do all they can to adjust demand to equal capacity supply by altering prices or promotion. In the long-run, which would include periods at which enterprises might make a decision to close down for 'off-season', industry supply will be more elastic. This is accomplished by:

- temporary closure out of season, or permanent shutdown, if enterprises are faced with MR falling below MC, or if off-season contribution levels are 'not worth the effort'
- new entrants to the industry, existing suppliers permanently expanding capacity, or doing so temporarily (by, for example, chartering extra aircraft or vessels) when market prices are high.

In practice, the temporary measures are usually associated with seasonal market variations. 'Off-season' does not normally mean that demand vanishes, but demand can only be sustained at much reduced prices. There are some exceptions to this, such as off-season in skiing areas, where snow capacity itself disappears, but sufficient price reductions in most areas of tourism can call forth demand of some sort. Suppliers obviously expect 'full' prices again in the following season. Permanent change in supply is occasioned more by long-term trends and supplier anticipations.

Inelastic supply and economic rent

Where supply is essentially fixed, increased demand can only be translated into rationing or higher prices, in which the increased return to the supplier is known as 'pure economic rent', as first shown by Ricardo in 1815. The potential for economic rent is high at unique tourism attractions, where even long-run supply is fixed. If products are sold commercially or are resaleable, economic rent is seen in action. Examples are scalp hunters' or touts' prices for Wimbledon tennis final seats or the Oberammergau passion play. Since many such attractions are public goods, they will be discussed further in Chapter 9.

Factors shifting supply schedules

A wholesale shifting of any supply schedule can be caused by changing market conditions for products in joint or competitive supply. With goods, joint supply normally implies by-products, such as wool and sheep meat, but there are few such cases in travel and tourism. Services are user-specific and rarely contain a by-product element. A version of joint supply only occurs where tourism products are also supplied to non tourism markets, and the demand is complementary; for example, a city hotel function room may cater for conference dinners on Wednesday and Thursday night, but provide an annual dinner dance for a local club on Friday and a wedding reception on Saturday. It thus provides what to consumers are three different products: a business tourism one, a non tourism one, and a local market/VFR one. If conditions in any of these markets change, willingness to supply in the others may be affected. If it is possible to serve all markets within capacity, then the products are virtually joint, but if total demand exceeds capacity, they are products in competitive supply.

In the short term, none of these factors affects supply willingness very much because of the inherent inelasticity. However, in the long run, capacity (and hence supply schedules) will shift. For example, during the 1970s and 1980s in English coastal resort destinations, relatively better prices and returns were often available to lodging proprietors from elderly residents seeking sheltered accommodations. The supply of traditional hotels and guesthouses for tourists was reduced as they were converted to nursing homes.

Changes in costs, including taxation, work through the same process. In the short run, travel and tourism suppliers facing cost increases will not adjust supply, but either absorb the increases with reduced profit or attempt to pass them on in higher market prices, depending on their degree of market price control. Industry-wide cost changes in particular (such as state 'bed taxes' at places of accommodation, or airport taxes) are immediately passed on to consumers (Hiemstra and Ismail 1993).

We shall now investigate more fully costs and supply economics for a number of major sectors in travel and tourism.

■ Carriage by air

Passenger air carriers measure output by *passenger seat kilometres (ps/km)*, with supply as *available* seat kilometres and consumption as *revenue* seat kilometres. The costs of a passenger-carrying airline can be divided into four broad groups as shown in Table 5.1 (Shaw 1985):

Table 5.1 Costs in passenger air carriage

	Average %
Airline-related (FC)	10
Route-related (SFC)	27
Flight-related (SFC)	45
Passenger-related* (VC)	18
	100

*including 9-11% ticket sales commission

Source: IATA airlines

Airline-related costs are inescapable fixed costs such as administration, reservations, marketing and group services. Route-related costs are incurred as soon as the decision to service a particular route is made, including the cost of aircraft (financing and depreciation), maintenance, and station costs such as providing check-in, offices and ramp handling at online airports. Route-related costs are therefore relatively fixed (semi-fixed costs or SFC). Flight-related costs are variable to the route but fixed as soon as the 'go' decision is made to operate a certain flight. They include flight and cabin crew, fuel (which is usually the largest single item, at around 30% of costs, to most airlines), airport and air traffic control charges. Passenger-related variable costs include meals, baggage handling and ticketing. Since sales commission is directly related to airfares it is more logical to regard the airline's return as a *net* price, leaving passenger-related variable costs at around 7-9%.

In the short-run, scheduled airlines are committed to operating licensed and advertised services, so that passenger-related costs are the only variable ones. Clearly then, the desired supply is that fixed by capacity (cax) on each flight. Profit and revenue maximisers then seek the highest revenue or *yield* from the flight, by using some of the following tactics:

• Setting market prices, airfares, such that total costs are paid for by a relatively low number of passengers (typically with a load factor of 55-60%). Given market segmentation, further seats can be sold at progressively lower prices, down to standby fares at VC level; all will be profitable (MR>MC).
• Ensuring that seat configuration in various classes uses inputs to create the optimum yield on each flight (see chapter appendix A).
• Selling each seat at the highest possible fare, by closely identifying the constraints on market segments and using them to cut into consumers' surplus. Additionally, international airlines use currency fluctuations to concentrate selling in those countries whose currencies have appreciated relative to their home currency (but where airfares have not yet been adjusted downwards). The use of Neutral Units of Currency (NUCs) in international airfares reduces this option but does not remove it (IATA 1988).

This supply activity, when coupled with cartel-type fare fixing agreements, can lead to a market situation such as that in Figure 5.4:

Figure 5.4 The marketplace for 'full-fare' air services

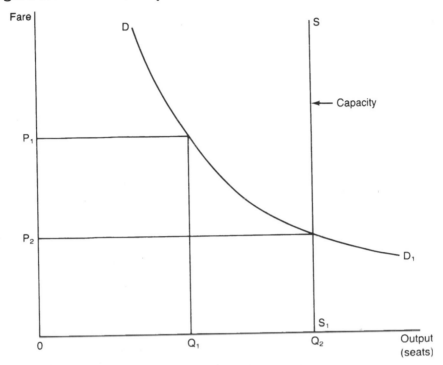

A 'normal' market equilibrium at airfare P_2 would fill capacity, clearing quantity Q_2 of seats. However, published airfares are held at P_1, selling only Q_1 seats and giving the airlines a load factor of $\dfrac{OQ_1}{OQ_2} \times 100$.

Remaining capacity $Q_2–Q_1$ can be cleared at discount fares down to P_2. Airlines' revenue is $P_1Q_1 + P_2(Q_2–Q_1)$. Why should airlines not simply fix fares at P_2? First because P_1Q_1 probably gives greater revenue than P_2Q_2, with small savings in VC as well; secondly, airlines have the option of expanding revenue still further with discount fares in marginal markets. Even deregulated, competitive air markets in the United States have rarely produced single-level low airfares (Civil Aviation Authority 1984).

One essential difference between scheduled and charter airlines is that the latter operate *de facto* with a flight as a unit of output rather than passenger seat or ps/km. A flight will only be guaranteed given a minimum pre-booked load factor (of, say, 90%) and therefore minimum guaranteed returns. Flights may otherwise be cancelled or consolidated. Whilst the 'normal' fares must be lower, to guarantee a high load factor, flight-related costs in essence become variable. Supply, in the form of flights, can then be much more readily adjusted to market needs—provided alternative uses can be found for aircraft and crews, and provided station-manning is flexible. For this reason, most charter airlines contract out station-manning, and rely heavily on cross-leasing of aircraft.

Charter airlines can therefore offer a dynamic response flexibility which scheduled airlines cannot, and which can serve recreational mass tourism needs well. Table 5.2 shows a comparison between business and recreational air travel ex-United Kingdom in 1992.

Table 5.2 Seasonality of air travel demand ex-UK, 1992

	(international trips) Business travellers		Recreational travellers	
	%	index	%	index
1st quarter	24	96	12	48
2nd quarter	27	108	28	114
3rd quarter	21	84	39	156
4th quarter	28	112	21	84
	100		100	

Source: UK Department of Transport, International Passenger Survey

Disregarding volume and actual fares, it can be seen that mass leisure tourism demands high seasonal flexibility, which charter airlines can provide. In fact a high proportion of the United Kingdom's recreational tourists used these services, from such airlines as Britannia and Air 2000. Realistic, feasible alternatives can be provided only by major scheduled airlines with large, variable-use fleets as have developed in the United States since deregulation.

In the long run, airlines vary supply through route changes and through fleet and system alterations linked to cost changes. Costs per unit of output (available ps/km) change with different inputs (such as new aircraft offering higher average productivity per unit of output), or by changing route systems to obtain economies of market sharing and to offer 'new' products. A good example is the use of a hub-and-spoke route system either domestically (Hanlon 1989) or internationally, using sixth freedom rights (Hanlon 1984, Williams 1993; see Chapter 10 of this text) to increase the 'supply of routes' to a theoretical $n(n-1)/2$ with a system of n spokes. Over the past three decades system efficiency coupled with cost savings brought about by aviation technology have been driving forces in allowing consistent expansion of supply in air carriage despite periods of fuel cost explosions and poor financial returns to many individual airlines.

■ Cruising

Ocean or waterway cruising has long been an accepted tourism product. Many cruise enterprises developed out of line voyage shipping companies, and the product concept moved gradually from transportation to that of a 'moveable resort', containing accommodations, catering and attractions. Unlike airlines, there is no standard unit of output, with products varying in location, duration and style. Short-run supply is extremely inelastic, as the only method of expanding supply in one area is by charter, usually from another line, which may take months to negotiate. Equally, owners of vessels are loath to lay them up in adverse market conditions, as many of the fixed costs remain. Consequently cruise lines attempt, like airlines, to keep their craft in revenue-earning service as much as possible (see chapter appendix B).

Modern cruising operations are very different from those operating before the 1960s (Kane 1984). Typical 'cruise products' may be compared:

Cruises before the 1960s	Modern cruises
long duration	7–14 nights duration
long distance	short distance
departure from generating area ports	departure from warm-water ports (often fly-cruises)
most time at sea	most day time in ports
used ex-liners	purpose-built vessels

Whilst changes in cruising have partly been a reflection of changing demand, many developments have been in response to cost considerations.

The three major cost areas are the capital investment in vessels, fuel costs, and labour. The first is fixed and the other two become fixed on a decision to proceed with a cruise, with some qualifications. Fuel can be saved by cruising more slowly, operating on a shorter itinerary and spending more time in ports. In the long run, fuel productivity is increased by using newer, more fuel-efficient vessels or by re-engineering older ones. The former liner *France* was given a much smaller and cheaper propulsion system when she was refitted as Norwegian Cruise Line's *Norway*, as she no longer needed speed in transatlantic crossings. Operators also make long-run labour cost savings by:

- hiring crews with lower wage rates, such as crews from Greece or the Philippines
- substituting capital for labour with labour-saving equipment on modern vessels and bought-in foodstuffs
- reducing service levels where they are no longer seen as an immutable product characteristic by consumers.

During the 1990s, cruise lines are attempting to become more efficient and competitive by ordering more new vessels, and by maintaining occupancy rates on cruises at high levels—of 85% or more (Baum 1993). There has been consolidation as cruise lines find economies of scale in production and marketing, and the development of 'mass market' cruise businesses, especially in the Caribbean, such as Carnival and Royal Caribbean cruises (Hobson 1993).

■ Hotel and motel accommodation

The lodging sector is characterised by its diversity. Not only is there a wide range of accommodation types for tourists, but the location, ownership and varying cost structures cause a variety of supply responses to market conditions.

The majority of hotels and motels possess a fixed supply of rooms available for letting, and if they are profit, volume or revenue maximisers, they will ideally wish to sell all their capacity—a 100% occupancy rate. In this they are like airlines. However, establishing a measure of output and supply is complicated. First, occupancy may be measured in three different ways:

- a *basic occupancy* rate measures the percentage of rooms used on a given night by guests
- a *bed occupancy* rate establishes how many guests are physically accommodated as a percentage of maximum capacity; for example how many double or twin rooms (which internationally account for over 80% of hotel rooms) may be let as singles
- a *revenue occupancy* or *yield* figure compares room revenue on one night with the theoretical maximum; every room will have a full-price or published *rack rate*, but many may be let at discounts for various reasons.

An example shows the difference:
Hotel X has 100 twin rooms each with a rack rate of $100. On one night:
    30 are occupied by couples at rack rate
    30 are occupied by couples at a special group discount rate of $70
    20 have single occupancy at $60.

$$\text{ROOM OCCUPANCY} = \frac{80}{100} \times 100 = 80\%$$

$$\text{BED OCCUPANCY} = \frac{140}{200} \times 100 = 70\%$$

$$\text{REVENUE OCCUPANCY} = \frac{6\,300}{10\,000} \times 100 = 63\%$$

Secondly, rooms may deliberately be let at less than market rates (and possibly at a loss) to cross-subsidise food and beverage, function or other operating areas, or simply to maintain cash flow in the off-season. A profit-maximising supply is therefore foregone in favour of other objectives.

In general hoteliers would wish to supply 100% of their rooms, at full bed-occupancy and full revenue-occupancy. This is because their cost structure, like that of airlines, contains a large fixed costs component (see below). However, they may sometimes face a choice of selling fewer rooms at full rate or more at a discount (for example when a tour group with monopsonist buying power—able to negotiate very low prices—is a potential customer). There may be a choice between selling 40 rooms at $100 each, or 90 rooms at $50 each; but the extra revenue of $500 may be more than swallowed up by increased variable costs, such as cleaning, laundry and power, which vary with room occupancy (Van Dyke and Olsen 1989). In seasonal tourism destinations, a distinction may be made as regards overall 'supply': in low season hoteliers take on the block group bookings, but they may be reluctant to do so in high season because of the better chance of selling rooms at rack rate later. Computerized *yield management* systems are increasingly being used here to aid decision making. (There is clearly room for improvement: in the United States, for example, the hotel industry only achieved an average occupancy rate of 67%, at an average room rate of US$80, during 1993.)

It is difficult to generate an 'average' cost picture for lodging worldwide, owing to the growing use of uniform accounting methods which do not allocate overheads between rooms, food and beverage and so on (AHMA 1986). Nonetheless, a generalised picture of worldwide average lodging costs is presented in Table 5.3:

Table 5.3 Worldwide average lodging cost breakdown (%)

	FC	VC	Total
Labour (direct and indirect)	20	20	40
Financial charges, depreciation & fixed property/fittings costs	30	–	30
Energy and maintenance	5	10	15
Laundry, linen and disposables	–	10	10
Other	5	–	5
	60	40	100

Source: adapted from Horwath International 'Worldwide Lodging Industry' 1993, and Arthur Andersen.

Whilst Table 5.3 can offer no more than a general guide, owing to the highly disparate nature of the industry and consequent high level of cost variance, there is no doubt that labour is a major input in lodging enterprises, and that fixed costs (FC) generally exceed short-run variable costs in total.

The difficulty many hoteliers face is that labour levels are an indicator, and probably corollary, of service quality which in turn characterises individual lodging establishments and allows them to command price differentials. This may not be a great problem in low-wage economies such as those in South and South East Asia, where guests are often confronted with a staff/guest ratio of over 3:1 in international hotels; it is more serious in high-wage economies. Hotels and motels do not have the luxury afforded to cruise ships of registering their property in a flag of convenience country and hiring crew from the lowest-wage-paying country, under that country's labour market conditions. Consequently hotel companies, like others, substitute labour-saving capital equipment and industrially produced inputs for their own expensive labour, which unfortunately tends to replace variable costs with fixed costs. Supplying at full capacity becomes even more important and pricing policy reflects this (Rogers 1976).

Pressure *in the other direction* (to convert fixed to variable costs) has produced an increasing separation between hotel/motel ownership and management. Before the 1960s most hotel companies owned their own properties. It is now normal, though, for medium and large establishments to be owned by property companies, and for the hotelier to operate with a management contract or lease. Most well-known chains such as Hilton, Hyatt, Marriott or Sheraton operate the bulk of their hotels this way. (Most other properties operating under these names are franchises.) This acknowledges that there are two businesses operating in *different markets*. The property company seeks an investment vehicle, especially in cities and major destinations, with capital appreciation and rental or profit-sharing returns. The hotelier is relieved of fixed-cost finance payments, and provided a fee or rental can be linked in some way to profit or revenue (Pannell, Kerr, Forster 1988), the cost becomes semi-variable. There is then more flexibility in supply decision-making.

■ Natural and historic attractions

One way in which tourist attractions can be categorised is:

A   events
B   specifically designed permanent attractions
C   natural and historic attractions.

The supply of events (type A) may be recurrent or volatile, depending on the event's nature. Golf classics, Rio's Mardi Gras and the Olympic Games are recurrent, an Expo or a royal wedding may not be. The supply of type B attractions is largely dependent on location. In a popular tourism destination there is a potential 'walk-in' demand and economies of concentration, which not only may produce a supply of small purpose-built attractions, but reinforce the commercial potential of large ones: The Walt Disney Co. builds theme parks in Florida, California and Paris rather than Iowa and northern Poland. Sometimes a successful type B attraction can be built at a stopover or as a 'monotony breaker' along a travel route. This is less important in, say, European countries where distances are relatively short and North American or Antipodean visitors are astonished to fall over historic or natural wonders every few kilometres. By contrast, a European tourist to Canada or Australia is ill-prepared for such vast distances with little of interest—in these countries, almost *any* attraction can be a successful product.

The supply of natural and historic attractions for tourism occurs in two stages:

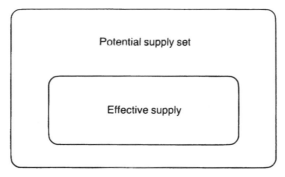

First there is a relatively *finite set* of possible attractions in any one destination. This may not be totally fixed, as fashions in demand may change so that places not previously considered worth visiting may become 'touristic'—for example some older industrial cities in Great Britain. Given a pattern of demand, however, this set of products (which is here termed *potential supply*) is extremely inelastic.

Secondly, not all potential attractions are actual ones. Owners or managers must:

- be willing to provide them for tourist use
- provide a use-management system (which could be something as simple as access or information).

This results in an *effective supply*, which of course is a subset of potential supply. A state government owned forest or wilderness area may be a potential attraction, but is only in effective supply if visiting is permitted and access provided. The situation is similar to privately-owned Hollywood film stars' homes or European castles.

Effective supply establishes the short-run maximum amount of attractions available, and within that the level of desired supply is accomplished via visitor management methods. These may include access control or promotion, as at the Pyramids of Giza, Egypt; control of circulation systems such as in the Tower of London (Murphy 1985), or insistence that golf players use electric carts; zone management; or control of opening hours. These are all *supply rationing* methods (compared with variable pricing which works directly on demand) and tend to be associated with controlling excess demand, especially at peak periods.

For most managers of historic and natural attractions the major costs are labour. Labour inputs may include direct visitor services (such as guiding), attraction maintenance, and conservators. Only the first group are a variable cost, and many attractions in high-wage economies replace labour-intensive systems with automatic turnstiles, audio cassette guides, and other audio-visual information systems. Cost saving is equally important for user-oriented attractions; for example, Euro Disney reduced staffing by about 10% in 1994, in response to a US$900 million loss in 1993.

■ Air tour operation

Air tour operation originated principally in Europe in the early 1950s as a supply-driven sector (Holloway 1989). At that time, many airlines had a surplus of seats caused partly by the addition to fleets of aircraft converted from former wartime stock, and partly because airlines did not have the sophisticated segmentation and fare differential systems now used. In consequence, many scheduled flights operated continually with empty seats. This opened the way for tour operators to act as *wholesalers/retailers* by buying vacant seats *en bloc* at a considerable discount. The price would be less than published airfares and at anything down to the level of variable costs, which, as was seen above, could be very low with actual prices being determined by the relative bargaining power of tour operators and airlines. In order to protect their full-fare markets, airlines began to impose conditions on the resale of seats by tour operators, some of which are still in effect today. The principal condition often was (and is) that the air travel could only be sold as a component of an *inclusive tour (IT)* incorporating destination accommodation and/or other services. This made tour operators into *manufacturers* building ITs as discernibly separate products. Tour operators then carried the business risk of selling product stocks themselves.

In buying accommodation for their ITs, tour operators bargain, as they do with airlines, to secure discounted prices. Relative bargaining power dictates final prices, so that, for example, a tour operator which offers to block book in a brand new untried hotel will secure a very cheap rate; the hotelier has both a guarantee of demand from the start and some customers, who may return later paying full price. Final negotiated prices may also depend on:

- the season and the hotel's occupancy rate
- whether the operator books, and guarantees payment for, a set block or *allocation* of rooms, or merely books on an *ad hoc* basis (the former results in cheaper prices for the operator but a semi-fixed cost, compared with a variable cost for the latter)
- continuity of the operator's demand, where demand in low season is a strong bargaining counter not only for low rates, but also protecting the operator's allocation in high season.

From purchasing blocks of seats on scheduled services as inputs, some air tour operators progressed to chartering whole aircraft, often on days when aircraft were standing idle owing to scheduling methods. Although the potential saving to the operator on individual seats is less, the operator can gain the same advantage overall as charter airlines, by working with a very high load factor. In this way many tour operators, especially in the United Kingdom, Scandinavia and Germany, built up volume of production to the stage where they bought their own aircraft and established charter fleets. Large operators also own bus fleets, attractions and sometimes their own accommodations.

In purchasing inputs, especially air carriage, the tour operator's objective is to obtain a *program series* of ITs. With a charter IT (ITC or CIT) for example, this means regular weekly or two-weekly departures, where this week's outward flight brings home last week's tourists, and accommodation is used continuously. It is often less easy to have this regularity with ITs using scheduled services (ITXs or inclusive tours by excursion), but the principle otherwise holds good.

Table 5.4 shows a sample statement of an air tour operator's revenue and costs:

Table 5.4   Sample income/expenditure percentages for an air tour operator

		%
Gross IT (trading) revenue		100
less commission on sales		10
		90
Airfares	47	
Accommodations	35	
Taxes and ground transfers	2	
Other costs & overheads	5	
		89
Net trading profit		1
add		
Profit from insurance & excursion sales		2
Interest on prepayments & surplus on foreign exchange dealing		2

Source: Japanese outbound air tour operator X

The table above reveals two key things. First, many operators do little better than break even on trading directly in their IT products, owing mostly to competition. Many obtain as much, or as in this case more, profit from interest received on deposits and prepaid holidays, from dealing in foreign exchange, and from selling 'add-on' products. Secondly, air travel and lodging are the two major input costs. These more than anything dictate tour operators' supply. A feature or product characteristic for many ITs is an overall price advantage to the tourist compared with purchasing individual components. This advantage has been found in some cases to be around 15%

(Sheldon 1986:United States basic air ITs to Hawaii) up to perhaps 40% or more in Europe. If operators lose cheap input prices they may be less willing to supply. Indeed, this may occur seasonally when airlines and hoteliers do not wish to sell to tour operators anyway as they can clear all their products direct to consuming tourists at full prices. The result is a potential *backward-sloping supply schedule* as in Figure 5.5:

Figure 5.5   A supply schedule for air ITs

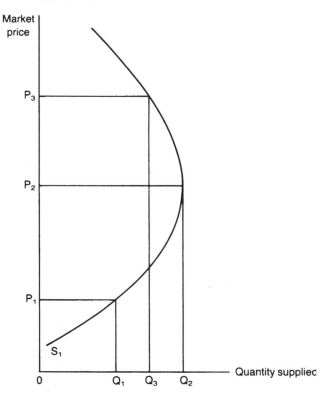

Along tour operation supply schedule SS_1, a market price P_1 calls forth supply $0Q_1$ of ITs. If market price rises to P_2, supply will be increased to $0Q_2$, but market price P_3 means that

(a) tour operators' margins are squeezed, and
(b) travel and lodging suppliers are not interested in selling to operators, so the supply of 'components' dries up.

This assumes that all market prices (whether for selling direct or through tour operators) move together, which is normally the case. As a result, operators are forced to reduce supply to $0Q_3$. The intense competitive challenges which result, especially in Europe, have been well documented (Bywater 1992).

■ Controls on supply

Controls are placed on supply in travel and tourism by both government authorities and the various sectors' own trade associations. The controls may be both long and short-term in effect. Governments establish controls principally through *licensing and grading*. Licensing systems operate in many areas to regulate the number of suppliers and the products which they supply, both nationally and internationally. For example, national governments negotiate bilateral agreements to determine international scheduled air routes and the capacities of seats to be offered, including how those capacities will be shared between countries; individual governments then license specific carriers to provide set proportions of those capacities. National governments may license domestic air carriage (and also other carriage) in a similar way.

This form of regulation has been justified for reasons of orderly competition, protection of national carriers' business, control of standards, providing services on uneconomic but socially desirable routes, and other political and diplomatic ends. During the 1980s, pressure to remove license restrictions or deregulate was strong, stemming from air service deregulation in the United States. European deregulation has followed.

Other forms of licensing include those for travel agents, tour guides (Shaw *et al.* 1988), foreign exchange dealing for tourists and a range of other activities where the aims are primarily either to enforce service quality standards or to protect consumers against losses following financial misdealings or failure. Consumer protection applies to the travel agency and tour operation sectors of many countries, and is accompanied by various kinds of financial bonding. The economic effect is to create barriers to entry, to make markets less contestable, and therefore restrict supply, so that such systems are frequently adopted by trade associations (on behalf of their existing members) as well as by governments.

Grading systems can also indirectly affect supply. In lodging, for example, some countries adopt what used to be the Spanish system of tying permitted hotel and motel rates to grading. A lodging proprietor may then restrict supply of one grade of accommodation in order to concentrate on another more profitable one, or shut down altogether if not permitted to charge whatever rate is considered necessary to meet objectives.

The influence of these controls and other, more direct, ones such as planning restrictions or straight price control on travel and tourism market places will be examined in Chapter 6.

An example of linear programming in aircraft configuration

Assume that an airline wishes to establish its supply of different classes of travel on an aircraft of fixed size with established crewing levels. It may offer:

First class	**F**
Business class	**J**
Economy/coach class	**Y**

where the profits per unit (seat sold) on a particular route are:

F: 6 (currency units)

J: 4

Y: 3

A profit-maximising objective function may then be expressed as:

Maximise: $6F + 4J + 3Y$

Assume two main constraints:

(1) There are 500 square units of space available for cabin configuration, and the space requirements per seat are:

F: 8 square units (seat pitch x width gross)

J: 6   "   "

Y: 5   "   "

(2) There are 360 minutes of cabin crew time available on each flight, and it has been calculated that passengers in each class require the following amounts of attention each:

F: 10 minutes per passenger

J: 8   "   "   "

Y: 3   "   "   "

These constraints may then be expressed as:

$8F + 6J + 5Y =< 500$ and $10F + 8J + 3Y =< 360$

or

$8F + 6J + 5Y + S = 500$ and $10F + 8J + 3Y + C = 360$

where **S** and **C** are *slack variables* in the use of space and manpower respectively.

Non-negativity constraints are also required—that is, all variables must have positive or zero values.

Linear programming (here using LINDO) yields the following optimal solution:

Profit	=	313.85
where F	=	11.54 (11 or 12 seats)
J	=	0
Y	=	81.54 (82 or 80 seats)

With 11F and 82Y, 2 units of space and 4 staff minutes are slack; with 12F and 80Y 4 units of space and no staff minutes are slack. Interestingly, under these conditions it is not worthwhile supplying business class seats at all, and a sensitivity analysis shows that profit per unit in J class would have to increase by 15% to 4.6 in order to merit a change.

Cruising schedules

Cruise companies endeavour to keep their vessels in revenue-raising service as much as possible. This example is of three vessels operated by Royal Caribbean Cruises, for 1994:

Majesty of the Seas
dep Miami 17.00 on 2 Jan and the same weekly all year to the Western Caribbean
arr Miami 08.30 one week later. *Turnaround in port: 8.5 hours*

Sovereign of the Seas
dep Miami 17.00 on 1 Jan and the same weekly all year to the Eastern Caribbean
arr Miami 08.30 one week later. *Turnaround in port: 8.5hours*

Monarch of the Seas
dep San Juan 22.00 on 2 Jan and the same weekly all year to the Southern Caribbean
arr San Juan 08.30 one week later. *Turnaround in port: 13.5 hours*

These three large vessels (each of over 73 000 tons gross) each carry around 2 300 passengers and 825 staff. Disembarkation, in port maintenance, bunkering, provisioning and embarkation are carried out very quickly to enable the maximum time in revenue-earning service.

Study questions

1 Examine the factors that differentiate between short-run supply and long-run supply in tourism.
2 Why is factor-substitution often a problem in tourism production?
3 Identify four examples of operations in travel and tourism production where there are short-run fixed capacities. How do managers optimize productive efficiency in these cases?
4 Show how marginal revenue is important to a carrier or lodging business with heavy fixed costs.
5 In what way is an airline's concern with yield likely to influence its attitude towards selling in different tourist markets?
6 Assume a 100-room motel faces a cost structure like that in Table 5.3. With occupancy rates of 40%, 80% and (potentially) 120% at three different seasons, what short-run production and marketing decisions would you recommend for each season?
7 Distinguish between potential and effective supply of historic attractions for tourism.
8 Why may inclusive tour operators have a potentially backward-sloping supply schedule?

Equilibrium in tourism markets

■ The establishment of partial equilibrium

In a market economy, the price system should operate, in markets for each product, to equate the quantity of those products that producers are willing to supply with the quantity that consumers are willing to demand; that is to say *scheduled* supply and demand must be equated (Samuelson 1989). Theory states that if prices are too high for this to happen, suppliers will be unable to clear all they produce through markets, and therefore price or quantity supplied must be reduced. If prices are too low there is excess demand, and buyers will 'bid up' prices which will draw forth a greater supply. All else being equal, for each product in an economy there will be a unique equilibrium market price and quantity, representing a partial equilibrium in the aggregate economy.

The sum of all partial equilibria in an economy determines two things:

- *general* equilibrium (of all interdependent markets)
- the allocation of resources to those who are willing and able to pay, by methods using the most economic inputs or factors.

In practice, the operation of price mechanisms to achieve a market-clearing equilibrium is rarely as simple as this. There are monopolistic imperfections and restraints on free trade in most markets; governments and other authorities intervene; and producers and consumers rarely sell and buy with the perfect knowledge of marketplaces that theories suggest they should have. In addition, markets are dynamic rather than static, so that constantly changing conditions may never permit the attainment of a stable equilibrium position.

■ The problems of identifying equilibrium in tourism

Identifying equilibrium in travel and tourism markets poses two particular problems: the geographical nature of the activity, and divergent perceptions of the product by suppliers and tourists.

Equilibrium analysis usually relates to a national economy. Whilst over 90% of the world's tourism—measured in tourist nights—is domestic, very few economies are closed to international tourism, and to many national markets inbound or outbound international tourism is very important, especially in money terms. Therefore the tourism market in any one country is a blend of domestic and international demand, and the international component may well be relatively more significant than foreign trade in most goods relative to the economy's domestic markets. This complicates the supply relative to any major generating area (demand), and the demand relative to any destination area (supply).

If there are **n** national economies in the world, the total number of travel and tourism 'markets' will be **n(n–1)** international plus **n** domestic. As an analogy to the principle of few major variables exercising the most discernible effect, for most economies there will be few significant tourism demand generators or tourism supplying destinations. Assuming worldwide **g** notable generators and **d'** destinations, the total number of tourism markets is **gd'** international plus **n** domestic. Since demand conditions vary constantly between the **g** generators, and supply conditions vary between the **d'** destinations, any simple partial equilibrium in travel and tourism is in practice difficult to arrive at.

Figure 6.1 Perceptions of the travel and tourism marketplace

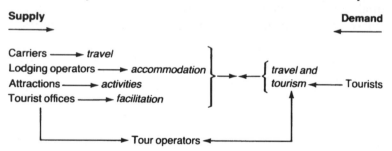

Secondly, there is the need to recapitulate a problem discussed briefly in Chapter 1—that of divergent perceptions of tourism between suppliers and consumers. Since most consuming tourists consider a business or a vacation trip as a single (albeit major) purchase, then it should be possible to identify a single, coherent demand side to establishing an equilibrium position. As has been seen, however, suppliers very often tend to view things differently, in the context of individual product sectors.

The perceptual conflict is demonstrated in Figure 6.1, which gives some examples of suppliers and the views they may have of the products they are supplying, compared with those of tourists. Debate continues about what a 'tourism product' really is (Smith 1994).

In a market economy which is essentially driven by effective demand, one way to resolve the divergence is to assume that demand for each of the sectoral products—attractions, lodging and so on—is a *derived* demand emanating from overall travel and tourism markets. In some cases this demand is solidly routed via tour operating middlemen; in others the 'middleman' may be implied. The result is that disequilibrium in one sector may easily, via overall tourism markets, cause disequilibrium in others; hotel accommodation shortages in a destination can mean airlines lose demand on routes to that destination, and the reverse is equally true. So many suppliers (particularly airlines) have diversified into related sectors such as lodging, leading to an integrated supply (Hudson 1969 and Hudson 1972).

It is an inherently straightforward step then to examine the market equilibrium in any one sector of travel and tourism as a *partial* equilibrium, contributing in some way to a *general tourism equilibrium*. The latter may not be directly identifiable, but can be assessed indirectly through measurement of each sectoral partial equilibrium, in the same way that the general equilibrium of an economy as a whole is made up of the partial equilibria achieved in the economy's constituent industries. Although the remainder of this chapter is principally concerned with these partial equilibria, for the various sectors of travel and tourism, we must remain mindful of the aggregate 'tourism equilibrium' balancing a (fragmented) supply against an integrated demand (see Leiper 1993).

■ Factors causing shifts in equilibrium

Given the general nature of tourism supply (outlined in Chapter 5) and demand (outlined in Chapter 3), a generalized view of equilibrium in a travel and tourism market might appear as in Figure 6.2:

Figure 6.2 assumes a short-run situation where demand for tourism in a destination market *in total* DD_1 reflects price 'stickiness' caused by differentiated product attributes and imperfectly competitive suppliers. Supply SS_1 reaches a capacity quantity at Q_c, and the load factor or occupancy rate is $0Q_e/0Q_c$ % at an equilibrium price level of P_e. If there were sufficiently long horizontal sections of both the demand and supply schedules at P_e, it is possible that there would be no unique equilibrium quantity Q_e, but rather a range of quantities which could be regarded as satisfying equilibrium.

Effects of taxation on tourism

Governments frequently impose (or reduce or remove) taxation on tourism products, both to raise revenue and to discourage or encourage the consumption of particular types of tourism. Some examples are:

- airport departure tax
- 'bed' tax (hotel room tax)
- permits for entry to destination areas
- entry/transit visas
- exit visas
- duty free goods (tax reduction or removal).

Figure 6.2 Equilibrium in tourism

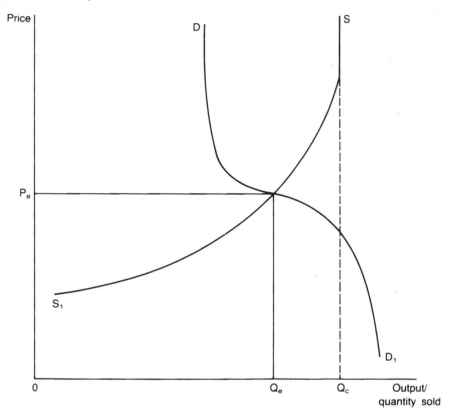

These types of tax may effectively change the price of the travel and tourism product to the consuming tourist. The amount of the price change will depend on the type of tax and its incidence. Any tax on something which would otherwise be free, and which is collected directly by the taxing authority, such as a fee-bearing entry permit to a national park area, of course falls directly on purchasers, with the total price of the tourism product increasing by the full fee amount. But where a tax is imposed on an item which is already priced to sell commercially in the marketplace, sellers may not be able to pass on the full tax amount to buyers unless demand is totally inelastic. This is demonstrated in Figure 6.3. To consumers, supply SS_1 shifts upwards to $S*S*_1$ to reflect the imposition of a tax such as bed tax. The new equilibrium position depends on the elasticity of demand over the range under consideration.

If demand is relatively inelastic, hoteliers are able to pass on most or all of the tax in higher rates; but with elastic demand, they will be forced to absorb the tax themselves in order to compete.

Research has found, as shown in the example in Figure 6.3, that the incidence of such tax tends to be shared between suppliers and tourists (Mak

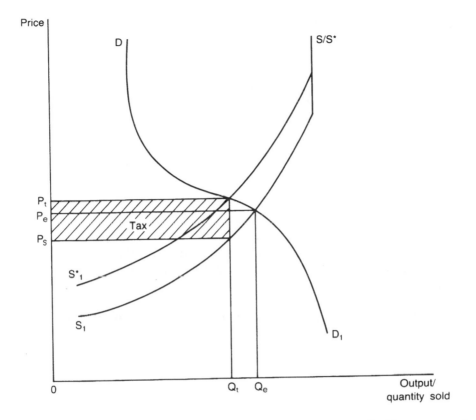

and Nishimura 1979, Mak 1988). Here tourists are paying P_t–P_e extra, and suppliers absorb P_e–P_s, now receiving P_s as a net price. Hiemstra and Ismail (1993) have found that for hotels in the United States, demand for rooms drops by 4.4% in the face of a 10% price rise, and that the tax burden is shared, 6/7 by hotel guests, and 1/7 by suppliers. This is highly significant, especially in a place such as New York City, where the total tax rate on hotel rooms whose rate exceeds $100 (almost all of them!) was 21.25% in 1992–93 (Wolff 1993).

Removing tax (such as duty on normally dutiable items) does not, on the whole, boost tourism where duty free purchasing is regarded as an 'extra' by consumers, but it occasionally has a significant impact (the reverse of that above) where there is an element of duty free driven tourism. Examples are cross-channel trips between the United Kingdom and France, and specific trips to duty free ports such as Hong Kong or Andorra. Not only is duty free shopping a significant tourism product—the Allders International duty free supermarkets at Heathrow Airport, London are reputed to have the second highest retail turnover of any shop in the United Kingdom—it may also subtly redirect tourism flows: many tourists traveling via the Middle East choose airlines which stopover at Dubai because of the very cheap prices on duty free products.

Equilibrium and price controls

Tourism cannot provide as many examples of intervention to control prices as can basic commodities and consumer necessities. Nonetheless, there are occasions when governments intervene in specific sectors to establish set prices, price bands or maximum or minimum prices. Domestic airfares in many countries are still controlled, lodging rates may be price-banded in line with compulsory classification systems, and of course foreign exchange is frequently subject to controlled rates. There is no problem when controlled prices are in line with what a free market equilibrium would set; but where this is not true an excess demand or oversupply can result.

As an interesting example, assume that international tourists visit a country whose currency, the *zilch*, is fixed artificially high. Tourists are unwilling to convert as much of their home currency, say dollars, as they would like because of the high rate. This is demonstrated in Figure 6.4, where the would-be free market equilibrium supply and demand for zilches (for tourist purposes) is shown at P_e.

Figure 6.4   The effect of an artificially high controlled tourism exchange rate

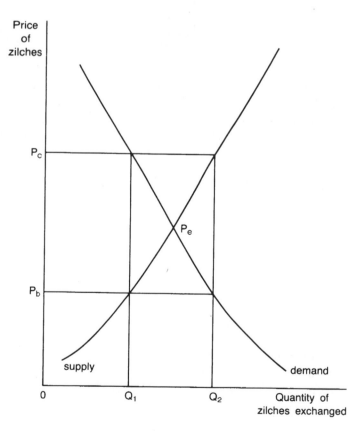

If the controlled exchange rate is held at P_c zilches to the dollar, there is an 'oversupply' of zilches in the sense that tourists are only prepared to buy Q_1 zilches with their dollars, and $Q_2 - Q_1$ represents an unfulfilled willingness by suppliers in the destination country to 'earn' more tourist dollars. This oversupply in the official foreign exchange market may be countered by a black market trade. To balance the oversupply of $Q_2 - Q_1$, a black market rate of P_b would be required to create extra demand for $Q_2 - Q_1$ zilches by tourists. Many countries have seen black market rates for tourists at less than half of official exchange rates.

Although the above analysis covers only one aspect of visitor spending, there may be significant effects on equilibrium in *total* travel and tourism to that country. If there were no black market, tourists could be less inclined altogether to buy visits to that country, and so not just the currency, but lodging and all tourism facilities, may be oversupplied.

Rationing to allocate travel and tourism resources

There are some travel and tourism markets in which price plays little or no role, and in which it is therefore very difficult to establish what is an equilibrium level of activity. In particular, this is the situation in those centrally planned economies where tourism is viewed as a social right; this has for many years been defined as *social tourism* (Hunziker 1951). Social tourism schemes ration out vacations and other tourism opportunities by government or trade union allocation, usually to workers or to underprivileged groups. Governments in these economies decide what facilities and expenditure to commit to social tourism programmes, so that tourists themselves have little choice in demand, but acquire tourism free or at a token price.

Social tourism rationing cannot identify an equilibrium position, since supply response to market conditions does not exist, and latent demand can only begin to be made effective through political lobbying. Any efficiency-maximizing planners will at least attempt to ensure that capacity in accommodations, carriage, recreational facilities and so on will be fully utilized all the time, even if this means mid-winter beach holidays for some. In turn this may lead to more enlightened planning and feasibility studies for acceptable, all-year tourism products.

■ The dynamics of equilibrium in tourism

As in many other markets, equilibrium in travel and tourism is not a static position but changes over time. Analyzing the dynamics of supply and demand here is of particular use in two situations: seasonal shifts in the short run, and the processes of long-term tourism development. In both cases there are disturbances to markets which may or may not result in some form of equilibrium stability.

Assume a hypothetical short-run situation where travel and tourism suppliers have no clear idea of likely coming seasonal demand for their products. They may attempt to pitch prices to fill capacity, but find that demand falls very short at those prices. How can this market approach equilibrium?

Given the pressure exerted on producers by cost structures to supply at or near full capacity, travel and tourism markets tend to exhibit conditions leading to *Walrasian stability* in the short run (Henderson and Quandt 1971, Paraskevopoulos 1977). That is, adjustments are made through the price system rather than suppliers attempting to change quantities supplied (the *Marshallian stability* condition). In this (Walrasian) case fares, room rates and so on may be cut, but at the same time seasonal demand increases produce an excess demand. Suppliers respond, probably after an adjustment lag, by raising prices again, but once again these may not find equilibrium. Given relatively inelastic supply, the result is a standard dynamic cobweb of oscillations, as depicted in Figure 6.5, leading to a stable equilibrium (or rather a set of equilibria for different seasons), at least until seasonal patterns change.

Figure 6.5   Dynamic cobweb of lagged adjustment in tourism markets

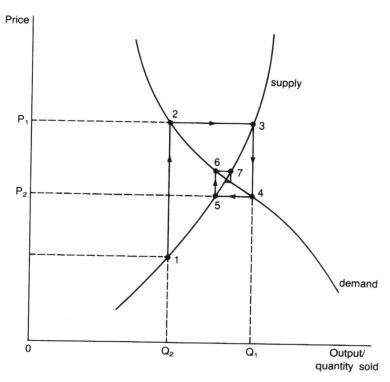

With the original price level set at P_1 in the *expectation* of demand Q_1, tourists actually demand only Q_2. When this happens, suppliers adjust price to P_2 which stimulates demand. (If seasonal demand is added, the whole demand schedule also shifts to the right). Provided supply is inelastic compared with demand, the oscillations progressively reduce to a stable short-run equilibrium.

Long-term dynamics

During a period of tourism development for a particular destination, or sometimes at the other end of a destination's life cycle (a period of decline), the lags between supply and demand responses may be greater, and eventual stable equilibrium may not occur. Assume that a government or private developer initiates a tourism development of some kind in time period **t'**, having undertaken a feasibility study to assess the viability of the investment (see Chapter 13). Let this be termed development **A**. On completion in time period **t'+1**, the development is marketed —that is, there is a supply. Because of the nature of tourism products, high demand may not arise immediately, as tourists who cannot sample before purchase wait for word-of-mouth recommendations before making a buying decision.

If the development is successful, demand may increase rapidly in period **t'+2** as positive referrals by opinion-leaders are quickly disseminated through personal contacts and the media to the 'fashion followers' who will rush to the new development. Prices may have been fixed and publicized in advance, so that a sudden excess demand cannot be cleared by price increases. Development A is now seen to be unable to satisfy demand, supernormal profits may appear to be available for new entrants, and in period **t'+3** developments **B** and **C** are built. By the time B and C join industry supply in period **t'+4**, A has raised prices to 'skim' profits, demand has fallen a little, and the combination of A, B and C produces an oversupply again.

A, B and C may now promote, possibly co-operatively, to encourage the 'early mass' tourist market. If successful, period **t'+5** may see another excess demand for tourism, inducing yet more entrants. The process is summarized in Figure 6.6.

This ratchetlike development effect is often found in travel and tourism development, for example with golfing and leisure resort development in Hawaii, mass-market transatlantic air services, and international hotels in Singapore. The chance of an eventual stable equilibrium market depends on:

• the nature of demand schedules (Samuelson 1989), where if, say, supply and demand exhibit equal elasticity, oscillations around equilibrium may persist
• the length of the lagged adjustment time periods, and whether suppliers have sufficient time to adjust prices or reconsider development plans *before* disequilibrium occurs.

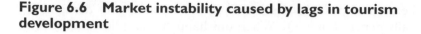

Figure 6.6   Market instability caused by lags in tourism development

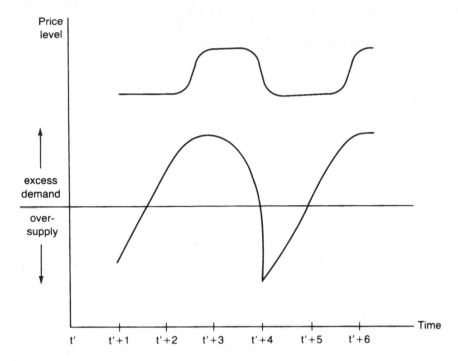

Although many developers and other tourism entrepreneurs entering new markets utilize sophisticated feasibility techniques, and highly complex investment appraisal models are available (see, for example, Powers and Powers 1977), the nature of the travel and tourism sector, its inherent attractiveness to new entrants and decreasing market regulation are strong factors causing development disequilibrium. Eventual stability is not always certain.

■ Long-term cycles and tourism in general equilibrium

As has been seen, travel and tourism markets make up part of the general economy of both generating and destination areas. Where these are different economies, as with most *international* tourism, tourism markets are interacting with different areas of those economies, and calling on different resources, as depicted in Table 6.1.

Table 6.1   Resources called on by travel and tourism

In generating areas	In destination areas
consumer incomes	land
consumer time	property/buildings
labour for selling/	labour for lodging/
marketing/transport	destination services
capital: investment in	foodstuffs
transport equipment	fixed capital investment
business travel time/	marketing expenditure
expenditure	lodging & operational
selling enterprise	enterprise

Whilst the economic activity in these two areas, and the resources called on, are not by any means wholly mutually exclusive, there are many differences, and it is misleading to refer only to tourism in destination areas as being of consequence to other sectors of the economy (including unpriced sectors) as some texts do. In *domestic* tourism, of course, these classification problems do not arise.

Within destinations, tourism competes with sectors including agriculture, forestry, general retailing and housing for factors of production such as land and property. A disequilibrium in any one of these may have consequences for tourism and vice versa; for example, an excess supply of sugar in Barbados and other Caribbean states in the 1960s caused many entrepreneurs to reallocate their skills, as well as local land, labour and capital, towards destination tourism, which for a while then became oversupplied. Tourism also competes in other sectors through demand for products; many analysts of the impact of tourism in less-developed countries have noted that food markets may be pushed out of equilibrium as tourist demand for food is added to local demand. However, in other ways tourism markets may *complement* other destination sectors—the effects of complementary equilibrium can be examined from a semi-macroeconomic point of view by input-output analysis.

In generating areas there is a major interaction between tourism and other economic activity through labour markets (supply of labour) and leisure preference. Potential tourists, both business and recreational, must spend time as well as money to purchase travel and tourism, and time is their own 'product', to be committed in some ways such as to a minimum working week, but elsewhere subject to *reservation demand* (Baumol 1977) where people wish to reserve some time for themselves. It has been noted that as wage rates rise, people's reservation demand for their own time is subject to substitution and income effects. They are encouraged to substitute more work for leisure if leisure becomes more expensive (that is, if the opportunity cost of leisure rises as wage rates rise), but income effects are often stronger, and the reverse of those for normal consumer products; as wages rise people can afford more, and may choose more leisure. Frequently this leisure time is used for increased tourism.

In generating-area economies therefore, disequilibria such as excess demand for some products may cause employers to wish to expand supply, requiring more labour, and perhaps the offer of higher pay. In a 'satisfied labour' market, this may simply result in a higher demand for leisure and tourism.

With business tourism, demand may be generated when other sectors are *in depression*, as producers decide they need to send sales forces out to generate demand for their products (depending on their own cashflow and selling method preferences). When most sectors are booming, there may be less of a desperate need to 'put sales people on the road'.

Since the travel and tourism sector is therefore sometimes competitive with, and sometimes complementary to, other sectors in both generating and destination economies, its cyclical nature can often run quite differently from that of a general economy. This has sometimes been a major factor in government decisions to stimulate a tourism sector. Its contribution to general equilibrium, assuming a Walrasian-type model can exist, may also vary substantially from year to year. The following chapters examine the general role of travel and tourism in a macroeconomic framework.

Study questions

1 Explain how it is possible to identify equilibrium in tourism when there are divergent product perceptions by suppliers and consumers.
2 Do tourism taxes fall on tourists, or suppliers?
3 Show how controlled exchange rates may influence tourism market equilibrium.
4 What could cause the dynamics of equilibrium in tourism to become unstable?
5 Find a local example where tourism shares a resource with some other activity. If the other activity has excess demand, or excess supply, what happens to tourism market conditions?

Growth and change in tourist demand —the case of central Florida

The state of Florida is, after California, the second most highly-visited of the United States. It attracts over 40 million tourists a year, about 7 million of whom are international visitors. Tourism is the state's largest industry. Domestic visitors spent an estimated US$49 billion in Florida in 1991, creating 1.5 million jobs (and so employing 24% of the total labour force). Through the 1950s and 1960s, Florida became renowned particularly for its sunbelt attractions to the senior citizens' market, with the greatest destination emphasis on Miami and other parts of Southeastern Florida. Many visitors came to stay, with the result that the state has the highest proportion of retired residents in the United States.

During the 1970s and 1980s, development emphasis shifted to Central Florida, around the city of Orlando. One of the primary catalysts was the construction of over 20 theme parks, especially Walt Disney World. Rather than attracting senior citizens, these products have catered mostly for families with children, and spawned a huge lodging industry within the local area. They have also become a major base attraction for international tourists, thus generating growth in traffic and terminal facilities at the local airport.

The 1980s and 1990s have seen the growth of conventions and meetings tourism. This has developed, partly because there is lodging and meeting space available in off-season periods, and partly because many delegates (about 70%) wish to combine business with recreational activity, accompanied by partners or perhaps their whole families. The Orlando region hosts corporate meetings, conventions of associations, and trade shows and exhibitions.

Tourism Statistics Central Florida

Year	Tourist nos. Florida	Tourist nos. Central Florida	Hotel rooms Central Florida	Occupancy rate (%)
1988	36.7 m	10.8 m	64 500	76.5
1989	38.6 m	12.0 m	69 500	82.0
1990	40.9 m	13.6 m	76 300	77.6
1991	40.3 m	13.1 m	82 500	71.6
1992	41.0 m	14.0 m	88 000	73.0

The 1992 figures are estimates. The decline in tourist numbers and occupancy in 1991 was mainly due to the Gulf War. Of Central Florida's room capacity in 1992, about 13 500 rooms were in hotels primarily serving conventions and meetings markets, together with about 1.5 million square feet of meeting and exhibition space. Conventions and meetings tourists numbered some 2.5 million.

Major theme park visitation (1991)

Park	Owner	Visitors (millions)
Walt Disney World / EPCOT / Disney-MGM Studios	Disney	28 m
Universal Studios	MCA-Universal	6 m
Seaworld	Anheuser-Busch	3.4 m

Aspects of tourist demand

Senior citizens have the longest length of stay, but with fixed incomes their demand is often price-elastic. Demand is higher for Southeast Florida than for other areas. Aggregate demand, however, is relatively stable, and long-term growth is likely due to the 'greying' of America. Competitive destinations are those offering a similar pattern of climate and recreation.

Families travelling to Central Florida, mostly to visit theme parks, stay on average 6 days. Half of these use a hotel or motel, and 70% or more arrive in a private vehicle. The vacation purchase is likely to be made from discretionary budgets. Demand is seasonal in relation to school and college vacations. Theme park entrance charges are a major item, and it is important that they are 'known' in advance. There are fewer competing destinations in the large theme park market.

International visitors frequently use inclusive tours, with discount prices negotiated by operators, so that revenue received per person may be lower. However, they create demand for airport services, public transportation, auto rentals, and spend more on souvenirs than domestic visitors. Demand conditions in individual generating countries may vary, so that a fall in demand in one market may be compensated for by growth in another.

Conventions and meetings delegates stay for shorter periods, averaging 4.2 days, but price elasticity of demand is likely to be lower, especially if expenses are deductible. Demand varies with business activity in the United States rather than with personal income levels. In 1989 the Orlando Convention and Visitors Bureau found that delegates spent an average of $623 per person during their visit. Orlando is one of the United States' most popular convention cities, but there are many possible substitutes.

Overall, some 60% to 65% of visitors are from the Northeastern United States, so total demand is sensitive to changing economic conditions in that region. Because of the demographic structure of Florida, there is a shortage of labour in many sectors of tourism, so that expansion is easiest where there is a low labour input need for increased production.

Discussion question

What are the main constraints on demand for tourism in Central Florida? Which, if any, are common to all markets, and which differ between markets? Are all markets of equal economic benefit to the destination?

Tourism supply in Prague, the Czech Republic

Communism, together with its centrally-planned command economy, was toppled in Czechoslovakia in 1989, during what has been called the 'velvet revolution'. Privatisation of the economy began in 1990, through the Act of Private Enterprise and the Acts on 'small' and 'large' privatisation passed through legislature in 1990 and 1991. Privatisation has continued, through a period in which the country split into two: the Czech Republic and the Republic of Slovakia. The number of private enterprises in existence has more than doubled annually since 1990, and the Czech stock exchange opened in 1994.

The capital, and largest city, of the Czech Republic is Prague, a city with medieval heritage and capital of the former kingdom of Bohemia. Its physical heritage, together with its historical, cultural and locational importance, have made Prague into a major tourist-attracting centre within a very short period of achieving open access to and from Western European countries. Prague is within two hours' drive of Germany, Austria and Poland, and within a day's drive from Italy, Switzerland and Hungary. It is estimated that between 40 and 80 million people now visit the city annually (including day visitors), of whom 6 million or more are international visitors staying at least one night. In addition to recreational tourists and excursionists, there are increasing numbers of business tourists, as the Czech economy opens up to international investment and competition.

To meet this demand, there is a range of suppliers, from state-run organisations, through newly-privatised businesses and new entrepreneurs, to foreign-owned or foreign-backed suppliers. The ability to supply, the industry structure (of each sector), and the suppliers' objectives vary between sectors.

Basic historic attractions

The major attractions of Prague are public buildings and monuments from the 14th to 16th centuries and the 19th century. In the city central area, there is a well-defined 'tourist zone' which encompasses the Old Town, centred around the Old Town Square, the 14th century Charles Bridge over the Vltava River, and the area across this bridge, known as the Lesser Quarter, leading up to the Prague Castle and cathedral complex on its hill. Most of the monuments are either church-owned or state-owned. The owners are responsible for upkeep, which is expensive, and entry may or may not be free. For example, there is general free entry to the Prague Castle and cathedral complex, but within the complex there are six specific attractions where users pay (the cathedral crypt and steeple, the powder tower, the St George Basilica, the Old Royal Palace and Royal Gardens). Prices are low: Combined entry to all six attractions cost about US$2 in 1993–94. Other museums, churches and so on are scattered around the city.

Accommodations

Prague possesses about 3 300 international-standard hotel rooms (1993 estimate by Pannell, Kerr, Forster), including those in internationally-affiliated chains such as Diplomat, Inter-Continental and Penta. Planned developments by Holiday Inn, Marriott, Hyatt and Conrad did not proceed, principally because of the uncertain investment climate and complexities of Czech procedures on private investment. The 15 or so major 'A' grade hotels are accompanied by another 20 or 30 'B' grade establishments, some of which are very traditional European style. Because of relative shortage, occupancy rates are high and room rates vary between US$80 and US$250—relatively expensive by European standards for the quality offered. Prices include 23% value-added tax.

In addition, there are backpackers and other hostel accommodations, ranging from cheap rooming houses (around US$15 per person) to 'hotels' established by universities and suchlike in their residential accommodation complexes, at around US$50 to US$100 per room.

Finally, many private householders let rooms in their residences, mostly through touts, soliciting at transport exchanges and other areas where tourists arrive. 1993 prices were around US$10–15 per person. In high season, accommodations are easy to sell.

Restaurants, cafes and bars

Food and beverages are mostly available in traditional Czech establishments such as a 'pivnice' (beer hall), 'vinarne' (wine cellar) or restaurant. They are relatively few, and meals are relatively expensive. Macdonald's, pizza houses and other Western style establishments have opened since 1990, but not in large numbers. New investment in food and beverage outlets is slow, apart from outdoor cafes in places such as the Old Town Square. In many establishments, as in many hotels, service standards demand more patience from consumers than would be the norm in Western Europe or North America. The service economy is underdeveloped throughout the country, and there is no recent tradition of full-time or part-time employment in tourism. For example, the Czech Republic and Austria are neighbouring countries. In 1993, tourism employed:

- 4.8% of the Austrian workforce, but
- 0.9% of the Czech workforce.

Transportation

Public transport is still mostly government-owned. State railroads (CSD) and bus systems (CSAD) operate to and from Prague. Prices are cheap by international standards—around US$1.50 per 100 km. Within the city, a modern Russian-built metro (subway) system, and older trams and buses provide comprehensive services at around US$0.13 per ride or per hour. A small number of Czech enterprises have started to provide tourist excursion buses at much higher fares (although many tourists arrive and travel around on their own excursion buses from other countries), and there is an increasing supply of private enterprise taxis. These are licensed, and operate at set fares.

The Czech airline CSA has been 40% owned by Air France and the European Bank for Reconstruction and Development since 1992, is buying newer aircraft, and is attempting to be a competitive supplier against Western airlines. Prague airport is still State owned. The airport authority is expanding the facilities, with the intention that the airport becomes a main European hub.

Agencies, tours and foreign exchange

The state-owned tourism office, CEDOK, was broken up in 1992–93. Its business included inbound and domestic tour operation, tourist buses, 90 travel agencies and four Prague hotels. The business was privatised in 1993.

More notably, there are scores of new, small private travel agencies and tour businesses emerging, often with minimal capital outlays. Some, for example, offer three or four-hour walking or minibus tours around Prague for around US$5–6. Others specialise as agents for private accommodations, on commission. Many congregate in leased premises around the tourist zone or near the central railroad station. The same is true for perhaps 50 to 60 foreign exchange dealers, in their small shopfront offices, who compete with established banks. Exchange rates varied enormously until 1990, between official high rates for the Czech koruna and very low black-market rates. Since then, the deregulated market and competition ensure that rates are very similar.

Shopping, souvenirs and entertainment

In the 'tourist zone' of Prague, there are a large number of souvenir outlets and retailers of Czech products such as Bohemian crystal. Prices and quality vary. Along the main pedestrian 'tourist trail' from the Old Town to the castle, and particularly on the Charles Bridge, there are up to 200 hawkers, buskers and merchants with stalls. These must each hold a license from the city authority, but compete with each other with open prices in a lively and noisy free market.

Tourist entertainment varies from state- or church-sponsored arts events and festivals to privately run cellar style jazz clubs and discos. There are 12 casinos, the bulk operated by German and Austrian businesses. Gaming taxes take 70% of net revenue for the government. Real revenues have fallen since 1992, suggesting that there is oversupply of gaming establishments in the city.

Discussion question

In Prague, which sectors of tourism supply seem to represent constraints on tourism markets, and why? What general factors have allowed suppliers and competition to flourish in some sectors, but have inhibited supply in others?

Tourism growth and national economies

■ Introduction

Having examined some of the microeconomics related to travel and tourism, and in particular the roles of tourists in demand and tourism organisations in supply, this chapter now turns to address some of the wider aspects of tourism in the economy—the *macroeconomic* role and consequences of tourism.

In many economies, the travel and tourism sector has for some time been recognised as a major area of activity which both draws upon the resources of those economies and affects their nature and development. Additionally, governments have increasingly seen fit to use tourism as a subject or agent of macroeconomic policies. Tourism often has a high involvement in policies related to employment levels or the balance of payments, whose significance in modern macroeconomic management is high.

■ The national economy

The size and value of a national economy is normally expressed as the total value of all goods and services produced by that economy during a specified time period, such as one year. For convenience, we can call this value a country's *Gross Domestic Product*, or *GDP*, although this simplifies a few calculations about the exact sources and uses of some of these goods and services. The two main elements of GDP are goods and services produced for *consumption* (C), or use in their own right, and those produced for fixed capital formation or *investment* (I) in capacity to produce further goods and services.

This simple definition GDP = C + I assumes that an economy is closed to foreign trade. As this is an unrealistic assumption for almost all economies, we should include the value of all *exports* (X), but exclude that of all *imports* (M), of goods and services during the chosen time period. The definition is then improved a little, and reads GDP = C + I + X − M.

Many macroeconomic statistical series use *Gross National Product* or *National Income* as the defined measure of a national economy. These involve further refinement in measurement; Gross National Product (GNP) excludes from GDP such factor receipts as property income from overseas, on the grounds that this money has really been generated in the overseas, rather than the home, economy. National Income can be defined as the net amount earned by the economy's factors of production, which means deducting the value of assets 'used up', or capital consumption, from GDP. Because, however, different series and reports use different measures, we shall mostly use GDP as our measure of a national economy.

Travel and tourism is likely to figure in all aspects of GDP. First, most expenditure by tourists would be regarded as consumption spending (C), if it is for domestic tourism or for the home-provided elements of an international trip. Secondly, expenditure by businesses on buildings, plant, equipment and so on to provide tourism services is part of investment (I), much of which is likely to be government expenditure, especially on infrastructure. Thirdly, a tourist who is spending money in a foreign country or travelling on transportation services owned by other countries is in a sense 'importing' services. This expenditure is a leakage from the national economy. Finally, the reverse situation provides an 'export', when a country can sell its transportation or tourism services to international tourists from elsewhere.

■ Factors affecting tourism's contribution to GDP

Variations in tourism's roles in, and contributions to, national economies in different countries are caused by a number of factors. Some of these are demand-side factors (that is, the importance of tourism is partly determined by the strength of domestic and inbound demand for local tourism), but the ability of a tourism sector to expand within an economy to satisfy these demands and create more depends more frequently on supply-side factors. Tourism in this respect is no different from any other sector.

It is possible to identify five major factors which determine tourism's role in GDP. In each case it is likely to be the *nature* of these factors *within the tourism sector relative to other economic sectors*—or the 'average' situation within an economy, rather than their absolute values, which are determinants.

I   The stock of resources

Economic activity depends first and foremost on the stock of resources available to use as factors of production. In traditional economic terms, these include the resources of land, labour, capital and enterprise. As seen in Chapter 1, travel and tourism make some special calls on particular resources concerned with land and its attributes, and the uniqueness or simple possession of these attributes can ultimately dictate whether or not an economy is likely to be able to support a tourism sector.

The role and activities of modern tourism, however, demand far more than just land attributes. Most tourism involves some element of service, which requires a competent and willing labour force. Whilst many jobs in the industry may not require a very high level of traditional skills or qualifications, the presence or absence of a pool of labour with a positive *attitude* towards tourism and tourists is of vital importance (De Kadt 1979). Equally, an economy's willingness and ability to supply the capital investment required for a tourism industry, in the shape of infrastructure, hotels, transportation and so on, will influence the size to which that industry can grow.

2   The state of technical knowledge

Many less-developed countries have regarded tourism as an easy industry to develop, because it demands relatively low technology compared with many other industries, and skills which can be easily mastered. Unfortunately, as tourism worldwide has grown and become more sophisticated, high-value contributions to GDP by tourism have tended to become associated with higher technologies. Examples range from the ability to operate fleets of large cost-efficient aircraft with the associated technology in reservations and passenger handling, through to technical innovation in providing more interesting, all-season attractions. When technical advances are applied to existing inputs of other resources, they enhance the productivity of the industry concerned and hence its contribution to GDP.

Certainly there will always be a place for low technology tourism, particularly whilst there are market segments which deliberately seek out the simple or natural life (current fashions in 'ecotourism' support this view), but dominant cultures in tourism-generating areas will ensure that returns within tourism sectors will continue to be high where supported by good technical knowledge and applications.

3   Social and political stability

Non economic factors, particularly cultural and political ones, have long been recognised by economists as vital in determining the capability and growth of sectors in an economy. In tourism this is especially important. Since 'consuming tourists' must go to the 'factory' to buy the product, social and political conditions in that 'factory' will directly influence the acceptability of the product and therefore the success of the industry. We may continue to buy goods imported from a country in political turmoil but are unlikely to want to visit it.

In fact, social and political stability has been cited as a *characteristic of the tourism product* (Van Raaij 1986, Woodside and Lysonski 1989), which for many tourism segments directly influences demand. As social and political conditions may be far more variable in a destination than, say, the stock of productive resources, they are more likely to be responsible for short-term fluctuations in the value of the tourism sector.

4   Attitudes and habits

Another major non economic determinant is that of psychosocial values, both of suppliers and consuming tourists.

First, the attitudes of a host population towards tourists, and in particular those of workers within the tourism sector, are an important facet of the tourism product, and their influence is similar in nature to that of social and political stability. A purchaser of a pair of shoes probably cares very little about the morale, attitudes and motivations of the workers in the factory that made them, but a tourist will be directly affected by the attitudes of those supplying tourism services face-to-face. Negative attitudes in Spain during the 1970s, for example, began to have such a serious effect on tourism that the government ran promotions advising 'be nice to tourists—they are your bread and butter'.

Secondly, on the demand side, tourism consuming habits are important. Two generating markets with similar levels of income may, all things being equal, have different *propensities to travel* (Burkart and Medlik 1981). This may be a function of cultural and traditional values, attitudes, or the quality of climate and physical surroundings at home. The propensity to travel will influence domestic tourism and the development of the sector in any destinations closely linked to those generating areas.

5   Investment

Economies which possess a good stock of resources available for use in tourism may have a head start in developing the sector, but the level of investment or *fixed capital formation* which an economy undertakes is increasingly important. Compared with heavy manufacturing, for example, tourism has not traditionally required such substantial investment in plant and equipment per dollar of output, yet some areas of the industry are becoming more demanding of fixed capital formation—notably passenger carriage, accommodation and infrastructure.

As will be discussed in Chapter 13, some investment is required to replace worn-out capacity, such as replacing old aircraft or worn-out hotel furnishings. However, an industry which is both heavily influenced by fashion trends, and hosts its customers in its 'factory', must inevitably invest in new and expanded facilities as part of its competitive strategy. An economy's ability and willingness to provide finance for such investment influences tourism's role in that economy. This in turn depends on savings patterns, the nature of financial markets, and rates of return available in tourism compared with other industries, coloured by general perceptions of the sector and government support for it.

■ Problems in measuring tourism's contribution to GDP

Estimating the value to an economy of any sector is always a tricky procedure. Estimating the value of a service sector is perhaps even more difficult than with goods, owing to the non tangible nature of products. Tourism is particularly difficult because of the fuzzy definitions of services included in it. This is true even where reliable government or industry association statistics exist (which is not the case in many states).

Despite these difficulties, most countries still attempt to provide an estimate of the value of tourism, for comparative and planning purposes. This value will be a summary of *private commercial transactions* openly accounted for. As such it may be satisfactory comparatively with other industries or countries. However, it will be inadequate to permit an accurate assessment of the 'real value' of the sector, because it will omit some positive and negative items, the most important of which are:

- unpaid services
- non accounted services
- notional costs
- public and private revenue distribution
- balance of payments anomalies
- social costs and benefits
- public goods.

Unpaid services are those performed for no payment, or a payment in kind or reciprocity. If no payment of any kind is made, one can argue that no economic activity has taken place even though the service exists, but an economic transaction certainly exists for a reciprocal or barter payment. For example, VFR tourists receive 'free' accommodation from their hosts; if they reciprocate or give their hosts some other services or 'presents', there is a true but unrecorded transaction.

Non accounted services are those which take place and for which payment is received, usually in cash, but are not accounted for formally. This may be to avoid taxation, wages regulations or for simple convenience; the overall result is sometimes designated the *black economy*. Non accounted services are very common in travel and tourism, particularly in hospitality, taxi driving, souvenir selling and so on, where there is often much part-time work, gratuities and second jobs or moonlighting. Many researchers have attempted to estimate the size of the black economy, but by definition this is almost impossible.

Notional costs are those which relate in principle to activity A, but are accounted for within activity B. One example in tourism comes from second home ownership. If a vacationer buys a second home, which appears simply as a once-and-for-all property purchase, that home may be used for vacations. Owners then pay no recurrent accommodation costs, but may be considered to be paying a 'notional rent' to themselves equal to the commercial rental value of their properties. This is part of the 'real value' of tourism.

Public and private revenue distribution concerns the distinction between sourcing and using revenues earned by the private sector in one area, but spent by the public sector in another. For example, if a government levies a tourist tax and uses this revenue in expenditure on agricultural support, it must be decided whether tourism includes the gross value of transactions, while agriculture includes nothing, or whether tourism includes the value net of tax, with the tax being included under agriculture. Otherwise there would be double counting.

Balance of payments anomalies in areas such as tourism investment, repatriation of earnings, and foreign exchange values of tourism revenues expressed in floating currencies, cause measurement problems. This will be discussed in Chapter 10.

Social costs and benefits are the differences between the value of private commercial transactions and their value to an economy or society as a whole, including third parties. Travel and tourism brings benefits, but imposes costs, on third parties in many ways, in such a way that the *social net product* of the sector may be quite different from the *private net product*. It has been suggested (Samuelson 1989) that this can be accounted for throughout an economy by using the Nordhaus-Tobin measure of Net Economic Welfare for an economy rather than GDP. Social costs and welfare resulting from tourism are receiving increased attention from economists (Clarke and Ng 1993). This issue will be taken up in Chapter 9.

Public goods are in a sense part and parcel of social benefits, and will also be reviewed in Chapter 9. Governments are increasingly aware of the 'value' to society of, for example, national parks, outstanding scenery or heritage buildings, for which no tourist entrance price has hitherto been charged. The 'real value' of tourism might include the notional prices that users may be willing to pay, multiplied by the number of users.

■ International comparisons of tourism in GDP

Given the need for caution in the above areas, it is possible to identify only broadly the 'real value' of tourism to an economy, but it is at least possible to make some reasonably realistic comparisons between private commercial transaction values. Table 7.1 shows a summarised set of figures based on travel and tourism receipts and published GDP figures for a number of major economies.

Table 7.1   Estimated contribution of tourism to GDP
1992 figures in standardised US$billion ('000 m)

	International receipts	Domestic receipts	Total	GDP	Total/ GDP %
Australia	4.4	14.0	18.4	325	5.7
Belgium	3.7	1.0	4.7	230	2.0
Canada	5.8	20.0	25.8	605	4.3
France	23.6	65.0	88.6	1400	6.3
Germany	12.0	35.0	47.0	1950	2.4
Italy	22.0	35.0	57.0	1330	4.3
Japan	4.0	19.0	23.0	3600	0.6
Netherlands	4.5	2.0	6.5	325	2.0
Spain	21.7	18.0	39.7	620	6.4
Sweden	3.0	3.0	6.0	270	2.2
Switzerland	7.7	7.0	14.7	270	5.4
UK	13.5	20.0	33.5	1200	2.8
USA	53.9	360.0*	413.9	6050	6.8
Average					4.3

Sources: adapted from NTO/ individual countries' statistical offices, WTO and IMF data.

[Note: great care should be taken with comparisons in this table as different countries include different elements in tourism expenditure, different methods of data collection are used, and some figures, such as United States domestic tourism expenditure, are government estimates. *Estimates of the value of United States domestic tourism range from US$280 billion to US$650 billion]

The data in Table 7.1 are derived mainly from receipts for travel and tourism expenditure. Domestic tourism receipts would be part of C + I (consumption + investment expenditure), whilst international tourism receipts measure the destination income contribution of tourism (that is, they are part of X). Replacing international tourism receipts with international tourism spending *elsewhere by nationals of the countries concerned* alters the figures in the sense that they show tourism's share of the use of GDP rather than contribution to it. Table 7.2 summarises the changes.

Differences between tables 7.1 and 7.2 reflect the balance of payments on a country's external account (see Chapter 10), so that those in the left column of Table 7.2 are net tourism generators, and those on the right net destinations. In these economies, which are not only amongst the economies with highest GDP but also with the highest expenditure and receipts on travel and tourism, the contribution of the sector to National Income tends to be in the range of 2–7%, the exception being Japan. Japan has a huge and highly diversified economy, and tourism has until recently been a relatively 'un-Japanese' activity in terms of work ethics and holiday-leave taking. Coupled with this, high relative prices in Japan and language and cultural difficulties have not been conducive to a high level of recreational international tourism to Japan, and the contribution of less than 1% to Japanese GDP reflects this.

Table 7.2   Effect on measuring tourism and GDP by residents' expenditure rather than receipts (i.e. replacing international receipts by international expenditure)

Contribution increased			Contribution reduced		
	change	to		change	to
Belgium	+1.7%	3.7%	Australia	−0.1%	5.6%
Canada	+0.8%	5.1%	France	−0.9%	5.4%
Germany	+1.0%	3.4%	Italy	−0.6%	3.7%
Japan	+0.6%	1.2%	Spain	−2.7%	3.7%
Netherlands	+1.0%	3.0%	Switzerland	−0.5%	4.9%
Sweden	+1.1%	3.3%	USA	−0.2%	6.6%
UK	+0.5%	3.3%			

Sources: as Table 7.1

On the other hand, countries such as France, Spain, Switzerland and the United States have for many years been amongst the world's leading international tourism destinations, which means that tourism makes a rather greater contribution to their national economies.

Many smaller economies of course have a higher tourism contribution, particularly from international tourism, and where few alternative industries exist, as in some Caribbean and South Pacific island states. (For current data see the *Revue de Tourisme* (Tourist Review), AIEST, St Gallen, Switzerland, or *International Tourism Quarterly*, EIU Publications, London, UK.) It has not been unusual in such economies to find tourism accounting for 10–25% of GDP (Demas 1965, Britton 1980, Sathiendrakumar and Tisdell 1989), where tourism is likely to be one of two or three staples of the economy. Extreme examples are 52% (of GNP) for the Bahamas and 58% for Antigua (Archer and Fletcher 1990). Such a level of dependence is relatively unhealthy, leaving GDP vulnerable to single-sector climatic, political or trade cycles.

If we compare the *net values of tourism* between economies, the picture is changed, particularly for countries which are tourism generators but not major destinations. Net value of tourism includes:

domestic + inbound − outbound tourism expenditure

which mirrors the concept of C + I + X − M in GDP. Some net contributions are shown in table 7.3.

The tourism sectors of Belgium, the Netherlands and Sweden show a net drain on GDP since outbound tourists spend more outside those countries than the combined expenditure of domestic and inbound tourists.

Tables 7.1, 7.2 and 7.3 in practice allow different comparisons: 7.1 shows the contribution of the value of tourism production, 7.2 the 'demand' on GDP or National Income of tourism expenditure by residents, and 7.3 the

Table 7.3   Net contributions of tourism to GDP

(domestic + inbound – outbound expenditure)	% of GDP
Australia	4.4
Belgium	–0.4 (a net drain on GDP)
Canada	2.5
France	5.4
Germany	0.7
Italy	3.2
Japan	0.0
Netherlands	–0.5
Spain	5.6
Sweden	–0.1
Switzerland	3.3
UK	1.2
USA	5.1

Source: as Table 7.1

net contribution to national accounts. Care must be taken in analysing any such figures to ensure that the correct series is chosen for analytical needs.

Globally, tourism contributes around 4.0% of the world's gross product by value. More than 75% of this is domestic tourism, heavily influenced by receipts and expenditures in major economies such as the United States. 4% may appear small, but it is comparable with the global value of major industrial sectors such as mining or transportation. Some estimates suggest that tourism will account for 8% of world gross product by 2010 (Source: WTO, Chase Econometrics), which may well make it the world's largest 'industry'.

■ Methods of measurement

Measurement is a major problem in analysing tourism's contribution to GDP. Outside a black economy, it is relatively easy to measure the total output value of, say, agriculture—particularly in an economy with regulated marketing boards or production quotas and guaranteed prices. Travel and tourism services however, even if they can be identified as such, are sold directly to thousands and millions of individuals who themselves may not be identifiable as tourists. Services and goods may be sold at varying prices, and records may be inaccurate. In addition, different countries use different methods of measuring the value of travel and tourism expenditure/ receipts.

Tourism analysts have identified four main basic measurement methods (Frechtling 1987a):

- direct observation of expenditure
- direct observation of receipts
- surveys of tourists
- household surveys.

In addition, *simulation models* can estimate expenditure, and there are some specific extra methods available to regulated economies, such as *bank returns*.

Direct observation of expenditure

Ideally, to follow tourists everywhere and record their expenditure would provide an accurate record of a consumption approach to GDP contribution. This is patently impossible, and would even be difficult to accomplish for a sample of tourists whose results could then be multiplied by total tourist numbers. The only feasible alternative lies in getting a sample of tourists to diarise their own expenditure.

Direct observation/census of receipts

A direct income approach to valuation results from aggregating all sales receipts figures from tourism enterprises. This information may come from government trade ministry census returns or tax returns, rather than from direct point-of-sale observation. Analysts have noted that whilst tourism sales values by travel businesses or carriers are reasonably accurate, values from entertainment, recreation, lodging and similar businesses are less so, simply because many suppliers cannot distinguish fully between sales to tourists and sales to non tourists.

Surveys of tourists

En route or in-destination sample surveys of tourists are used widely in tourism value analysis. They can be fairly reliable except for recall bias, and unfulfilled intentions (in a survey carried out when a tourist stay is unfinished-ed). For those passing through entry or exit points to a destination, *gate methods* are available—that is, entry or exit surveys. These are popular for use with international tourists at exit ports. Another problem is that to multiply expenditure by tourist numbers is easy enough for international tourists, where immigration records are held, but domestic tourist numbers are frequently no better than a 'guesstimate'.

Household surveys

It is possible to estimate tourism expenditure at the generating point by household surveys, in which general household expenditure can be disaggre-gated and tourism spending isolated. Coupled with an analysis of business travel expenses from tax returns, these can provide a reasonably reliable picture of tourism-generation expenditure.

In practice many analysts combine the above methods, and may further build them into simulation models of various kinds. For example, a known breakdown of tourism and non tourism spending in a travel sector can be applied to estimate the tourism component of expenditure in a lodging sector, or one can multiply known process of tourist products by estimated visitor numbers. Most such models are *aggregative models*—that is, they build up a total value for travel and tourism from individual sector or local area expenditure. A good example is the *Travel Economic Impact Model* of the United States Travel Data Centre (see Frechtling 1987a). Alternative approaches include *disaggregative models*, which like input-output models usually involve other sectors of the economy, and *difference or estimation models*, such as Kreutzwiser estimation (Smith 1989). The latter assesses local community 'buying power' or consumption C_l and compares this with actual local total consumption expenditure C, attributing the difference to expenditure by tourists C_t. That is, $C_t = C - C_l$.

Bank returns

In some circumstances, other methods of tourism value measurement are available. In economies whose foreign exchange controls are tight, and where incoming international tourists must spend in the local currency (assuming import and export of that currency is not permitted), the total value of personal foreign currency exchanges reported by banks often provides an estimate of foreign tourists' spending.

In summary, the reliability and accuracy of any of these measurement methods is doubtful, so many analysts use more than one method to cross-check results.

◼ Tourism growth and its effects on an economy

A simple representation of an economy such as that in Figure 7.1 shows the major flows of goods and services, or money in exchange, and the major component 'players'.

In Figure 7.1, monetary flows are defined as follows:

C = consumption spending I = investment G = government spending
Y = factor payments (incomes) M = imports T = taxation
S = savings X = exports

So far, we have identified the bulk of travel and tourism value in the economy through C and I, for domestic recreational and business tourism expenditure, X for inbound international tourism, and M for outbound international tourism. These tourism expenditures circulate throughout an economy, and the sector may also be important in other areas.

Tourism receipts by businesses are transformed into payments for factors of production—rent, wages, interest and profits—which swell income (Y) and

Figure 7.1 Diagram of a simplified national economy

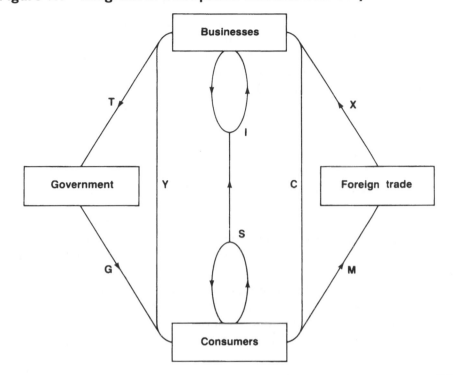

provide consumption tax and income tax revenue (T) to governments. The *recirculatory* effects of changes in the value of tourism will be examined in the next chapter. Other direct injections and leakages also take place through travel and tourism. Governments may stimulate development of a tourism industry through grants and loans, and by undertaking their own fixed investment (G); if the capital required is obtained from capital markets by government or private businesses, there is a direct increase in I. Outbound tourists take expenditure out of an economy equivalating an import (M), but the method of funding trips may also affect the economy: tourists intending long expensive trips may put aside money towards the trip for some time, either in advance or by credit instalments afterwards. In the short term this may represent increased savings (S), and less consumption of other items.

Airlines and tour operators also affect short term capital markets in the same way. By obtaining payments in advance for many types of ticket and ITs, but postponing their payments to suppliers as long as possible, they maximise saving on short and medium term money markets. At the beginning of the summer peak European holiday period, up to US$4 billion ($4000 m) may be supplied in this way.

As tourism grows, the effects vary in different flows in the economy, according to the structure of the economy and changes in the type of tourism. Some of these effects will be examined in Chapter 8.

The effects of inflation

Tourism's role within a growing economy can be altered by inflation. Classical economic theory holds that production of most goods will be stimulated by the anticipation of rising prices, partly to ensure that input factors are acquired as soon as possible before their price rises, and partly in anticipation of selling output later at higher prices. Because of the 'instant' production and sale of most tourism services, however, tourism production rarely responds in the same way. Firms making investment decisions will also discount their potential cash flows by the expected rate of inflation, which may reduce their willingness to invest. In addition, if consumer price increases run ahead of increases in incomes, then a higher proportion of consumption (C) will be needed for buying basic everyday goods and services, leaving less for (discretionary) tourism expenditure.

Inflation also alters the balance of domestic and international tourism. If prices at home rise, tourists may be more inclined to take foreign trips as substitutes, diverting expenditure from C to M in our model—see also Chapter 10.

Finally, tourism itself may bring demand-pull inflation to a destination economy or region. Pressure of extra demand where supply is inelastic translates into higher shop, accommodations and transport prices. This effect has been widely noted in research papers and is discussed in Chapter 8.

■ Forecasting the value of tourism

In order to provide for policy and planning, many governments and other institutions attempt to forecast aspects of tourism activity. In the context of GDP, the most important forecasts are those of tourism demand (in numbers of tourists—domestic, inbound and outbound), and tourism expenditure either in absolute terms, or relative to the rest of GDP. The variables are usually:

- numbers of tourists
- total expenditure or per capita expenditure
- tourism market shares, or
- the tourism sector share of GDP.

It is important to ensure that the variable selected relates directly to the forecast data need (Sheldon 1993). Forecasting expenditure is valuable in finding tourism's *relative contribution* to income or GDP; forecasting tourist numbers is more helpful in assessing the call that tourism will make on *resources*. Five main methods are in use for tourism forecasting of this kind. They are depicted in Figure 7.2 (and discussed more fully in Var and Lee 1993).

Qualitative methods are perhaps the least well-known in tourism forecasting. They include brainstorming, executive consensus and Delphi methods, and

Figure 7.2   Basic tourism demand/value forecasting methods

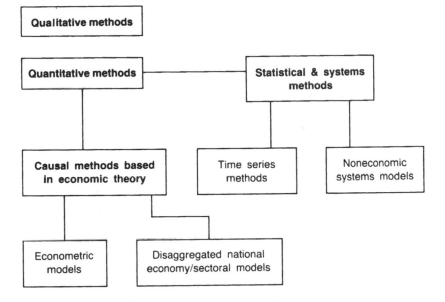

have tended to be used most by commercial organisations in predicting their own demand, such as IATA for air traffic demand. They are sometimes considered less rigorous than quantitative methods (Archer 1987, Var and Lee 1993), but are appropriate where data is insufficient or unreliable for quantitative forecasts. They have been used to forecast tourist numbers in places such as Canada, the United States and Thailand.

Quantitative forecasting divides broadly into techniques founded in economic theory and techniques which are purely statistical or borrow 'systems' from other disciplines. In forecasting terms, comparison of their usefulness can only be made on their accuracy of prediction rather than explanatory or analytical elegance, so that causal model forecasting is not always superior to straight statistical techniques. Statistical techniques include time series analysis of various kinds, with trend extrapolation and seasonal analysis (BarOn 1975) being of major importance; they also include systems models such as spatial models (gravity models, intervening opportunity models and so on), Box Jenkins I, market share analysis and analogous simulation models (Renoux 1973).

Almost all of the above methods are univariate or bivariate, and apply to a single dependent tourism variable, normally either tourist numbers or tourism expenditure. They are rarely used in other aspects of tourism's contribution to, and pull on, GDP. For these variables, and for simultaneous forecasting, causal economic theory based models are more popular (Martin and Witt 1989). These models are normally either econometric forecasts of single variables or sectoral models, whereby tourism values may be forecast as sectors of disaggregated national economy values.

Typically, econometric models include price levels, foreign exchange rates, consumers' incomes and dummy variables for special events in specifying determinants of demand or tourism flows (see, for example, Loeb 1982, Witt and Martin 1987). Often the purpose of such analyses is explanatory rather than predictive, but results are frequently very good in predicting international tourism (Witt 1992)—perhaps less so domestically. Some models attempt to link tourism with the rest of an economy; this is the case, for example, with the Dutch Ministry of Economic Affairs tourism market model (Van Dijk *et al.* 1991). Sectoral analyses may include input-output models (see Chapter 8) or multiple interactive econometric models of an economy (such as the Cambridge model in the UK or ORANI in Australia). These models not only look at tourism demand but also at sectoral investment, income, taxation collected, and other transactions which make up the total contribution of tourism to the economy. Both single variable econometric models and multi-sectoral analyses are likely to use lagged effects of determinants in their formulation, creating 'rolling' forecasts (Fritz *et al.* 1984).

Since the role of most tourism forecasting is to provide reliable 'future data' to help tourism and economic policy decision-making, it follows that forecasters are more concerned with predictive accuracy than with explanatory power and statistical elegance. High technical standards of econometric modelling do not necessarily improve the forecasting ability of such models compared with more naive methods (Witt and Witt 1990), so that a mix of methods is sometimes more appropriate (Witt 1992). Accuracy is not cheap, however, so that lower cost (and more understandable) methods sometimes prevail, such as using simple spreadsheet methods (Sussman and Fletcher 1994).

The most sophisticated modelling can also be of value in planning an 'ideal' contribution of tourism (or any other sector) in terms of opportunity costs of resources used, commercial returns by sector, risk spreading to avoid an economy's vulnerability to the trade cycles of particular industries, and any other important policy requirements. The results of forecasting on an 'as is' basis can then be compared with the (presumed ideal) contribution of tourism to an economy in order to help government planning for the sector.

Study questions

1 Define GDP. How can it be measured?
2 Identify the major factors determining tourism's contribution to GDP in the country in which you live.
3 Demonstrate how there is an interaction between a country's economy and its population's propensity to travel.
4 Why is it difficult to measure tourism's contribution to GDP?
5 Suggest reasons for the differences (in both domestic and international tourism contribution to GDP) between the Netherlands and Spain (see Table 7.1).
6 Compare the four main methods of measuring tourism's value. Why do you suppose they might yield different results?
7 Identify one example of tourism's value in each of: C, I, G, T, X, M, S and Y.
8 Critically assess the likely accuracy of each method of forecasting tourism.

CHAPTER

8

Employment and income creation

The value of tourism expenditure is by itself fairly meaningless. It is the nature of the economy within which it is spent, and the use that is made of the money, that determine its ultimate usefulness. Analysts have concentrated on tourism's effects on *income and employment*, although there is increasing interest in the way tourism can influence other things, such as investment and price levels.

■ National income

Standard macroeconomic analysis such as that based in the work of Pigou or Hicks identifies both classical and Keynesian features which determine and influence the size and volatility of an economy's national income. These include the levels of saving and investment, the pattern of consumption, prices and interest rates, government and external sector imbalances, and the degree to which resources (including labour) are fully employed at any one time. Since tourism activity is involved in most of these areas, it follows that it can have direct influences on national income, especially in those countries such as Spain, Bermuda, Cyprus or other island states where tourism represents a sizeable proportion of GDP.

In a basic closed economy (or one in which the government plays a neutral role, and there is a zero external trade balance) the level of national income is determined by the total value of consumption (C) and investment (I) in any one time period. Income distributed may be spent on further consumption or saved (S). The total C + I or C + S may or may not yield full employment. Assume that people at some point wish to consume more—that is, the *propensity to consume* increases. This may be because of expectations of later price rises, a change in social attitudes, or other reasons. The effect may be an increase in general prices if producers do not wish to produce more or the economy is already at full employment (demand–pull inflation), or producers may expand output to meet the increased demand, and so GDP and national income increase. If businesses wish to increase their investment in fixed productive capacity (perhaps because they anticipate good future demand, or to take advantage of new technology) the economy will, all else being equal, expand to provide the new investment products, and later expand again through output of all products from the new investment. This once again may expand national income.

In an economy where government plays an active budget role through taxation (T) and government expenditure (G), and where export and import levels (X and M) do not balance, net *inflows* or *injections* to the economy (G – T > 0 or X – M > 0) are likely to have the same effect. A net export surplus allows foreign investment to build up (Samuelson 1989), or the acquisition of later imports without cost. However, net positive government expenditure, like increased consumption, may be financed through credit—which may not only be inflationary, but may drive up interest rates and affect business investment. Net *outflows* or *leakages* from an economy (G – T < 0 or X – M < 0) can reduce the value of national income as money flows out to government or to foreign suppliers—the latter becoming creditors to the economy.

Investment decisions, which will then induce further expansion in national income, are influenced by the need to replace worn-out productive assets, but also by interest rates and expectations. A government's monetary policy can control both of these, as it can go some way towards controlling the general level of consumption through consumer credit and the supply of money.

■ The distribution of national income

Not only is the size of national income, including *per capita* measures, important to an economy, but so is its composition and its allocation (distribution), as is demonstrated by Figure 8.1.

A large and diversified economy will have many productive sectors and little sectoral concentration. It will be less vulnerable to cycles and specific slumps than a small economy based on few sectors. This has a particular importance for the value obtained from developing tourism.

The way in which national income is then split up also helps determine the size of the economy. For example, two economies with similar populations may start with similar GDP in time period 1. Suppose in country A the distribution of incomes is very even, as is the distribution of shared wealth in productive capital. People are likely to spend and save in similar ways, other things being equal, and economic growth should smoothly reflect the

Figure 8.1   Composition and distribution of national income

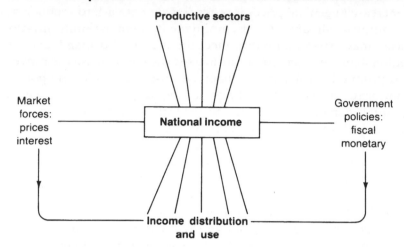

country's marginal propensities to consume and save. Suppose, however, that country B's production is in the hands of few individuals or businesses, and that it is highly automated, requiring plenty of capital but little labour. Economic growth probably depends on export markets or reallocative government fiscal policies; propensities to save amongst the majority of the population are probably zero, and imbalance-based political instability makes prediction of country B's future national income very risky.

Whilst classical economic theory assumes that income distribution will, through market forces, correct itself to reflect the marginal productivities of factors of production, economists have shown that this does not always happen (Kaldor 1955). Because of market imperfections, social systems, regional imbalances or other reasons, a 'steady state' income distribution can exist which does not reflect marginal productivities. Policies for development, including tourism development, may then promote not just income generation, but normative goals of income distribution (see, for example, Lin and Sung 1984).

■ The direct value of tourism to employment of factors

In the above contexts, travel and tourism has a significant impact in many economies. First, it is a sector of relatively recent development in many economies, and is still showing growth in most. Most countries now identify travel and tourism as a discrete productive sector of their economies, which was unusual until the 1960s or 1970s. Secondly, because travel and tourism can assume many different forms, from backpackers' 'meet the locals' experiences through business trading and convention centres to segregated exclusive up-market resorts, an economy may need only *minor structural changes* of resource reallocation into tourism. This attracts governments looking for development opportunities. Thirdly, tourism can often be developed specifically in locations and with resources which have little alternative economic use (that is, low opportunity costs), such as picturesque landscape locations with no mineral resources and little agricultural value. This allows the direct employment of land as a factor at little marginal cost.

The direct (and indirect) impacts of tourism on an economy are one of the most intensively researched areas of tourism analysis (Mathieson and Wall 1982, Eadington and Redman 1991). In particular, many writers have concentrated on local impact studies and tourism in less-developed countries. There are some general principles which apply in virtually all cases, which will be examined here.

The direct value of domestic tourism

Within an economy, domestic tourism expenditure normally counts as part of C + I, and therefore is principally a reallocation of consumers' or producers' spending from something else. It does not therefore provide an injection of fresh demand and money. The reallocative effects will depend on answers to the following questions:

1 What was the opportunity use of the cash spent on tourism? i.e. what would tourists have done with their money if they did not make tourist trips?
2 Do tourists 'spread out' their spending spatially (regionally)?
3 Are the destination areas generally less well off than generating areas in terms of incomes and employment?
4 Do trips induce tourists to return permanently?

The first question provides a key to the value of domestic tourism in a couple of important ways. First, if the alternative to domestic tourism were foreign tourism expenditure, then by spending domestically there would be a form of *import substitution* (see Chapter 10), reducing the leakage of M and actually increasing C + I. This directly benefits national income. The same is true if the alternative to a domestic trip were spending on imported goods. Secondly, if, rather than buying tourism, people bought goods and services at home (such as home improvements or entertainment), income and wealth would tend to be concentrated in the areas which would otherwise be generators.

The answers to the second and third questions carry this a little further. If domestic tourists spread their activity spatially, there is a redistributive effect on income and employment. Concentration or 'localisation' of tourists can be measured (Defert 1966, Pearce 1987), and highly localised domestic tourism tends to create local excess demand, price increases (see later), and may actually reduce real incomes in destination areas. If destination areas start with underemployment and comparatively low incomes, tourism will create employment and may raise incomes, depending on the structure of the tourism labour market. This means:

- there can be a reduction in government spending (G) as unemployment payouts are reduced
- there may be an increase in taxation revenue (T) from newly earned incomes, although this depends on threshold tax rates and the opportunity use of tourists' expenditure
- marginal propensities to save may fall slightly, as tourists' spending transfers income to less well-off recipients who would tend to have a higher propensity to consume.

The fourth question frequently provides a key to long-term development of tourism destinations and hence to the spatial redistribution of economic activity. Tourists have visited coastal destinations in many countries, liked them, and retired there—providing a permanent demand base. Others who are entrepreneurs in 'footloose' industries may decide to relocate their businesses to pleasant areas they have visited as tourists; an example is the relocation of research, computer and electronics firms to California and Florida (Doering 1976). Such moves in the United Kingdom, backed by government policy, have decentralised economic activity from London and other major cities, and unless firms have taken all their staff with them the moves have created local employment, frequently at national award wage rates.

The direct value of international tourism

The main direct benefit to national income of inbound international tourism is the injection of money and demand from an external source. This is equivalent to an increase in exports (X) regardless of whether the spenders are recreational or business tourists. The major difference between tourism revenue and goods export revenue is that the latter often generates an overseas credit, similar to an increase in I, whereas in most cases tourism expenditure physically takes place inside the receiving country on goods and services which are normally regarded as consumption items.

Other than international balance of payments effects, which are summarised in Chapter 10, two other major impacts may result from inbound tourism:

- demonstration effects
- pressure on price levels.

Demonstration effects from international tourism have been studied over a long period (for example, Bryden 1973). Particularly in less developed countries, residents observe and learn the lifestyles and consumption patterns of inbound tourists, and may seek to emulate them. In economic terms this may engender changes in consumption patterns, and result in, say, a higher propensity to import those consumer items which tourists are seen to have.

Therefore M rises and partially offsets the value of increased X, a phenomenon researchers have noted in places as distinct as the Caribbean, the
Canary Islands and Fiji.

Where tourists come from a country with generally higher incomes and
price levels than their destination, they may bring *price pressures* with them.
This is a form of imported inflation, but differs from the normal concept (that
high priced imports increase local costs), as it works through extra demand
pressures and the demonstration effect. Figure 8.2 shows the effect on the
local general price equilibrium if large numbers of tourists arrive.

Figure 8.2   Tourism-imported inflation

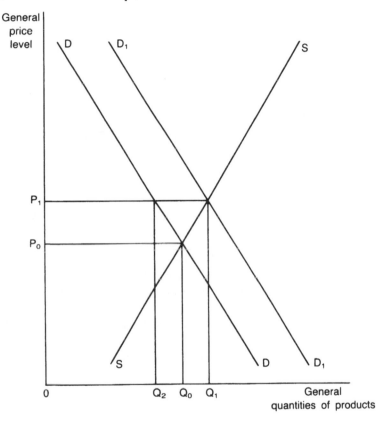

In the absence of international tourism in this economy, the general equilibrium
is at P_0Q_0. The arrival of relatively rich tourists shifts demand from DD to D_1D_1,
moving the economy to a new equilibrium at P_1Q_1 —more products are traded,
but at a higher price. Unfortunately, local consumers are disadvantaged, as they
may now only have quantity Q_2 for themselves at price level P_1.

In practice, locals probably also receive these higher prices to the extent
that they are responsible for local supply, and there will be increased
employment and income. However, at least some of this well-being is likely
to disappear in higher prices, and locals wishing to sustain their living
standards may force prices (and total demand) up yet further as they compete

with tourists for available supplies. This has happened with foodstuffs in many parts of the world, with property for second homes in places such as Spain, Wales, Denmark, the Caribbean and Hawaii, and even with everyday artefacts which become souvenirs.

One result of 'rich tourist' arrivals may be the development of dual markets with separate prices for tourists and locals. Sometimes these are officially sanctioned, as with property rentals in many states; elsewhere dual markets may develop informally through product differentiation (souvenir hawkers congregating only at tourist attractions and selling at relatively high prices despite bargaining), or through 'spot the tourist' methods of price discrimination. In this way incomes and employment are generated without exposure to inflated prices.

Finally, there may be a range of individual direct impacts in specific circumstances; a good example is the contribution to taxation (T) made by tourists to Monaco who gamble in the Monte Carlo casino. In fact this contribution, which is mainly from international (non-Monegasque resident) tourists, provides all of the government revenue required in the state.

The direct value of travel and tourism in generating areas

Very few researchers have attempted to analyse the value, if any, of tourism to generating economies. Certainly any international tourism activity means a reduction in national income in these economies, as travel away represents a leakage (M). However, *mass tourism generation*, at least, is likely to produce:

- employment in travel agencies, tour operators, transport undertakings and enterprises engaged in marketing destinations
- investment by carriers and tour operators, and the possibility of developing multinational tourism enterprises
- a possible fall in seasonal price levels whilst tourists are away and demand is slacker
- increases in short-term saving (S) as people 'put by' for trips, or businesses hold pre-payments on money markets
- a source of taxation revenue (T) on those items purchased before or on departure.

■ The distribution of tourism-generated income

The direct (and indirect) impacts of tourism expenditure depend on the ways in which the receipts are allocated—which in turn depend on the ownership and resource utilization of the tourism supplying sector. Intensity of use of

Figure 8.3   Use of factors in tourism production

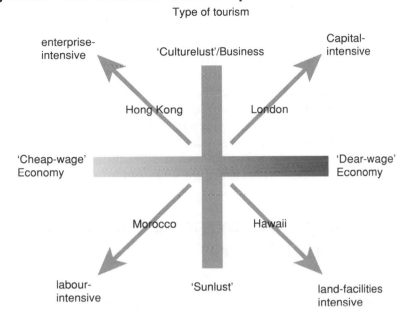

Type of tourism

enterprise-intensive

'Culturelust'/Business

Capital-intensive

Hong Kong   London

'Cheap-wage' Economy

'Dear-wage' Economy

Morocco   Hawaii

labour-intensive

'Sunlust'

land-facilities intensive

factors of production depends not only on factor productivity but also on the type of tourism provided. Figure 8.3 provides a very rough guide to the basis of production expected in different cases.

The horizontal axis in Figure 8.3 shows—as an example only—a continuum from an economy where wages are relatively cheap compared with other factors of production to one where they are relatively dear. On the vertical axis lies a range of tourism types, from the business or culture centre to the destination principally offering sun, sea and sand. Destinations tend, all else being equal, to possess a tourism sector whose income is distributed in relation to the intensity of factor use. Thus for $1 spent on a trip to Morocco, more employment is likely to be generated (though not necessarily a higher number of cents taken out for wages) than with a trip to London, where the dollar is likely to be 'used' more in returns to capital such as financing hotel property costs or paying for phone calls.

The distribution of returns to factors of production in tourism therefore depends not only on the marginal productivity or efficiency of each factor, but also on the type of tourism. In 'sunlust'-based less developed countries, tourism normally provides increased employment, though not always with high wages, which increases C directly. In higher-wage economies, tourism development may mean a call on land and fixed investment, for sophisticated transport systems, resort development and gazetting of National Parks. This ties up revenue in financing investment (I) (including land holding), and the effects of tourism on the economy then depend on who supplied the capital and what they do with the interest income.

In tourism generally, as with other industries, capital–labour ratios are changing to reflect the use of increased technology and, as demands grow, the increasing costs of land and land-facilities in relatively fixed supply. However, the process of labour replacement in travel and tourism is slower than in many other industries, because of emphasis placed both by producers and consumers on the characteristic of *personal service*. Where this is considered important (whether in travel agencies, airline cabin service, hotel restaurants or TICs), labour inputs will remain high. Thus even in a high wage economy there will still remain labour-intensive tourism enterprises such as the Ritz Hotel in Paris or American Express special business travel services. If consuming tourists want this service characteristic, they are usually prepared to pay for it, and direct employment and the allocation of income to wages remain high.

■ Secondary employment and income 1: tourism multipliers

One of the most discussed areas of tourism in relation to a country's economy is that of the impact on secondary employment and income, and hence the 'flow through' caused to that economy other than in direct or primary effects. A number of techniques have been used for assessing secondary impacts, of which the main ones are *tourism multipliers* and *input–output analysis*.

Tourism multipliers have been developed over some years based on largely Keynesian principles of the recirculation of a proportion of income by recipients into consumption spending, which then engenders further income and employment (Archer 1977, Holloway 1989, Frechtling 1987a). The basis of a simple multiplier is that a direct injection of cash into an economy, by, say, international tourism expenditure, means a higher income for suppliers of tourism services. This will be distributed partly as wages and salaries, rent, interest and profit, and partly as *indirect income* to suppliers of goods and services needed by tourism enterprises. The latter indirect income, distributed to food and beverage suppliers, electricity and phone companies, fuel distributors, printers and so on, is also distributed in further factor and supplier payments.

Recipients of all the above increased incomes then may spend or save these increases. To the extent that they choose to spend on goods and services produced in their home economy, a round of transactions creates increased *induced income* for the secondary suppliers, who then themselves have more to spend, and so on. The principle is summarised in Figure 8.4.

The value of the simple multiplier shows the total amount of income, or whatever variable is being measured, in relation to the initial injection or tourism expenditure. In the example in Figure 8.4 the initial expenditure is $1000, of which $500 is re-spent in the economy from indirect and induced

Figure 8.4   A basic tourism multiplier at work

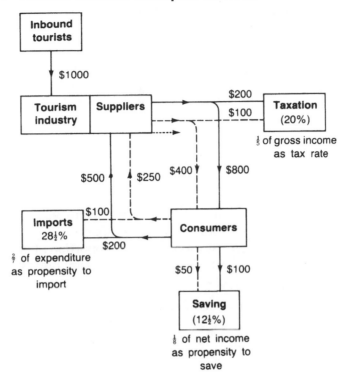

income. Of this $500, $250 is recirculated, and so on. The total value of income created, over some time, is the sum of the geometric progression:

$$\$1000 + \$500 + \$250 + \$125... = \$2000$$

As the total income value of $2000 is twice the initial expenditure of $1000, the value of the multiplier in this case is held to equal 2. The value of 2 is directly related to the re-spending habits of income recipients; on each round they re-spend one half of extra income, defined as the *marginal propensity to consume* (MPC). The value of the simple multiplier is the reciprocal of [1 – MPC]:

$$\textbf{Simple Multiplier} \quad = \quad \frac{1}{1 - \text{MPC}}$$

Leakages

The reason why only a proportion (in this example one half) of extra income is re-spent in the local economy is that other calls are made on that income, which remove part of the flow from being re-spent in local transactions. Primarily these calls are:

- taxation on income
- that part of extra income which people choose to save—the *marginal propensity to save* (MPS)
- expenditure on imports.

These losses to the direct re-spending chain are leakages from extra local consumption–income circulation. Since they represent that part of the chain which equals [1—MPC], it is possible to make an alternative formulation of the multiplier:

$$\textbf{Multiplier} \ = \ \frac{1}{\textbf{MTR} + \textbf{MPS} + \{[1 - \textbf{MTR} - \textbf{MPS}] \times \textbf{MPM}\}}$$

where

MTR is the community's marginal tax rate, and we assume the government does not immediately re-spend this on consumption
MPS is the marginal propensity to save, as a proportion of gross income
MPM is the community's marginal propensity to import, as a proportion of consumption expenditure.

Let us invent a fresh example, of an economy where MTR = 20%, MPS on gross income = one fifth, and MPM on consumption expenditure = one sixth. (This differs from our example in Figure 8.4, where MTR was 20%, MPS was 10% of gross income or 12.5% of net, and MPM was 28.5% of consumption.) In this new example:

$$\textbf{the multiplier} \ = \frac{1}{0.2 + 0.2 + \{[1 - 0.2 - 0.2] \times 0.167\}} = 2$$

Although the value of the multiplier has in this instance ended up as the same as that in the example in Figure 8.4, the pattern of leakages is a little different.

Tourism income multipliers

In tourism impact analysis, most multiplier calculations have been applied to income generated, and the multiplier concerned may be termed the tourism income multiplier (TIM). There are two different basic formulations of TIM (Archer 1977, Archer and Fletcher 1990). So far we have assumed that all the original tourism expenditure turned straight into direct and indirect income, but this may not be the case. Some of it may immediately leak into payments for transport operated by foreign carriers, food and beverage imports to satisfy tourist needs, profit and interest payments to foreign-owned or foreign-financed lodging and tour operators and so on. So it is possible to relate TIM either to the total initial tourism expenditure:

$$\textbf{TIM} = \frac{1}{\textbf{leakages}} \qquad\qquad (a)$$

or to the direct and indirect income created by the initial expenditure after deducting direct import leakages:

$$\mathbf{TIM} \ = \ \{1 - \mathbf{MPM_t}\} \times \frac{1}{\mathbf{leakages}} \tag{b}$$

where $\mathbf{MPM_t}$ = the marginal propensity or need to import goods, services and factors to provide directly for tourists' needs.

Formula (a) is sometimes known as the *ratio* or *unorthodox* multiplier, and formula (b) the *normal* or *orthodox Keynesian* multiplier. Both are used, but results should not be compared. Examples of impact assessments using TIM are given in chapter appendix A. It is important to realise that multipliers should only be used to measure the value of *additional* (marginal) income created by *additional* tourism expenditure. Researchers (for example, Archer and Fletcher 1990) have noted how multipliers are sometimes misleadingly and inaccurately used to relate total tourism expenditure to total income.

■ Employment and other multipliers

Whilst TIM is perhaps the most useful tourism multiplier, the concept can be applied to other economic activity, to describe the total impact and relate it to that directly caused by tourism. Some of the main multipliers are:

- The tourism **employment multiplier**. This relates total extra employment created to direct tourism employment brought about by increased tourism arrivals.
- The **transactions multiplier** identifies the increased volume of business activity by sales turnover value, in relation to initial tourism expenditure. In a sense this is like TIM before provision for MTR and MPM, and is sometimes confused with TIM. It should relate however to *gross turnover* rather than *net incomes*.
- The **output multiplier** is similar to the transactions multiplier, except that it includes the value of all goods and services produced rather than sold; that is, it may include additions to inventories.
- The **capital or asset multiplier** assesses the increase in value of an economy's stock of assets, in relation to either tourism investment or tourism expenditure. The important proportion here is not just MPC but MPC and MPI, the marginal propensities to consume and invest. If all saving is translated directly into investment by a perfect capital market, then MPS is the salient proportion from each round of consumption-generated income.

Again, some of the many examples of these multipliers from tourism impact literature are given in chapter appendix A.

Dynamics and factors influencing tourism multipliers' value

As with any multiplier effect, it takes time for the 'rounds' of activity generated by initial tourism expenditure to permeate throughout an economy. Analysis can account for this either by specifying a time period, such as one year, and including only those effects which take place within that period (static analysis), or by examining successive time periods where lagged effects from preceding periods are added to each new period's increased tourism expenditure effect (lagged dynamic analysis).

The value of any tourism multiplier, and in particular of TIM, depends first on the spending patterns of tourists, and secondly on the propensities noted in the formula. A refined multiplier should disaggregate expenditure by type of tourist, because they have different spending patterns (Liu and Var 1982, Var and Quayson 1985). For example, convention delegates may spend a greater proportion of each dollar on accommodation than backpackers; the delegates' spending may be worth more in employment but less in income if the delegates' hotel is foreign owned. A final multiplier will then be the weighted sum of the multipliers for each tourist segment, the weighting according to that segment's total expenditure.

Of more importance is the degree of leakages from income in the destination economy. In measuring tourism multipliers in a large national economy such as the United States, MPM is seen to be relatively low, most taxation is actually re-spent within the economy and is therefore not really a leakage, and national tourism multiplier values are high. In a regional or local 'economy', taxation may flow to authorities outside the region, as may payments for goods, services and factors. These are then leakages to that 'economy' of MTR and, technically, MPM. Regional multipliers are therefore lower than national ones (Sadler, Archer and Owen 1973), although the initial injection of tourism expenditure includes not only that of international tourists but also that of domestic tourists from outside the region.

In addition, regional economies in particular are subject to an apparently high multiplied value of income or employment which is not really newly-created, but actually *diverted from other activities*. Domestic expenditure may have taken place anyway, but not on tourism; employment generated in tourism may not mean new jobs—merely different ones. Clearly, one would expect a net economic benefit anyway, since under these circumstances tourism must have a higher opportunity cost than any other activity from which resources are diverted, but to suggest that all employment and wealth generated is newly created is misleading. Tourism is often more important in redistributing employment and wealth. The larger the region studied, the greater the chance that employment and wealth have been redistributed—within the region—by tourism rather than created (Johnson and Thomas 1992).

One criticism of multiplier analysis is that it assumes constant marginal propensities or *linearity* throughout indirect effects in an economy. This implies stable trade patterns, linear production and consumption functions, and no constraints on expanding the economy. Again in a small local or regional 'economy' these may be justifiable assumptions, but are probably not justifiable in a large national situation.

In practice, researchers have found a wide range of values for tourism multipliers (see chapter appendix A), from virtually zero to over 2.0. Evidently, an economy with a high MTR—not quickly recirculated by the taxing authority —and a high MPM will not benefit greatly from induced and indirect effects. If the tourism industry itself is owned, financed and supplied from outside the economy, even the direct income and employment is dissipated. Thus small countries with a narrow economic base which have sought to introduce tourism as a development catalyst have often been disappointed. The total value of tourism income depends, perhaps paradoxically, on the diversification of an economy's structure and hence its ability to supply most of its goods, services and factors itself (Burkart and Medlik 1981).

■ Secondary employment and income 2: input–output analysis

Whereas a multiplier analysis attempts to estimate the aggregate secondary effects on an economy resulting from a direct injection such as increased inbound tourism expenditure, input-output analysis tries to show how those effects work through an economy, based on the specific supply and demand interactions between different industries or sectors.

Input–output methods as a tool of economic analysis were developed to a relatively sophisticated state during the 1950s and 1960s, and are based on the notion of *transactions* between all producers and consumers in an economy (Leontief 1966). This includes those producing sectors which are consumers of other sectors' output. The concept was originally used for economic planning, but has increasingly been used, and often misused, in other ways.

To build up a set or matrix of transactions it is necessary to:

- define industries or sectors
- identify the total output of each sector and the breakdown of where it goes—that is, whether it goes to other sectors or to consumption *per se* (final demand)
- identify the total inputs of each sector acquired from other sectors, and in particular what marginal inputs are required to make a marginal increase in output.

Most input–output tables use money values, although it is possible to calculate in terms of employment or even land use.

In offering input–output analysis to measure the secondary economic effects of tourism, it is normal to try to isolate travel and tourism as a separate sector (Blaine 1993), although sometimes it is merely included as part of final demand (Morison and Powell 1988). To illustrate, let us assume a simple economy of six sectors: minerals, agriculture, manufacturing, construction, tourism and other services. Table 8.1 then shows a sample *transactions matrix* for this economy.

Table 8.1   A sample transactions matrix

Producing sector	Consuming Sector						Final demand	Total output
	1	2	3	4	5	6		
1 Minerals	5	5	15	10	3	5	7	50
2 Agriculture		2	4	15	2	2	12	40
3 Manufacturing	10	5	20	10	5	5	25	80
4 Construction	5	2	10	3	10	8	12	50
5 T & Tourism	2	2	5	2	2	5	22	40
6 Other services	4	3	8	5	5	5	20	50
Value added	22	19	7	18	13	19		
Total input	50	40	80	50	40	50		310

In this example, the travel and tourism sector accounts for 40/310 of GDP (13%); of its 40 unit output value, 22 units are for final consumption—such things as recreation and VFR. The sector sells two units to the minerals industry—probably business travel—and so on along the row concerned. As a producing sector, travel and tourism requires three units from minerals, two from agriculture and so on down column 5, with the value added of 13 representing the difference between input purchases and value of output (that is, factor returns).

Assume final demand for travel and tourism is lifted by four units as the result of increased inbound visitors. This requires a 10% increase in the value of the travel and tourism sector, which means increased inputs and value added. If we assumed linearity in production, all figures in column 5 would increase by 10%; for example, tourism would now require 11 units of construction. This in turn raises the output required from construction to 51, as well as output from other sectors which in turn require further inputs. The size of the final boost to the economy as a whole depends on the inter-industry transactions requirements. Of course, in practice a more sophisticated model must allow for non linearity in requirements as marginal inputs change, and for rows covering leakages, such as inputs of imports.

To predict directly the secondary effects of increased tourism expenditure, it is possible to use a *direct requirements matrix* which shows the inputs required per unit of output for each sector. For travel and tourism, for example (sector 5 in the table), with a total output of 40, construction inputs are 10, and the requirement per unit of output is 10/40 or 0.25. These input coefficients are shown, for the same example, in Table 8.2:

Table 8.2   A sample direct requirements matrix

Producing sectors	Consuming Sectors					
	1	2	3	4	**5**	6
1	0.1	0.13	0.19	0.2	**0.08**	0.1
2	0.04	0.1	0.19	0.04	**0.05**	0.06
3	0.2	0.13	0.25	0.2	**0.13**	0.1
4	0.1	0.06	0.13	0.06	**0.25**	0.16
5	**0.04**	**0.06**	**0.06**	**0.04**	**0.05**	**0.1**
6	0.08	0.06	0.1	0.1	**0.13**	0.1

It is then possible to see the impact of a $1 increase in tourism expenditure, providing the same assumptions as above are made. The $1 increase means *indirect* spending of 8c for minerals, 5c for agriculture and so on, and the spending generated by resulting demands on these sectors is the flow on of *induced* expenditure. The mathematics of the procedure are adequately presented in many texts (for example, Jensen and West 1986).

Many researchers have attempted to use input–output analysis in tourism, with varying degrees of success (see chapter appendix A). Two major problems are:

• the paucity of data, particularly at a regional level
• specific difficulties with the nature of tourism, such as determining what is and what is not part of the travel and tourism sector.

Additionally, because of the nature of supply schedules in much of tourism, fixed inputs are often under used—hotels or buses operating at half capacity for example. Short term increases in tourism income may be used in paying off loans, or saved as temporary windfall profits to pay bills when demand is slack again, so marginal input coefficients would be tiny. If the industry is already operating at full capacity, increases in demand and direct expenditure could trigger a much more substantial need for new construction, more goods and more services, so that marginal input coefficients change rapidly. This highlights a problem of the technique: it is more suited to static than dynamic analysis. Production functions which change rapidly, as they do in many parts of travel and tourism, require complex computing and data which is frequently unavailable.

Despite these problems, multiplier studies and input–output analysis have tended to be the most widely used means of examining secondary impacts of tourism on an economy. Other methods exist, such as economic base models (Archer 1977), which are variations on these methods, but have not proven to be significantly more useful.

■ Labour markets and employment

Relative to other sectors, travel and tourism has often been shown to be a high employer of labour per dollar of sector income. Thus many authorities have considered tourism development as ideal in soaking up unemployment in regions which have few other employment opportunities, even if those regions have a high income. (This may come about where a region possesses a high value-added but capital-intensive industrial structure with a heavily skewed distribution of resulting income, and few jobs.)

The job value of travel and tourism depends on how one measures employment, and the nature of local labour markets. The *number* of people employed in the sector at some point during the year is likely to be high for four main reasons:

- relative labour intensity
- many low-wage occupations
- much part-time and casual employment
- seasonal peaking.

Labour intensity

As mentioned earlier, some areas of travel and tourism are labour intensive. This is true of front-office situations in travel, lodging, restaurants, souvenirs and small scale tourism activities, and especially in low wage economies. The major reason is the traditional importance of personal service, accompanied by the fact that in many of these areas labour-saving equipment and automation have only been late arrivals. Transport, tour operation and 'back-of-house' activity have, by contrast, a much higher capital-labour ratio in general. Thus in restaurant businesses, it is common to find more capital intensive methods being introduced in food production, but staff numbers being maintained in food service (Kirk 1989).

Another feature of labour intensity in travel and tourism is that of small-scale entrepreneurial activity in 'niche' areas of activity. As tourism production is so fragmented in most economies, there is room, in many roles, for specialists who are largely *labour-only* or *labour-mainly suppliers*. Examples include very large numbers of hawkers and souvenir sellers in cruise ports or at tourism attractions in less-developed countries, scalp hunters or touts at major sports or arts events or outside revue bars in cities from Bangkok to Las Vegas, some cab drivers and instant 'guides' and 'fix-it' people (try Egypt or India). Often technically self employed, their capital investment is usually negligible. Their income is often dependent on pestering ability; it is earned in cash and not declared. Nonetheless they are working in the tourism sector.

When tourism destinations are developed, labour intensity varies according to the type and stage of development (Erbes 1973), and has been found in some cases to be less than in other industries. That travel and tourism creates jobs should not therefore be taken for granted.

Low-wage occupations

Tourism does not necessarily create both employment and income to the same extent. In most economies wages in the tourism sector are low relative to other industries for a number of reasons:

- many jobs are unskilled
- many jobs are *treated by employers* as unskilled even if some level of skill, say in customer service, is really called upon but not recognised
- many employees are transitory, and labour turnover is high
- unionisation and collective bargaining are often weak
- as a result of the transitoriness of labour and weak unionisation, even where minimum wage regulations do exist employers often flout them without reprisal
- in areas where there are few or no alternatives to tourism, there is zero or negligible opportunity cost associated with employment within the industry. With no competitive jobs available, tourism is a monopsonist industry in buying the services of labour, and depresses the price accordingly.

Average wages in hospitality, travel and retailing in North America, Western Europe and Australasia are 5-35% below national average wages (source: government departments of employment statistics and OECD 1992), although wages may of course be higher in secondary employment created by indirect and induced expenditure (Farver 1984). Supplementation of wages through gratuities in many jobs is regarded as normal practice in North America and Europe; there may therefore once again be a discrepancy between recorded incomes and actual receipts.

Where tourism is being newly expanded in less developed countries (LDCs), wage levels are often very low since there may be a large supply pool of labour, which is anxious to secure 'quality employment' in tourism. Employers may also argue that they must spend on basic training, as recruits may not possess even simple reading skills or knowledge of tourists' customs. On the other hand, tourism has sometimes been developed, in the Caribbean for example, where labour supply was quite inadequate (Cleverdon 1979), forcing up wages for both tourism jobs and competing industries.

Higher wages apply where internationally transportable qualifications restrict supply. Qualified passenger airline pilots, chefs with completed apprenticeships or European-trained hotel managers can command high wages internationally; pilots in particular are also often unionised. Even travel consultants with IATA fares and ticketing qualifications can obtain similar real wages internationally.

Part-time and casual employment

There is a distinction between the number of workers employed in the travel and tourism industry and hours of work completed. In virtually all economies a considerable number of workers are part-time, and more are casual, working only for temporary periods when employers consider that final demand warrants taking on extra staff. The use of part-time and casual employees is dictated by two factors:

- with many fixed-capacity enterprises, using part-time and casual labour enables employers to alter some labour cost from fixed to variable
- the nature of most travel and tourism activity requires 24 hour working, or at least work beyond normal business hours; this in turn means split shifts and/ or part-time extra work.

Many such workers are 'moonlighters' taking second jobs, or people not normally reckoned to be in the labour force, such as students. Again, the contribution that tourism makes to economic activity through this type of employment is difficult to assess, as much goes unrecorded.

Seasonality

In most recreational tourism destinations, seasonality means there are effectively at least two labour markets: one for permanent workers throughout the year, and a second market for peak season work. As with casual work, seasonal employment may draw in 'marginal workers', and if demand pressure is high enough, wages may increase. This may draw labour away from full-time employment in other sectors (Mathieson and Wall 1982), forcing up seasonal wages in those sectors or reducing their viability.

Seasonality occurs not only in direct tourism employment but also in indirect work generated by tourism activity. In free labour markets the result is often substantial temporary migration of workers, with consequent shifts of regional income and induced expenditure.

■ Summary: tourism and an economy

The commercial economic value of tourism to a country (presently disregarding economic costs and other externalities, which will be dealt with in Chapter 9) depends therefore on its resources and its structure.

Structure determines *how* a tourist dollar is allocated, in factor rewards, payments to suppliers, taxation, imports and so on. It also fixes the secondary value of inbound tourism, through indirect and induced effects on other parts of the economy. A large and diversified economy, with little government intervention and some spare capacity in factors of production, will tend to benefit most from injections of tourism expenditure.

Resources possessed determine *how many tourists and how much expenditure* there will be to start the system off. Successful destinations, and to a certain extent mass generators, depend on touristic comparative advantage. This advantage is perhaps not the classical advantage of cheaper comparative labour costs, but more the Heckscher-Ohlin view of advantage in productive factor endowments and production intensities, for tourism (Chenery 1961, Moroney and Walker 1966)— see also Chapter 10.

Empirical findings on secondary effects of tourism expenditure

There has been a considerable amount of empirical research into indirect and induced effects of tourism on income and employment, principally using multiplier and input–output analysis. Five good summaries are:

Cleverdon (1979) pp. 32–45; Mathieson and Wall (1982) pp. 68–82; Murphy (1985) pp. 90–99; Archer (1989); Archer and Fletcher (1990).

As expected, national multiplier values tend to be highest, ranging from around 2.5 (Canada: TIM) to 0.8 (Philippines, Bahamas: TIM). Larger, diversified economies such as the United Kingdom, Canada, Australia, Pakistan and Greece have yielded orthodox multiplier values in excess of one, whilst LDCs and small island states face considerable leakages. Their TIM values range around 0.7–1.2, although employment multiplier values are higher, reflecting low wages. Transactions multipliers are also found to be higher. In Bermuda, for example, the transactions multiplier was found in 1989 to be 2.66, but the value of TIM was only 1.17 (Archer and Fletcher 1990).

State and local secondary impacts are less, once again demonstrating higher leakage rates. In particular, values of unorthodox TIM have ranged between 0.25 and 0.8 in regions such as Gwynedd, UK, Victoria, British Columbia and Dade County, Florida (Mescon and Vozikis 1985). The value of TIM may even be zero if all tourism facilities are owned from offshore, and all goods and services need to be imported. Again, transactions and employment multipliers have higher values.

Recent analysis mostly uses relatively sophisticated input–output models to calculate effects, or where production methods and price levels change at the margin, more composite multi-sector economic models such as ORANI in Australia (Australia, IAC 1989). However, specific *ad hoc* disaggregated multipliers are still used. A typical formulation might be:

for **j** tourism industry sub-sectors:

$$\mathbf{TIM} = \sum_j \left\{ \mathbf{K} \left[1 + \mathbf{K}' \left(\frac{1}{1 - \mathbf{K}''} \right)^n \right] \frac{\mathbf{S}_j}{\mathbf{TE}} \right\}$$

where
   $\mathbf{S}_j$ = tourism industry sub-sector j (for example, lodging)
   $\mathbf{K}'$ = indirect leakages
   $\mathbf{K}''$ = induced leakages
   $\mathbf{TE}$ = tourism expenditure.

A dynamic comparison can be used, with the same region or country at two points in time, to estimate whether tourism has an increasing total value through reduced leakages.

Study questions

1 Assess the contributory and distributive factors which determine the size of national income.
2 Why do governments sometimes view tourism development as an attractive way of boosting a national economy?
3 Examine the reallocative effects of domestic tourism in your country.
4 Are any 'demonstration effects' of tourism noticeable in your locality? If so, assess how they may have affected the local economy.
5 What is meant by a dual market? Why do dual markets occur in some tourism destinations?
6 The direct value of $1000 spent by a visitor to Germany and $1000 spent in India may be quite different in each economy. Show why.
7 Distinguish between direct, indirect and induced income from tourism.
8 Distinguish between orthodox and ratio multipliers, and examine why sometimes one is more appropriate, sometimes the other.
9 Find any example of a calculated tourism multiplier, and examine how accurate it is likely to be.
10 What is a transactions matrix?
11 Show how there may be a difference between the value to an economy of increased tourism expenditure in low season, and that in peak season.
12 Identify the reasons for low wages in many sectors of tourism employment.

CHAPTER 9

Unpriced values and externalities

▉ Introduction: non market economics

Orthodox or 'mainstream' economists (Samuelson 1989) restrict most of their microeconomic and macroeconomic analysis to the operations and outcomes of markets in which the interactions of suppliers and purchasers (perhaps with government intervention) determine economic activity. Many economists, and researchers in other areas fringing economics, are concerned with variables and processes which are part of this activity, but are generally outside commercial market workings. Such variables and processes include the allocation of 'free' resources or public goods, values, unpriced character-istics of products, the effects on third parties of trading between suppliers and purchasers, and so on. These are sometimes ascribed to *market failure*.

Chapter 1 introduced some of these problems in relation to travel and tourism. First, tourism is notable, compared with many other sectors of the economy, in that it calls upon many free resources or public goods in order to satisfy the wants and requirements of tourists. The valuation and allocation of these non tradeable items becomes important:

• if the pressure of demand within tourism and from other activities makes a hitherto free resource scarce; for example if demand for beach use rises, should an allocation mechanism exist (such as assigning property rights and charging a money price for beach use, as happens on many beaches in Italy and France)?
• where there is a cost (including an opportunity cost) involved in supplying public goods such as access roads, national parks or policing in destinations.

In these circumstances it may be important to know the real costs of supply, and to be able to measure the value of non tradeable items to tourists and other competing users.

Secondly, travel and tourism activity may impinge on third parties who are not part of the buyer–seller market. In this there is nothing unique about tourism. Benefits may be bestowed on others for which no payment is received, and costs imposed for which no payment is made. The benefits and costs are often known as *externalities* or *external effects* of market activity. Some are easily identifiable, as are the third parties affected—aircraft noise disturbing residents around airports serving tourism routes, for example. Others are less easily defined, such as the loss of a mangrove swamp when a tropical island resort is built, or fauna preservation through establishment of African safari parks. Which third parties benefit or suffer, and by how much? Do elephants or mangrove trees have rights, and what are they worth? The questions may sound almost frivolous at first sight, but some at least deserve serious answers.

By analysing externalities, the public or social benefits and costs of tourism may be added to, and subtracted from, its commercial market value to an economy. Governments may take steps to internalise the externalities through fiscal means, or at least have a clearer idea of the Net Economic Welfare (Nordhaus-Tobin) of travel and tourism as an industry compared with others. This is essential in welfare efficient economic planning.

■ Tourists' values

When tourists make a product selection for purchase, particularly a destination selection, the bundle of characteristics required to generate utility will include many which are possessed by, or are themselves, non tradeable items. For example, a group of American international recreational tourists identified scenic beauty and pleasant attitudes of local residents as the most important characteristics (of a list of eleven) for their trip (Goodrich 1977). Other major non tradeables might include:

- rest and relaxation
- geographic features (including access)
- climate (Rugg 1971)
- cultural surroundings
- social or business contact at meeting places.

Although these characteristics can all be incorporated into tradeable tourism products, none of them is *per se* a good or service regularly traded. They are generally public goods or 'free gifts of nature'.

If these items strongly influence tourists' propensity to spend on a total tourism product, it is important to assess what contribution they make to tourist utility, and hence what *value* is placed on them by tourists. In this sense we are attempting to measure *value in use* rather than *value in exchange*, where many characteristics in tourism would have a relatively low marginal utility but a high total utility to tourists. The values are good examples of what have been termed unpriced values (Sinden and Worrell 1979); that is, no market price attaches to the characteristics, but it may be possible to assess their value to tourists in money terms. The difference between value in use and value in exchange is illustrated in Figure 9.1:

Figure 9.1   Value in tourism demand

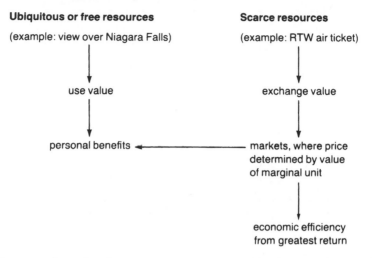

In the absence of market forces, many researchers have attempted to measure the value of utility or personal benefits generated by free resources. This involves non market estimation of benefits evaluation, or the calculation of *shadow prices* (Smith 1989). There is a considerable amount of literature on this topic relating to recreation, although less to tourism as a whole.

The value or shadow price of a characteristic in tourism to an individual consuming tourist can be estimated in different ways. The first and perhaps most obvious is to ask tourists in direct surveys what value they place, in money terms, on each characteristic. This is known as *contingent valuation modelling*, and is done by asking about either:

- willingness to pay—that is, to spend on acquiring the characteristics; or
- willingness to sell—that is, how much tourists would need to be bribed or compensated for the loss of a tourism benefit.

Direct questioning about willingness to pay and willingness to sell provides individual valuations which are only as accurate as survey methods, respondents' bias and other extraneous and subjective variables permit. In empirical studies, tourists nearly always provide a lower willingness to pay value than willingness to sell. Differences are also caused by whether consumers are questioned at destinations or at home in household surveys. Methodological studies such as Smith (1989) expand on these problems.

A second method of eliciting the value placed by tourists on unpriced characteristics is by indirect inference. The best known example of this is *travel-cost methods* (Clawson and Knetsch 1966). These methods can only be used for tourism destinations or attractions as a whole, rather than for individual characteristics. They make the travel cost incurred in reaching a destination a surrogate for the value placed by the tourist on that destination, assuming linearity in, and consistency of, responses to travel cost changes. (That is, the same number of tourist trips are always taken, but possibly to varying destinations, since if travel costs rise then destinations change in 'value'). The method is intuitively attractive, as for example in the Michelin Guides' assessment of restaurants' value (see chapter appendix A).

There are two main difficulties encountered in using travel cost methods to estimate tourists' values. The first is that the methods can only apply to a single endpoint of a trip. In the context of a business trip for a convention in Los Angeles for example, travel cost can be used to estimate the value of benefits expected from the convention *and other destination activities* as a lump, but not to value individual activities such as side trips to Hollywood, Disneyland, Long Beach and so on which might be taken as recreational extras. In valuing a single attraction, the same problem shows up if it is visited as part of a linear tour. On a sightseeing tour such as the 'milk run' in the United Kingdom (Holloway 1989), a tourist travelling from London to Stratford-upon-Avon is almost bound to visit Oxford en route, owing to geography. The marginal travel cost of a visit to Oxford in these circumstances is nearly zero, but few tourists would agree subjectively with this as an attraction valuation.

A second difficulty is found in defining what costs to include in travel costs. Evidently direct or variable costs of carriage should be included, but researchers disagree over the importance of including the cost of time taken (see below), and indirect or fixed costs—such as the proportion of depreciation on a family car used on a tourist trip in addition to everyday travel. Finally, travel cost approaches assume that tourists maximise utility by finding a known destination with a set of preferred benefits, and for a particular length of visit, always at the lowest cost (Forster 1989). This is unlikely to be true, as market imperfections mean that tourists rarely have perfect information about all destinations, and variety or change is in itself often a desirable tourism characteristic.

Hedonic pricing

Over recent years there have been many attempts to develop alternative methods of valuing unpriced commodities. They include von Neumann-Morgenstern preferences, point scoring, ranking and other non economic empirical measures (Sinden and Worrell 1979). The most promising approach expands on hedonic pricing, outlined in Chapter 3. When developed from a Lancasterian model, hedonic pricing can allow for an implicit or shadow price to be calculated for each important characteristic of a tourism 'product', by comparison between products with minimal differences. For example it might be possible to value the sun trapping orientation of a beach by comparing two similar and neighbouring beaches which face in different directions. This is a similar problem to the valuation of individual characteristics of *commercial* products, such as the different attributes of restaurants (Falvey *et al.* 1992). Hedonic analysis is limited (Brookshire *et al.* 1982, Edwards S 1987), but shows promise in this area.

The value of tourists' time

The full cost of any human activity is a sum of its market prices and the value of the time foregone from other uses. Time has thus been viewed as a resource used in the 'production' of activities (Becker 1965), and tourism is normally an extensive time user. Given a business travel or leisure 'time budget' **T**, an individual can allocate time into:

pure tourism activities (in destinations) $a_1, a_2 \dots a_n$
travel to or from destinations **t**
unallocated time (presumably at home) **L**

If each of these activities yields a stream of benefits, or *negative benefits* (*disbenefits* or *time costs*), then utility **U** can be maximised:

maximise $\quad U = U(a_1, a_2 \dots a_n, t, L)$
where $\quad\quad T = 2t + (a_1, a_2 \dots a_n) + L$

By assuming that a time budget relates exactly to maximum trip length we can omit L.

Some writers assume that a journey is a pure cost: that is, it yields negative benefits or a negative time value, and tourists will therefore trade off time against money in seeking either a closer destination or faster travel means. In this case the marginal productivity of time can be estimated from the ratio of travellers between A and B selecting a fast, timesaving mode of transportation and those selecting a slower one. It must be noted though that time 'saved' is merely available for immediate transfer to another activity rather than being storable; its value or shadow price would change according to the value of the other activity (Truong and Hensher 1985).

An alternative argument is that a journey itself can yield positive utility: 'getting there is half the fun'. This increases tourists' propensity to allocate time to the journey (2t in the above equation) and may reduce the time value of destination activities (which incidentally would not be picked up in travel cost models). In this regard, three different types of tourist and excursionist market segments have been noted (Cheshire and Stabler 1976):

- 'pure' visitors, who value time at a destination or attraction highly, and wish to minimise the journey time (negative benefits)
- 'meanderers', who gain positive utility from their journey

- 'transit' visitors, whose journey to a destination may be for an unrelated purpose, and whose visit to a recreational attraction is incidental; for example, international VFR tourists to Toronto happening to visit Niagara or the Algonquin Provincial Park, but who have not valued time travelling to Ontario principally for those visits.

It has been found (Walsh *et al.* 1990) that time may have a positive utility or value for people on short, scenic trips, whereas as the journey becomes longer and perhaps more tedious, the value declines and becomes negative.

The value of time allocated to activities a_1, a_2 .... a_n within destinations is a simpler opportunity–time–cost tradeoff, which can be found from systematic recording (Pearce 1988).

■ The total value of public and non tradeable goods in tourism

In principle, it should be possible to find out what values individual tourists place on a destination or characteristic. By summing these values a shadow demand schedule should appear. The total use-value is then the aggregate consumers' surplus under the demand schedule. This is represented in Figure 9.2 by the area $0P_1Q_1$:

Figure 9.2   Shadow valuation of a non market tourism good

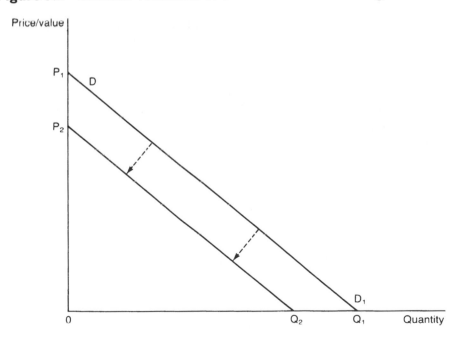

For a completely 'free' good such as the enjoyment of a magnificent view or witnessing a Mardi Gras carnival, the consumers' surplus is a value over a zero money price. The only alteration to value may come from a shift in the shadow demand schedule and a change in consumers' surplus to, say, $0P_2Q_2$. This cannot happen intrinsically with *pure* public goods, whose consumption by one individual leaves the quality and quantity of the good unchanged for others; an example might be buoyage and coastal navigation marks for pleasure boats. With *mixed* public goods, however, consumption by one individual can at some point reduce the utility of others, and hence their individual valuation (Burns 1988). Traffic congestion in popular destinations and recreation sites reduces tourists' willingness-to-travel values in this way. Whilst destination services are then allocated between consumers on the basis that those whose utility is most adversely affected by congestion will drop out of the market, the *total value* of the destination is reduced, as no-one escapes the congestion disbenefits whilst continuing to make trips.

At some point there may be a policy decision to internalise consumers' surpluses into market prices. This may happen whether tourism attractions are privately owned or are within the public domain. The reasons may be:

- an ordinary commercial profit opportunity
- the need to recoup costs of providing some aspects of the tourism attraction (such as maintenance, conservation and information in national parks)
- an attempt to regulate allocation to consumers of, for example, a heavily congested attraction.

The decision to charge consumers at a publicly-owned attraction is commonly known as the *user pays* principle. During the 1980s and 1990s, many countries have seen an extension of the user pays principle into resources which were previously regarded as free or public. 'User pays' in tourism destinations is seen as particularly defensible, on the grounds that tourists are not permanent local contributors to the common wealth of resources, through taxation or voluntary effort.

Charging, at least by implication, introduces a supply schedule for the tourism attraction, which is likely to be inelastic over much of its range. Consider, for example, a marshalled car park at a location with free attractions and activities, the car park consisting of two fields. The supply of parking space is generally fixed by the capacity of the land, although at low usage times less marshals may be used and only one field opened. This translates into a simple, two-stepped supply schedule, which at other than low usage supply has zero elasticity. A more generalised version of this is shown in Figure 9.3.

If the owners of the tourism attraction or amenity introduce a price P_c, then their revenue will be $0P_cEQ_c$ taken from consumers' surplus $0P_1Q_1$. This reduces consumers' surplus to that area above the price level

Figure 9.3   Tourism goods with partial charging

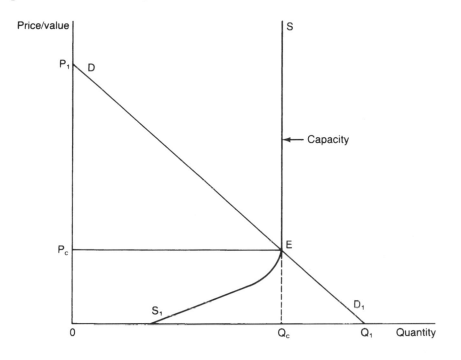

set, that is P_cP_1E. Notice that this has reduced the total public valuation of the attraction to $0P_1EQ_c$, since those tourists who valued their trip at less than P_c are now out of the market.

A feature of many tourism attractions and amenities is the large element of *pure economic rent* involved. Economic rent, as demonstrated by Ricardo in the early 19th century, occurs when supply of a commodity or factor of production is inelastic, and the revenue price received for the commodity or factor is not necessary to call forth further supplies (Samuelson 1989). In the above example, element S_1EQ_c of revenue relates to increased supply of the tourism attraction, and the larger element $0P_cES_1$ represents rent. A higher (non equilibrium) price could be charged, which might simply increase the value of rent (or *producers' surplus*, as it is sometimes known).

Rent is highest where there are no alternative uses for the resources employed in tourism. The existence of alternative uses, in aggregate rather than for a single attraction, would make supply elastic and therefore reduce the opportunity for pure rent. As noted in Chapter 8 however, tourism flourishes in many areas principally because it can utilise land, water assets, historic buildings and so on which have little value to other sectors. Their value to tourist perceptions is often further enhanced by the absence of conflicting industrial activity. Economic rent on public tourism resources is therefore high when user charges are imposed.

■ Net values and opportunity costs

Although tourism is frequently the only economic user of local factors of production, there may be other semi- or non economic uses for those factors. Is tourism then the most efficient user of these factors? In commercial operations this problem is solved by using markets and profits earned from the use of factors to determine their allocation, through production functions. In non market or unpriced sectors, tests of efficiency are less simple.

Examples of the choice involving tourism or non tourism use of factors, in the public domain, might include:

- zoning waterfront land either for open space to be enjoyed by residents, or to construct a tourist marina
- operating a museum collection or historic site either as a fully preserved entity for scholarly study, or as a tourism attraction, where combination is difficult
- applying scarce government funds to a National Tourist Office, or any alternative spending programme.

Tests of allocative efficiency in these and similar cases are within the area of *welfare economics*, whether or not third parties are involved as a separate group.

If a factor of production, or resource, is used for tourism, its basic welfare or social cost to an economy is its *opportunity cost*, or the lost opportunity of using it in the (presumably) next best activity. Evidently, to maximise general welfare, the opportunity costs of using resources in tourism must never exceed the benefits accruing, and should be minimised where there is choice. The criterion for efficiency in resource allocation is generally held by economists to be *Pareto optimality*; use of resources is said to be Pareto-optimal if no reallocation can increase one individual's utility without reducing that of others. If, by taking resources from tourism for example and employing them elsewhere, some people's utility could be increased without reducing that of others, then tourism allocations would be Pareto-non optimal. Conditions for Pareto-optimality are complex for public goods (Henderson and Quandt 1971), and very few attempts have been made to establish whether tourism in specific cases is the 'best' user of available resources. For example, Lake Okeechobee in Florida has seriously conflicting demands made upon it for tourism (sport—fishing), tomato irrigation, public water supply and so on. With or without its additional pollution problems, Pareto-optimal allocation of its uses is vital.

Differing approaches towards solving the above problem have been suggested. Since tourism involves a wide range of activities, values and impacts, a social welfare function approach (Arrow 1951) might be used to aggregate individuals' general utility values of tourism resource use compared with their judgments on other uses. Alternatively, benefit-cost analysis has been suggested (Gray 1982) as a method to establish the *net value* of tourism activity or resource use. This could be accomplished, for example, by summing all consumers' surplus and economic rent accruing to a tourism activity (the benefit), and treating as a cost those surpluses and rents which might obtain from alternative resource use. The difference would be net value.

In using any of the above analyses, a difficulty which is specific to tourism is that of determining whom to include in assessing value. (This is in addition to considering the effects of externalities on third parties, which will be discussed below.) Governments and other decision makers normally measure social welfare in relation to a local region or a nation. This is fine if all tourists are domestic, as all consumers' surpluses are part of the domestic economy's social welfare—and we may assume that tourism resources are publicly owned or owned by residents. If, however, some or all tourists are international visitors, their consumers' surplus 'flows out' of the economy, and the question arises as to whether the social value of tourism activity in an economy should exclude this amount (Clarke and Ng 1993).

Nationalists would presumably answer yes, and advocates of a single global society no. Since the 1960s, the general movement towards a solution has been by internalising consuming tourists' surpluses either into user fees or international government payments to support world heritage tourism resources. Cases in point include the sinking city of Venice, Italy, and the big game national safari parks of East Africa, where domestic social valuation alone might lead to non tourism uses.

■ The asset theory of tourism

The net value, or net social benefit, of tourism for a particular time period thus consists of all identifiable consumers' surpluses and producers' surpluses (economic rent); in Figure 9.3 this is the area $0P_1ES_1$. Again, this excludes external effects and other implicit costs (Sinden and Worrell 1979). These values are obviously highest where tourism attractions or destinations are unique, or command some degree of monopoly characteristics in tourists' perceptions. They are less where destinations are easily substitutable or at such great time/cost distances from generating markets that surpluses are low.

The 'stream' of surpluses produced by a tourism destination has been likened to the stream of income produced by commercial, productive assets. This view of destinations' basic attracting power has been termed the *asset theory of tourism* (Gray 1982). Touristic assets are immobile, and many can depreciate like other assets if they are not maintained. Depreciation may be physical wear and tear on beaches, parks, monuments, buildings and so on, or it may be non tangible depreciation in the reputation of a destination, caused for example by tourist congestion, overpricing or hostility to tourists from local residents.

Asset valuation for an aggregate stock of tourism attractions can be attempted by summing the streams of surpluses over the expected life of a destination (which may, for a unique natural attraction, be infinite), and discounting by an appropriate rate. This can be stated at its simplest, for a life of **n** time periods (**t**), by:

$$\text{Tourism asset value} = \sum_{t=1}^{n} \left[\frac{C_t + P_t}{(1+r)^t} \right]$$

where:

C_t is the consumers' surplus derived from valuations by visiting tourists in time period t

P_t is producers surplus or economic rent in period t (If no user charges are levied and/or there are public costs involved in providing and managing tourism assets, P_t could be zero or negative)

r is a discount rate probably related to anticipated inflation and the opportunity rate of return—if any—of using resources for non tourism purposes.

A valuation of this type ignores the *intrinsic value* of attractions, but summarises value-in-use for tourists.

Public asset valuation in tourism has rarely been attempted empirically because of the complexity in calculating values for a diverse, composite sector. The procedure can be valuable, however, in providing data for government decision making where tourism's importance is to be compared with that of other sectors.

■ Externalities

There can be very few economic activities, involving transactions in which commodities are supplied by one party to be acquired and used by a second party, which do not affect third parties in some way. If it is possible to put a money price on these effects, they can be termed *external economic effects* or *externalities*; that is, they are outside a specific market transaction. In legal, social and environmental terms the effects may normatively be considered 'good' or 'bad' on third parties; in economic terms an externality can be examined to see whether it causes a net increase or decrease in social welfare. The concept of external effects or externalities was first comprehensively explored by Pigou (1950), who noted that in the course of economic activity the utility of people other than suppliers or consumers of a commodity may be enhanced or reduced. An enhancement given 'free' is a social benefit, and a reduction not compensated for is a social cost.

Although to establish a valuation of externalities it is necessary to be able to measure them in money terms, they are mostly unpriced value effects, not dealt with in commercial markets. Externalities are usually divided into:

• social/ economic benefits which increase the welfare of third parties, in contrast to costs, which reduce welfare, and

- aggregate externalities of all economic activity or that of a particular sector, compared with marginal externalities which are related to a specific investment or economic development.

More researchers have concentrated on costs than on benefits, particularly in relation to travel and tourism, largely because benefits are frequently incorporated into secondary effects of multiplier studies. Most analysis also addresses externalities associated with specific development or sectoral growth, in order to examine marginal changes to, or consequent fresh impacts on, welfare. The best example of accounting for aggregate externalities in the whole economy is perhaps that of the Nordhaus-Tobin calculation of Net Economic Welfare (NEW), where:

NEW = GDP + Net Externalities (Nordhaus and Tobin 1972).

It is perfectly possible for NEW to fall as GDP rises—if third party costs increase at a faster rate than the change in value of commercial transactions. The reverse can also happen.

■ Classification of externalities in tourism

Many of the effects on third parties which tourism activity causes are by no means specific to tourism. For example, the costs of traffic noise to residents living on major highways, or of surface pollution caused by diesel oil and litter on coastal waters, could equally arise from tourism or from other commercial activities. There are, on the other hand, some externalities which arise directly out of the specific feature of tourism that purchasers consume at the point of production. These are externalities connected with the movement and temporary relocation of people. Most externalities are therefore people numbers related (including congestion, crime and physical wear and tear on assets—but also including better local amenities and communications).

In practice it is unworkable to isolate those externalities which are solely tourism-related from those which, though caused by tourism, could equally well be caused by something else. Any classification is likely to start with aggregate external costs against external benefits of travel and tourism. Various classifications have then been proposed, such as:

- environmental restructuring
- waste generation
- direct biological impact of tourists
- population dynamics
  (OECD 1981)
or:
- fiscal effects—generally falling on government
- quality of life effects—generally falling on individual residents (Frechtling 1987b).

For economic assessment, a more generalised classification of tourism's externalities might be useful, such as that in Table 9.1. Those affected are either individuals not involved in tourism, or governments and societies collectively. These, together with tourists and tourism suppliers (who may also, of course, be government authorities), make up the generally accepted 'four groups' in tourism impacts (Pearce 1989).

Table 9.1   A classification of tourism externalities, with examples

Who is affected		TYPE OF EFFECT		
		Economic Effects	Social Effects	Environmental Effects
Mainly Individuals	benefits	new transport links, new recreational amenities and shops, rising property value	positive demonstration effects (eg better health care, education)	enhancement of a view
	costs	falling property values, inflation	traffic and people congestion, higher crime, negative demonstration effects	spoiling views & landscape (visual pollution), noise, air & water pollution, litter
Governments and collective welfare	benefits	increased direct and indirect tax revenue	increased value of culture, reduced loss from migration	preservation of flora and fauna
	costs	maintenance of infrastructure tourism amenities if no user-pays system	extra policing health services, fire protection, sanitation & garbage	destruction of flora and fauna

The *types* of effects concerned are either directly economic (in which case their benefits or costs are generally measurable), or social and environmental impacts (which may or may not be measurable in money terms). Although social and environmental effects have been the concern of a very large number of researchers in tourism, the ability of economics to address these impacts is limited by valuation methodology.

■ Cost-benefit analysis for travel and tourism developments

Social pressures increasingly force the developers involved with any new investment project to assess externalities, where possible, as an adjunct to normal commercial investment appraisal. Thus, social and environmental impact studies are now a normal part of the feasibility studies for such developments as new resorts, airports or tourism attractions. The assessment technique most commonly invoked is cost-benefit analysis (or benefit-cost analysis, depending on the researcher's origin). Cost-benefit analysis involves:

1 identifying externalities
2 valuing them where possible in money terms
3 incorporating them as positive benefits, and negative costs, into some form of social account
4 summing the resulting 'net' costs or benefits into a net present value which can be subtracted from, or added to, the commercial or private value of a development, to form a *social value*.

Each of the four stages above presents special problems. Identification and valuation methods were developed rigorously during the 1960s, principally for public investments such as hospitals, highways and subways (underground railways), where commercial returns either do not exist or are insufficient to justify social investment on their own. In relation to Table 9.1, economic effects are relatively easily measurable, and techniques for valuing social effects are improving (Murphy 1985 pp.100-102, although this relates to aggregate tourism in Norfolk, England, rather than to a specific development).

Environmental impacts are still tricky to price empirically; partly because of the question of property rights. For example, if a new airport development for tourism purposes produces increased aircraft noise to residents, some compensation payment for sound proofing and inconvenience can probably be negotiated—the Kaldor criterion for social welfare optimisation—provided the airport is still viable. Property rights are clear.

If, however, the same development means filling a swamp and losing duck habitats (London's third airport proposed in the 1970s) or mangrove trees (Brisbane airport, Australia) on public land, unless governments assign property rights to ducks or mangroves the environmental loss is very difficult to assess in money terms. The only potential valuation is the amount that duck or mangrove lovers could successfully use to bribe developers not to go ahead—the Hicks criterion for social welfare optimisation.

The third and fourth stages of cost-benefit analysis, to complete social accounting and social valuation, are no simpler. Questions such as the rate at which to discount future externalities, and how to handle constraints such as situations where compensation or tax is impossible, have to be resolved (Prest and Turvey 1965). A useable social accounting method has to be chosen, such as:

- a social cost-benefit ratio, separate from commercial evaluations, which summarises net social effects alone; a good example was that of an early study into hotel development in the Caribbean (Bryden 1973), which concluded that increases in net social welfare from tourism development were poor, especially where non tourism alternatives were available
- a unified commercial and social accounting approach, which adjusts each commercial value, such as wage costs and revenue prices, by a factor representing the externalities involved; classic examples are applications of the Little-Mirlees method in development of the Trinidad Hilton (Forbes 1976) and the Seychelles Reef Hotel (Bevan and Soskice 1976). The Little-Mirlees method allows additionally for non optimal government decision making.

As with tourism asset valuation, cost-benefit analysis essentially provides shadow prices for non market values, either independently or as an addition to or subtraction from market prices. Again, as with asset valuation, the benefit prices are highest where there is zero or low opportunity cost—that is, little economic alternative to tourism development. The major difficulty with cost-benefit analysis is that it is empirically very complex, and often involves subjective valuation of externalities.

■ Optimising the total social value of tourism

Whilst cost-benefit analysis is useful in the context of individual development appraisal, it is misleading when it is used, frequently, to examine externalities in an aggregate way. Values can be assigned to externalities at any one time, but these values change to reflect marginal external impacts and fluctuating social priorities. This is especially the case with environmental impacts (Baumol and Oates 1979). That externalities exist, many economists argue, is evidence of market failure, and therefore market methods should apply continuously to handle them. This essentially means *internalising* externalities into the market prices paid and received by tourists and suppliers. Under this principle the user pays, the polluter pays, the benefactor receives. If all of tourism's external effects were internalised, market equilibrium would equate with social equilibrium, and contribution to NEW would equal contribution to GDP. (It has been suggested that there are cases where the social value of tourism is always positive. That is, it contributes to net welfare regardless of internalising externalities (Clarke and Ng 1993), but internalising will help to ensure more efficient resource allocation between tourism and other resource users.)

Unfortunately, internalisation methods are usually too clumsy to reflect true values. It is usually considered a function of a government to assign property rights, to identify externalities, and, where it wishes, to internalise via taxation or compensation. Governments can only simulate one side of 'the market', however—the 'supply of externalities'. In the absence of dynamic 'demand', government valuations are cumbersome. Thus, for example, a tax on motoring tourists (to internalise pollution and road wear and tear in a destination area) is unlikely to discriminate sufficiently against peak season users who cause the marginal breakdown of road surfaces, the marginally damaging noxious exhaust emission, and the marginal demand on road space that finally brings congested traffic to a standstill. It would be even more difficult to establish who should pay how much, and to whom, to internalise the cultural benefit provided in London by the existence of many live theatres whose commercial viability is assured by tourists (London Tourist Board 1989).

So whilst in theory it may be possible to assess the total contribution of tourism to the social welfare of an economy, we do not possess the means to make a practical valuation. Recognition of the importance of unpriced values and externalities in tourism at least warns us to treat carefully any statistics on the commercial importance of this sector to an economy.

The travel–cost value of restaurants

The Michelin Guides to hotels and restaurants, developed in France, rate restaurants considered to provide a superior dining experience with one, two or three rosettes, more or less irrespective of restaurant prices. The Guide's ratings are:

- one rosette—'a good place to stop on a journey'
- two rosettes—'worthy of a detour'
- three rosettes—'worthy of a special journey'.

The Guide's authors are thus in principle applying a travel–cost criterion as a measure of the value of an individual consumer's surplus: their willingness to pay for the travel/gastronomic experience in excess of the market price.

Study questions

1 Distinguish between free resources and public goods in tourism.
2 Amongst a group of colleagues, such as students, attempt to estimate a shadow price for some local attraction (currently free) by asking them their willingness to pay, *or* identifying the travel cost to visit the attraction.
3 Why is time spent on a tourist activity sometimes a cost but sometimes a benefit?
4 Identify the arguments for internalizing consumers' surpluses on visits to state-owned heritage attractions.
5 What is meant by Pareto-optimality?
6 The asset theory of tourism values a destination in relation to the stream of surpluses it may generate. Find examples which by this criterion would have a fixed asset value, and others which might depreciate or appreciate.
7 Find some examples of external costs or benefits of tourism in your locality or country. How could they be measured?
8 Examine the difficulties of applying cost-benefit analysis in tourism development.

The balance of tourism payments

Tourism's external account

■ Balance of payments terminology

Tourism has a major influence on many countries' balance of payments. We have largely defined tourism, in terms of money flow, as the spending (in the destination) of money earned in a generating area; internationally this means money earned in country A being used as payment for services rendered in country B.

In a sense the term 'balance of payments' is rather misleading to describe the summary of a nation's receipts and payments to and from other nations, as nearly always the two do not balance. A summary external accounts table is shown in Table 10.1.

Splitting the current account into visibles and invisibles is a traditional feature of national accounting to identify goods and services provided, but this may be an increasingly fuzzy distinction where services are frequently a corollary of goods supplied internationally. Capital movements are largely concerned with international investment, and with international government borrowing.

Many countries maintain data to represent foreign accounts for specific classes of goods or services. Hence at the very simplest level there may be a 'balance on tourism'—normally part of the invisible balance—which would be represented by:

receipts from overseas tourists visiting a country

less

payments abroad by that country's own outbound tourists.

Unfortunately, the net tourist expenditure result is a relatively meaningless figure, as it merely measures *final payments* by tourists for services and some goods in destination countries. To find out what tourism is really worth to a

Table 10.1   External accounts of a national economy

Receipts or income	*less*	Payments or expenditure	Result
Current account			
Exports of goods		Imports of goods	Balance of trade (visible balance)
add			
Invisible receipts		Invisible payments	Invisible balance
			Balance on current account
add			
Capital account			
Private and public capital inflow		Private and public capital outflow	Net capital movement
			Total balance of payments surplus [or deficit]

Surplus or deficit results are represented by net monetary movements.

country, or its real cost, we should include *all* international transactions which are necessary because of tourism (Baretje 1982). These include not only final tourism payments and travel payments, but also international payments for goods and services needed for investment in, and operation of, tourism industries. The result can be termed the *travel and tourism external account*.

■ Comparative advantage in tourism

The principle of comparative advantage, as a basis for international trade, dates back to the writings of Ricardo in 1817. That principle, which holds that trade is beneficial between any pair of countries where there is a *comparative advantage* in efficient production of any good by one country over another, regardless of *absolute advantage* (see, for example, Samuelson 1989), has rarely been applied theoretically to tourism services. But individual countries do possess specific comparative advantages which lead to international tourism flows:

- There may be specific base resources in certain countries which are a fundamental tourist attraction, as already identified in Chapter 1—for example, the Grand Canyon or the Eiffel Tower. Tourists from France may therefore exchange 'consumption' of the Eiffel Tower for 'consumption' of the Grand Canyon with tourists from the United States.

- Some countries offer all-round advantage in the production of tourism services, such as an attractive climate plus plenty of beach space and low labour costs. Spain and Mexico are good examples; Romania and Bulgaria directly 'exchange' tourism for goods from more northerly Eastern European countries.
- A destination country's geographic location relative to mass tourism generators may be such an important 'pull' factor that it pays that destination country to concentrate transferable resources into tourism, even from industries which are more efficient than they are in the generating countries. This is especially true of small, two or three industry economies such as some Caribbean countries.

In addition to comparative advantages, differing tastes, the constant desire of some types of tourist for new and foreign experiences, and *changing* international constraint conditions (such as variable exchange rates) all combine to provide an economic rationale for international travel and tourism.

Tourism analysis has in fact caused a reappraisal of international trade theory with respect to services, and in particular those which are not competitive with domestic services (Gray 1970). Tourists sometimes visit another country because its product is entirely different from anything available domestically, rather than merely because of a price advantage. They therefore make use of specific tourism resources or factor endowments possessed by the destination. This view is consistent with economic models of international tourism demand based on Heckscher-Ohlin theories (for example, Smeral 1989).

■ Tourism payments' statistics

Since international tourism payments are often an important component of invisible balances, governments and economists are interested in monitoring figures. In most cases all that is available, and used, is the simple balance of payments data on tourist receipts and payments—and frequently such data is unreliable (White and Walker 1982). This makes international comparisons very suspect, and the best that can be hoped for is internal consistency and reliability for an individual country.

There are three basic sources of tourism payments statistics:

- direct spending totals provided by tourists themselves
- indirect data gained from multiplying tourist numbers by average length of stay and by average daily spending
- exchange figures from banks and other financial institutions.

The first two rely on surveys (either census or more likely by samples) of tourists *in situ* or post-visit, and are therefore subject to the normal problems facing survey research methods. Much of this survey work is undertaken at international departure points such as airport gates, so is sometimes known as *gate methods*. Bank data is really only useful in countries with non convertible currencies and a prohibition on import and export of their currencies. With partial or no exchange control, it is impossible to monitor all cash movements and their uses.

The real value of international tourist payments is also altered in two specific circumstances. First, when VFR tourists travel, they are unlikely to spend much on accommodation, food and other services in their destination, these being items in the host family's (increased) domestic budget. Therefore tourism services in major VFR destinations are likely to be undervalued. Secondly, few balance of payments statistical systems are sufficiently accurate to take account of the real value of expenditure by tourists on inclusive tours purchased in the generating country. Although payments actually made directly by tour operators to destination suppliers will be evaluated, much may be channelled through multinational enterprises in third countries, or there may be contra payments. Again, tourism is often undervalued.

■ Travel receipts and payments

For clarity, we can now distinguish between *travel* payments and *tourism* payments in external accounts. Here, travel payments are defined as money paid for international carriage to and from destinations—primarily air fares. We shall define tourism payments as money spent on goods and services in destination countries: 'ground' services (even if this includes domestic air transport).

Figure 10.1   Air links and airline choice

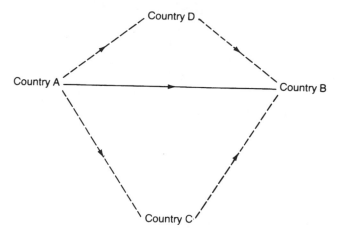

Travel is clearly a service, and therefore travel payments are part of invisibles. One of the problems, however, is that tourism destinations may receive nothing from travel. A tourist who is resident in country A and visiting country B may travel on an airline based in country A, or one based in country B, or in many cases one based in a third country C. On long-haul routes the tourist may indeed use more than one airline, based in more than one country. The reasons lie in bilateral air agreements, competition, and complexity of tourist itineraries.

First, A and B will have a bilateral agreement to share direct traffic between their countries amongst their own countries' airlines (see Figure 10.1). This uses third and fourth freedom rights of the air (see chapter appendix A for a description of freedoms of the air). Secondly, a tourist may want to visit both countries B and C, and given the same freedoms there is an option to use country C's airline on two sectors. Thirdly, country D's airline may be using fifth and sixth freedom rights to grab a market share of traffic from A to B by offering a (frequently cheap) virtual through service via its own country.

To take an example: Australia, through its main international airline Qantas, does not earn very much at all on the travel account from tourists arriving from the UK. In 1993:

30% of United Kingdom tourists used Qantas
27% used British Airways
8% used Singapore Airlines
35% used other means (mostly Asian airlines)
(Source: Australian Tourist Commission)

Singapore and other Asian airlines are clearly in the position of country D (Hanlon 1984, Poole *et al.* 1988); the destination country B (Australia) receives only about one third of total travel payments in this market.

Travel account policies therefore often seek to maximise foreign exchange earnings from international visitor flows. A destination country will carefully examine freedoms of the air which it grants, and attempt to maximise inbound use of its own airline(s)—something not always easy for less-developed countries but often tried. Generators will encourage their own outbound tourists to 'fly the flag'; other airline-operating countries in favourable intermediate geographical positions may try to get travel revenues from travellers who are not 'their' tourists. With increased deregulation of airline operations, even domestic tourists in some countries are now able to fly with foreign airlines.

The end result of the situation above is that there is frequently no relationship between the volume of tourist flows from one country to another and the value, to either country, of earnings on the travel accounts between that pair of countries.

■ Tourism receipts and payments

On arrival in destinations, tourists purchase goods and services ('ground' content) with money presumably brought with them and exchanged. The broad categories of product bought are:

• accommodation and food
• domestic transport

- tours/excursions and 'entrance to attractions'
- souvenirs and daily necessities.

As discussed in Chapter 8, one of the main concerns of a destination country is whether it owns the means to produce, and actually produces, the above goods and services itself. In many cases, this is becoming increasingly difficult as multinational enterprises and organisations based in tourist generators supply or take over supply of these products. We therefore see a flow of foreign exchange earnings on tourism products sold in destinations to *countries which themselves are not destinations*, but which provide resources, particularly capital, to tourism production elsewhere.

　　Values of tourism payments and receipts are also influenced by exchange rates. Figure 10.2 gives an example of how this can happen.

Figure 10.2 Exchange rate variations and tourism balances.

Date	Event	Current exchange rate	Japanese payment	US receipt
Jan	Japanese tour operator contracts US hotel at forward rate	YEN130=US$1 (spot=forward)	YEN65 000	US$500
Jul	Japanese tourist takes IT and YEN90 000 spending money to USA	YEN120=US$1	YEN90 000	US$750
Dec	Both countries total their tourism accounts	YEN100=US$1		
			YEN155 000	US$1250
	and convert to US$...		US$1550	US$1250

Figure 10.2 presents an admittedly extreme hypothetical example, but the principle is clear: in such accounting for international tourism payments, it is very difficult to arrive at reliable 'true' valuations of tourism for an economy.

■ Foreign exchange dependence on tourism

Given the above difficulties of valuation, it is perhaps only possible to regard published data on tourism payments and earnings as a rough guide; but it is possible to gain some idea of how dependent a country is on tourism earnings as part of its balance of payments. Table 10.2 shows the earnings of the 'big' tourism destinations:

Table 10.2   The tourism contribution to the balance of payments of major tourism destinations

Country	*billions of US$—1992*		
	tourism receipts	**total visible & invisible receipts**	**tourism % of total**
USA	54	726	7.4
Italy	22	267	8.2
Spain	22	111	19.8
France (1991)	21	359	5.8
UK	13	362	3.5
average			7.2

Sources: *IMF International Financial Statistics Yearbook 1993*, and *WTO Yearbook of Tourism Statistics 1993*

The 'top 5' international tourism earners from Table 10.2 on average are not highly dependent on tourism alone for their balance of payments inflows. With the exception of Spain they have earned less than 10% from tourism. This is because, on the whole, they are large and diversified economies earning foreign revenue from many sources. Spain is much more dependent on tourism—for nearly one fifth of its balance of payments revenue—which makes it more sensitive to changes in tourism demand and travel conditions.

At the extreme, Table 10.3 shows how highly dependent some countries *can* be on tourism receipts.

Table 10.3   Tourism contribution to the balance of payments in the most highly tourism dependent countries

Country	Tourism credits as % of total international credits (1991 unless stated)
Antigua/Barbuda	86.8
Bahamas	70.0
St Lucia	60.5
Barbados	56.5
Seychelles	46.9
Maldives (1992)	45.7
Western Samoa	41.3
Grenada	40.8
Jamaica	34.3

Source: *IMF International Financial Statistics Yearbook 1993* and *WTO Yearbook of Tourism Statistics 1993*

Such dependence on any single industry is likely to be unhealthy, as a change in market conditions or production difficulties can severely damage a nation's balance of payments. In many cases, tourism is less sensitive to market problems than are other activities such as primary industries, but over recent years we have seen political or weather problems cause serious disruption to tourism in such countries as Cyprus, Fiji, Grenada and the Seychelles. In these cases, a high tourism dependence is very damaging.

The level of dependence on a *single generator* is also crucial. Mexico, for example, is highly dependent on the United States for its visitors; South Korea on Japan; and Denmark on West Germany. Changes in the economic well being, or fashions, in the generator, as well as changes in the political and travel links between generator and destination, can then have a significant effect at the destination.

■ The effects of tourism development

As tourism developments in destinations have become less sporadic and more organised, so their implications for a national economy and its balance of payments have become clearer and more important. In addition, the supply of tourism products designed for international consumers has become the province, to a large extent, of multinational investors and organisations—see Chapter 11. So to assess the impact of tourism developments on a country's balance of payments, it is necessary to identify as many items as possible within the tourism external account, rather than just simple visitor foreign exchange receipts.

These aspects, for a hypothetical tourism development, are summarised in Table 10.4 (Bull 1990).

We must examine some of these items more closely. The initial *capital inflow* is likely to come from countries which are strong external investors—mostly rich, developed nations—and to be triggered either by prospects of higher rates of return in the destination than elsewhere (net of taxation or including investment incentives), or by some need for integration. This inflow is of course a once-and-for-all capital account movement, where the interest 'reward' outflows are recurrent.

Other recurrent outflows will depend on the degree of development and diversification in the destination economy, and hence its ability to supply goods itself to support the tourism industry (Burkart and Medlik 1981). Less diversified economies have a higher need or propensity to import, and thus greater outflows.

Naturally most destination governments hope that the *operational inflows* will easily pay for all the outflows and leave a net positive balance of I-O. Some researchers doubt that this benefit may exist (for example, Dwyer and Forsyth 1993), but clearly it is important to view the value of the inflows in

Table 10.4 Tourism development's effects on the balance of payments

Stage	Inflow to balance of payments	Outflow from balance of payments
Investment	Capital inflow (Capital account)	Dividends & interest (Current account)
Construction	——	Design & consultancy fees Import cost of materials
Operation	Receipts from foreign tourists Souvenir sales Taxes on foreign operators Wages received from foreign operators Saving from supplying domestic tourism product (import substitution)	Royalties & technical aid Imported materials and spares Imported consumer goods
Marketing	——	Overseas promotion Overseas based personnel costs
	Total Inflow (I)	Total Outflow (O)

relation to *all* tourism-related *and tourism-induced* foreign exchange effects, as detailed above. One notable inclusion is the saving from supplying a new domestic tourism product. Whilst this means no actual receipt from abroad, it implies that tourists domestically now have available a more attractive product than one overseas which would otherwise be in demand. This *import substitution* is analogous to the consumption of home-produced goods to replace imports. Of course the development will only be of interest to local consumers under the same conditions as a new ray on the demand graph in Figure 3.8.

As further developments take place, destination governments would hope that the I-O surplus ratio increases, as:

- the destination attracts an increasing range of inbound (foreign) tourists
- local support industries and employment skills become more sophisticated and competitive, thereby reducing the need to import
- unavoidable overseas expenses (such as NTO overseas promotion) cover an enhanced range of tourism products with little cost increase—i.e. there are increasing returns.

This has generally been true for countries such as Spain, Fiji or Tunisia, which have only reaped significant I-O benefits after several years of tourism development.

■ Policies for the balance of tourism payments

The governments of Japan, Taiwan, South Korea, Germany, Saudi Arabia and some others have for many years normally seen a large balance of payments surplus in their countries. Apart from dealing with pressure from less fortunate trading partners, their balances of payments need no strict policy. These countries pay their way, and are net creditors. On the other hand, a very large number of countries have to deal with balance deficits, including, increasingly, the United States. They do not pay their way. They must therefore embrace policies to reduce deficits or even obtain surpluses. In addition, in those cases where their own currency is not an acceptable form of international payment, they need ways to earn 'hard' or convertible currencies.

Using tourism to improve a balance of payments position in the above circumstances is popular. There are several reasons for this:

- *Negative* or prohibitionist policies to reduce imports, by such action as quota enforcement or increased tariffs, not only have possible injurious effects on the domestic economy (see, for example, Samuelson 1989) but may incur retaliatory measures from trading partners.
- Stimulation of domestic goods producers to increase exports may be a difficult process, especially where a country has few immediately exploitable comparative cost advantages. Also, the lags between stimulatory policy → increased production → sale of goods → shipment of goods → payments received may be so long as to be useless in making an immediate correction to a balance of payments deficit.
- Tourism is relatively easy to exploit *quickly*, providing no great infrastructure development is needed. Brief but intensive overseas promotional campaigns, the granting of new transport or taxation rights, or measures to reduce prices (by devaluation for example) can have almost instant effects in attracting more inbound tourists and their money. It is also relatively simpler and 'cleaner' than much new industrial development.
- Reducing outbound tourism by enforcing special taxation or severe exchange control does not normally attract retaliation, as it is not usually seen as a specific anti free trade weapon.

So a number of specific policies have been used to take advantage of these factors, which we may group as follows:

Promotional policies: overseas (usually NTO) promotions; special tourist price reductions (for example, a special tourist exchange rate; cheap 'tourist petrol' prices as used for some years in Italy); market repositioning to attract not more but higher spending, inbound tourists

Development policies: grants or tax allowances for businesses developing products to attract international tourists; infrastructure development, including transport links with generators

Regulatory policies: devaluation; exchange control/currency export prohibition; departure taxation for residents; strict negotiation in bilateral air agreements to preserve the largest share of travel receipts for home carriers; visa relaxation.

Combinations of these policies have been used by almost every country seeking to reduce a balance of payments deficit. They work by a mixture of demand-side and supply-side management, and of course are normally integrated into overall economic policy.

The freedoms of the air

To enable the orderly conduct of international air transport, governments negotiate bilateral agreements on air services and traffic rights. A large number of these agreements incorporate the 'freedoms of the air', the first five of which were defined by the International Civil Aviation Conference in Chicago, 1944.

First freedom
The privilege to fly over the territory of another state without landing.

Second freedom
The privilege to land in another state for non traffic purposes (for example refuelling, mechanical repairs only).

Third freedom
The privilege to set down in another state fare-paying passengers, mail and freight taken on in the state where the aircraft or airline is registered (Country A's airline may carry passengers from A to B).

Fourth freedom
The privilege to take up in another state fare-paying passengers, mail and freight, and to carry them to the state where the aircraft or airline is registered (Country A's airline may carry passengers from B to A).

Fifth freedom
The privilege for an aircraft or airline registered in one state and en route to or from that state to take up fare-paying passengers, mail and freight in a second state and set them down in a third state (Country A's airline, while flying a route A—B—C may carry passengers from B to C).

This freedom is often jealously guarded, and subject to much negotiation.

Sixth freedom (not formally recognised in Chicago 1944)
The privilege for an aircraft or airline registered in one state to take up fare-paying passengers, mail and freight in a second state, carry them via its own state, and set them down in a third state (Country A's airline, while flying Z—A and A—B may carry passengers from Z to B).

Many states, especially in Europe, the Middle East and Asia, do this, although some (such as Singapore) claim it is not a separate freedom, merely a combination of fourth and third freedoms. Nevertheless, their timetabling is often indistinguishable from that of a through service.

Study questions

1 Define these terms: invisible receipts, invisible balance, balance of payments deficit.
2 Is the sum of all inbound tourist expenditure less all outbound tourist expenditure a true picture of the tourism balance of payments? If not, show what is missing.
3 Demonstrate with examples the difference between absolute and comparative advantage in tourism.
4 Summarize the foreign exchange reasons for a country to want a national airline with fifth and sixth freedom rights.
5 Give three examples of how a country which is neither a generator nor destination may earn foreign exchange from tourism.
6 Explain the paradox that highly tourism-dependent economies may benefit from the sector relatively less than more diversified economies.
7 In general, would tourism *demand* management policies or tourism *supply* management policies act more effectively to support balance of payments management?

CHAPTER 11

Multinationals in travel and tourism

■ Types of multinational involvement

When an enterprise seeks to extend operational commercial activity beyond the frontiers of its home or 'parent' economy, it can be defined as a *multinational enterprise* (MNE). In fact this is a slight simplification, as some enterprises trade 'at arm's length' outside their frontiers or without incorporation elsewhere. Let us assume here that any transnational commercial operation (other than those which are just trading with foreign enterprises) is a MNE.

There are three main classes of foreign involvement which MNEs undertake. These are equity ownership, loan capital supply and non-investment management arrangements. In this discussion, 'parent' and 'subsidiary' are used in a general sense rather than with the restricted meaning found in company law.

Equity ownership

The most 'solid' form of MNE involves a parent company in country X either purchasing equity stock in an existing business in country Y, or setting up a partly or wholly owned subsidiary from scratch in that country. There is often a considerable distinction between enterprises acquiring controlling equity interests and minority ones. The former may involve 51% or more of stock, or *de facto* control through sizeable minority shareholding, perhaps larger than any other single holding. Many governments impose stricter controls on controlling interests than minority ones, often insisting that 51% of equity be held by their own nationals. This applies less in travel and tourism than in more sensitive sectors such as media or defence equipment, but is often still relevant. Again, for simplicity we may include under this heading direct branch offices in other countries, where it may be necessary under the laws of those countries to incorporate there.

Supply of loan capital

A lesser step, and one which some may argue is not true multinational enterprise, is for the parent in country X to lend money directly to a country Y enterprise, but not on an equity basis. There may, however, be a lien over the recipient enterprise's assets or some trading agreement which provides the parent company with an operational or production advantage, as well as earning interest. The contractual agreement may be sufficient motive for the parent company's interest, while not breaching ownership provisions set by country Y's government.

Non-investment management arrangements

It is very common in *multi-plant* enterprise, whether domestic or multi-national, to find a parent which operates a subsidiary under a management contract, or leases operating rights, or offers a franchise agreement. The enterprises in each country are separately owned, probably domestically, and may be financed from anywhere, but usually there is a single multinational trading name used.

Parent enterprises using non-investment management arrangements (NIMAs) do so mostly to obtain external economies of scale, especially marketing advantages. When domestic markets are too restricted to provide a background for strategic expansion, and where foreign markets are open to production and sale of similar products, international external economies may be valuable. Parent enterprises may also have superior production and marketing skills which they can 'export' to recipient countries, and gain advantages over wholly local competition.

■ Theories of multinational investment

Whichever form of multinational activity results, theory suggests that there are four main reasons for the original decision by an enterprise to transcend national frontiers. Each assumes that the enterprise is a long-term profit maximiser, and desires short-term profits or growth.

Conventional investment theory

If all economies were open to flows of capital and investment expenditure, then it might be expected that interest rates would reach international equilibrium, and that enterprises would seek to invest, anywhere, as long as the marginal efficiency of the investments exceeds the rate of interest. In practice of course, there are restrictions, imperfections and different degrees of risk internationally. However, conventional theory predicts that where free capital flows are still possible, multinational investment will take place on the same basis as domestic investment. This means that transnational capital movement will continue until the marginal productivity of capital (marginal efficiency over interest rate) invested into country Y equals that in the parent country X (MacDougall 1960).

The above may apply both to new investment in productive enterprise, and to *portfolio* investment—the acquisition of stock in existing enterprises. The determinants of the amount of multinational investment are: comparative interest rates, comparative yields obtainable, the 'openness' of economies to transnational investment and factor payments, and the degree of risk, or risk-spreading, involved. Thus United States and Japanese holding companies and property groups often buy into highly-performing tourism businesses around the world simply for direct financial returns.

Production advantages

A second possibility is that country X enterprises may secure advantages in production in country Y over local firms. If normal profits in the two countries are similar, then the MNE may be able to make above-average profits out of country Y.

The production advantages possessed by MNEs over local competitors may be superior technology, skills or management knowledge (Root 1978). Alternatively, country Y's authorities may offer special inducements in the form of cheap resources or tax advantages to the MNE. If the parent enterprise can combine production advantages with highly useable resources in a specific location, and internalise the management of all the activities and product flows concerned, it has a very powerful reason to act multinationally. This has been termed the *eclectic* theory of international production (Dunning 1979). There are good examples in the way that Western businesses have become involved in developing tourism in Eastern Europe since 1990 (Hall 1991).

Exploiting monopolistic advantages

Enterprises using NIMAs (see above) are primarily seeking economies of chain operation through horizontal integration, and will extend beyond national frontiers where markets are all-encompassing, or sufficiently similar, to warrant it. Most of these external economies are marketing ones, relating to international image, advertising and known product standards. Other more general chain-operation economies may be important internationally to an enterprise based in a small economy. For example, large Belgian, Dutch or Swiss enterprises are almost by definition multinational.

Monopolistic advantage at home may also come from vertical integration, in securing resource supplies or market outlets. Where those supplies or outlets occur in another country, an enterprise may buy or tie up trading agreements internationally to protect its domestic position (Caves 1971).

Large mining and oil companies have always done this, and the search for tourism resources is often equally as international as that for minerals. The quest for international vertical integration is greatest where enterprises are oligopolistic in their own country. The result may be 'bunching' of investments by more than one country X enterprise in country Y. Oligopolistic competition easily crosses frontiers.

Product life extension

A final theory for multinational investment suggests that an enterprise may expand abroad to extend or alter product life cycles. A product introduced some time ago in country X may now be nearing the end of its life cycle, but country Y's market may be a 'laggard' for that product. Rather than merely exporting all production to country Y there may be advantages in transferring production lines completely (Knickerbocker 1973). Classic cases of this have occurred with British and German car builders moving into India, Mexico and Brazil. Multinational product life extension applies to manufactured goods rather than services.

■ Reasons for multinational operation in travel and tourism

Whilst the majority (over 90%) of the world's tourism by volume of tourist numbers is domestic, international tourism counts for a very significant share of total value. As we have seen, when tourists buy the tourism product, they acquire a set of services (and some goods) which emanate from the generating

Figure 11.1   Total trip expenditure by hypothetical short-haul international tourist (%)

Generating Country		International Link		Destination Country	
Travel agency services	8	Air carriage	30	Lodging	22
Other services		Goods (e.g. duty-free)	5	Transfers & sidetrips	13
(e.g. information)	3			Personal and	
Taxes	2			souvenirs	12
				Taxes	5
Nontax total	**11**	**Total**	**35**	**Nontax total**	**47**

Source: adapted from tour operators' market research

country, the destination country, and perhaps some intermediate or stopover countries as well. A typical short-haul international tourist trip might involve the breakdown of expenditure as shown in Figure 11.1.

The products in Figure 11.1 are known to be largely complementary in demand. The supplier of any one knows, therefore, that demand for its product means there will be demand for the others. Consequently:

- if each of the products can be produced and sold profitably, a profit-maximiser has a ready incentive to diversify into those areas; for example an airline could make profit on 93% of the tourist's spending rather than on 30 or 35% by internalising all the other activities
- providing an IT consisting of two or more of the product elements—especially the main ones of air travel and lodging—has marketing and supply-preservation advantages (Holloway 1989),
- suppliers based in generating markets particularly can capitalise on knowledge of tourists' tastes and market trends in their own country by supplying destination products.

In addition, tourism enterprises have diversified not necessarily to maximise operation in existing total tourism markets but to stimulate further tourism development which may lead to growth opportunities in their 'home' business (Lane 1986). In the past this has generally meant new equity investment in other countries, but increasingly means taking part in a NIMA with local partners or forming international trading agreements, rather than multi-national enterprises. The rationale is to seek ways of utilising international business to improve profitability and growth of existing activity.

Pressure to develop into multinational operations in tourism is greatest in generating countries. This can be seen in the arguments above, and also from examination of the values in Figure 11.1. Assume for simplicity that enterprises A, B and C respectively own the travel and tourism resources in the generator, international link and destination. If each were able to acquire every enterprise supplying the tourist:

- A could earn revenue of 93 instead of 11—an increase of 8.5 times
- B could earn revenue of 93 instead of 35—an increase of 2.7 times
- C could earn revenue of 93 instead of 47—an increase of 98% (i.e. just under 2 times).

Enterprise A therefore has the greatest revenue, and presumably profit, to gain from internationalising.

In practice of course, the potential business expansion is nearly always less, as few enterprises would be able, or willing, to acquire and operate *all* of the tourism producers concerned, and they may well start with more than one. An airline, say, may already own a domestic retail travel chain.

A final alternative is for an enterprise such as a hotel or restaurant chain, not currently involved in either this generator or destination, to come into the system, usually by management contract or franchising. This would directly give them marketing advantages of geographic diversification as well as utilising more widely their production knowhow. The geographic 'homes' of most MNEs in travel and tourism are the United States, France, the United Kingdom, Japan and increasingly Hong Kong. This reinforces the view that multinational operation in the sector is strongly driven by tourism generation and by the wish to export investment capital.

The spread of West European and United States tourism businesses into Eastern Europe has been a good example of three factors combining: spreading production knowhow superior to that of existing local businesses; anticipating higher yields (marginal productivities) from growing Eastern European generating markets; and obtaining international operating economies. These have led, respectively, to franchising hotels in Eastern Europe, buying shares in travel companies, and strategic East Europe-West Europe airline alliances (Hunt 1993).

■ MNEs in air travel

Of all types of enterprise in travel and tourism, perhaps airlines have had the most obvious interest in multinational operation, and to a certain extent investment. Since the opening of the first international passenger air service between London and Paris just after World War I, airlines operating internationally have had to choose whether or not to operate their own branch offices at foreign ports or important off-line major cities. The alternative is a local agent.

To develop business from foreign ports and compete effectively with local airlines, the international airline may think a branch office is worthwhile, and may be forced by local law to establish an operating subsidiary. An alternative is a reciprocal arrangement with a local airline which provides joint marketing, joint ramp handling, interline agreements and the monopolistic advantages of an MNE. The logical development in pure airline business has been 'true' MNEs, in central reservations systems such as Covia/Galileo, Sabre, or Amadeus/Abacus, in insurance and emergency support, and in interline banking (bank settlement plans).

Multinational operation of flights themselves has been restricted by governments jealous of maintaining 'flag' airlines for political or diplomatic purposes. Some have prospered, such as SAS (Scandinavian Airline Systems) representing equity from Norway, Sweden and Denmark; others are developing in the less regulated air markets of the 1990s. The key development of the 1990s is that of airlines maintaining their individual entities, but operating linked services, such as 'codesharing' (featuring a single flight under two different flight codes). This enables each airline to *seem* to offer a much wider range of flights than they actually do—a marketing advantage, which offers the airline physically operating each flight production advantages from a higher load factor.

Airlines with hotels and other tourism businesses

When country X's airline flies passengers to country Y, it tries to maximise its *yield*, or revenue, by selling to residents of those countries in which it can charge the highest fare (see Chapter 5). The airline tempers this with the knowledge that it needs to specialise in the market of its own country, for political and business development reasons. Many of these country X passengers will require accommodations in country Y, and perhaps recreational tourism activities.

For many years, airlines have therefore kept a close eye on the adequacy of lodging and ground handling in the destinations to which they fly. They may then wish to expand local capacity, or control the supply of these services in pursuit of a trading advantage in carrying passengers to the destination. The first major example of an airline interest in lodging was Pan Am, which formed Inter-Continental Hotels as a subsidiary in 1946. TWA, United and several European airlines later followed into hotel equity ownership or NIMAs internationally. Since trading advantages vary between destinations and between airlines, *multiple* airline/hotel affiliations have become normal, with two or more airlines frequently involved in one hotel chain (such as Penta), or airlines linking with more than one hotel chain. This has been termed *polygamous* rather than *monogamous* linkage (Hudson 1969, Lane 1986), and has resulted in large but loosely interconnected MNEs in air carriage plus lodging.

Some airline-hotel links have followed 'historic' patterns of trade and tourism flows, such as:

Air France → Meridien Hotels worldwide
Canadian Pacific → CP Hotels (Europe & North America)
KLM → Golden Tulip Hotels worldwide
TWA → Hilton International Hotels (until sold)
UTA → UTH & Accor (Africa & Pacific).

Other links have generated travel as a result of airlines' route development providing fresh destinations for their passengers, such as:

All Nippon → ANA Hotels in the Pacific area
Japan Air Lines → Nikko Hotels worldwide.

In either event, joint airline/international hotel operation allows enterprises to sell complementary products in one transaction, to control supply availability, and to enable sophisticated marketing techniques such as frequent flyer and accommodation programmes. Where deregulation and increased competition have forced airlines to pull out of hotels and back into their 'core business', they have maintained agreements and alliances with hotel chains rather than formal mergers (Dev and Klein 1993).

To increase complementarity, airlines may extend activity into foreign local ground transport, tourism attractions or food (Byrnes 1985). The resulting operation is likely to resemble that of international IT enterprises (see below).

Airlines with travel agencies

Many airlines seeking to exploit monopolistic trading advantages may seek control of product distribution by acquiring travel agencies. It is very rare, however, for such acquisitions to be multinational, as airlines naturally tend to concentrate on domestic markets in which they have a large share, rather than foreign ones in which their share may be very small. These links therefore do not normally contribute to MNEs.

■ MNEs in travel agencies and related services

There are few examples of multinational operation in the travel distribution sector. A number of reasons can be identified:

- until recently, few technical (production) economies of scale have existed, causing little pressure to form chains
- marketing and management economics do exist for chains, but tend to relate mostly to discrete generating markets; travel service enterprises must specialise in the requirements of a particular generating market, and this 'production advantage' may not extend easily across frontiers
- licensing and qualifications legislation differs from country to country, often in ways which impede transfer of skills and knowhow—despite the ubiquity of methods in, say, IATA ticketing
- many travel businesses work as subsidiaries of domestic enterprises in other fields which have no interest in multinational operation, or work with limited capital and are therefore not looking for further investment.

Nevertheless, examples of multinational operation in travel services do exist. Probably the best known are American Express, Thomas Cook and Wagon-Lits Tourisme. These are all long-established enterprises involved both in travel agencies and other services, the complementarity of which makes multinational operation desirable. Thomas Cook, for example, developed from its British base (although it is now German-owned) to have 350 equity-owned branch offices in 25 countries, particularly English-speaking ones. Wagon-Lits Tourisme, originally the Belgian-based sleeping car and luxury train operator, has 415 offices in 33 countries specialising in continental Europe, Mexico and South America (The Wagon-Lits Company is now integrated with the Accor hotel chain). Thomas Cook and Wagon-Lits, which for many years were closely linked with each other, also have associates in other countries.

The rationale for such multinational operation is not primarily travel retailing, but the supply of services *which themselves are international*, or destination services which are linked with pre-trip services. Most of the 1000 American Express travel offices, for example, sell travel to local clients, to onward travellers, handle travel check and card financial business, and provide general in-destination tourism services. A similar situation applies where the retail travel agency is only part of another activity such as National Tourist Office services or shipping. Enterprises such as Balkantourist, Japan Travel Bureau, Cunard and CTC thus possess what are effectively MNEs in travel.

Like airlines, many other travel service markets require multinational operation. These include car rental companies, hotel reservation representatives, medical assistance, travel insurance and credit card companies. Sometimes this results in equity ownership MNEs, such as Avis, Hertz, Utell or Diners Club; elsewhere NIMAs exist. The reasoning, in both cases, is that part of the service to consumers will be supplied in one country and part in another, as well as global 'name' promotional economies. Extension of global economies of scale in the use of information technology and communications systems has also led to the internationalisation of travel information systems by enterprises such as the Reed Travel Group, combining OAG and Travel Information Group services in the United States, ABC Guides from the United Kingdom, Utell hotel reservations and other information and reservation services.

■ MNEs in accommodation

In assessing the role and impact of MNEs in tourism, more attention has been paid to those in the accommodation sector than any other. This is partly due to the high visibility of lodging chains as an element of tourism (and economic activity), and partly due to the larger international flow of investment. An airline's investment in foreign plant may be restricted to office and basic maintenance facilities; travel service enterprises also mainly require offices (and maybe transportation equipment), but hotels and resorts demand substantial fixed investment in land, buildings and equipment.

In the 1950s and 1960s most international investment by accommodation enterprises was:

- of American origin
- direct equity investment.

This has changed—towards NIMA bases of operation (Lee 1985, Dev and Klein 1993) and a far wider spread of origins. Major non-US based MNEs in the sector include Club Mediterranee, Accor and Meridien (France), Forte and Bass (United Kingdom), CP Hotels (Canada), Oberoi (India), Melia/Sol (Spain), Nikko, Aoki and ANA Hotels (Japan), and New World and Mandarin Oriental (Hong Kong). Major United States accommodation MNEs such as Holiday Inn, Westin, Sheraton, Inter-Continental, Hyatt and Hilton accounted for half of all foreign-owned or associated hotels worldwide in 1978 (Dunning and McQueen 1982), but expansion by non-US enterprises, as well as the acquisition of American hotel companies by foreign businesses (Olsen 1993), reduces this proportion continually. Demonstration effects of the economies of chain operation in lodging are largely responsible.

The move from equity investment to NIMA operation has been partially explained by the nature of direct investment costs compared with available markets (Litteljohn 1985), and partially by the fact that there is no need for parent enterprises to centralise and internalise investment (Dunning and McQueen 1982). The major benefits to the parent flow from operation rather than ownership, and there is no conflict of interest. Indeed it is not unusual for a hotel in country A to be owned by a country A enterprise, which is a subsidiary of a country B holding company (interest rates perhaps being lower in country B), and operated by a country C multinational operator under management contract. Any of these enterprises may in turn be linked with airlines or other businesses. Thus the enterprise has formalised, by separate ownership, the optimum acquisition of factor inputs:

- land and 'tourism resources' from country A
- capital from country B
- entrepreneurial skills from country C.

The country B company then develops as a development-portfolio or equity-owning but non-managing MNE in tourism, such as Kumagai Gumi or Daikyo of Japan; the country C operator such as Hyatt or Sheraton becomes the better known MNE hotelier.

Whether by acquisition or development, MNEs in lodging have one of the fastest growth rates of any sector in tourism; Club Mediterranee for example started in 1949 with one small village in Majorca, and have expanded over the years to operate 85 large self-contained complexes, in more than 30 countries. More recently, Japanese, Hong Kong and Korean-based groups have grown even faster (Shaw 1989).

■ MNEs in tour operation and cruising

Some of the earliest multinational involvements in travel and tourism were those of passenger shipping companies which inevitably needed to develop at least an agency presence in overseas ports served. This extended to the needs of:

• selling travel to residents of each country in which ships called (and maybe off-line countries too)
• purchasing supplies and bunkering in foreign ports

- acquiring factor inputs internationally to optimise production (for example, United States finance for a Finnish-built vessel, registered in Panama, insured in London, using Norwegian officers and a Filipino or Levantine crew).

The demise of most of the world's passenger line voyages has not altered these involvements, as the same needs have extended to cruising. United States, British, Scandinavian, Italian and Greek cruise companies operate in Caribbean and other ports (Hobson 1993) with German, Finnish and French-built vessels insured in London, registered and crewed from a variety of countries. Marketing activity is likely to concentrate on the United States, Canada, the United Kingdom, Germany and other European countries.

Many cruise companies operate enterprises in other sectors of travel and tourism; for example P&O-Sitmar, Cunard and Chandris all own hotels or resorts. Whilst they may or may not be linked operationally to cruising, they tend to increase the geographical spread of the MNE parent.

Mass international tour operation has developed principally from Western European, and more recently Japanese, bases. Most outbound tour operators start by using ground handling agents or inbound operators in destinations to provide destination services; expansion may provide economies of scale from providing their own ground handling, and possibly their own ground transportation and accommodations. These are often exclusive NIMAs. The rationale for this form of integration was seen in Chapter 4. Once again, the main pressure for integration comes from enterprises in generating countries, who potentially have the most to gain from operating their own 'production plant' in destinations (Caves 1971). It is common for German, Dutch, Scandinavian and British tour operators to undertake resort representation, ground handling, transfers and excursions in destinations to which they direct many customers. This is partly to limit the growth of new competitors (Bywater 1992). If demand is sufficiently large, they may also own or have exclusive NIMA contracts with hotels. Thus, Dutch operators own hotels in Torremolinos, Spain; TUI (Germany) and Thomson Holidays (UK) have at one time or another owned hotels and even cruise ships in the Mediterranean area. Japanese operators spread similarly across popular destinations in East Asia and the Western Pacific.

With the odd exception such as Canadian Pacific, multinational integration of tour operating activities has not been a feature of North American enterprises, principally because of the different structure of outbound travel markets. There is also the presence already of many Canadian or United States-owned resorts, hotels and tourism facilities in major destination areas such as Mexico and the Caribbean.

In practice, the distinction between tour operators with their own destination plant, international hotel chains and airlines with hotel links is specious in regard to multinational operation. They all supply the same markets with similar products, and as MNEs are likely to have the same requirements of their operations in host economies.

■ Effects on host economies

Since the early 1980s, studies of the effects of MNEs on tourism on host economies have produced a generous literature, largely due to the seminal work of Dunning and McQueen (1982). There are five basic areas of concern to a host economy—defined as any national economy in which a MNE has an economic presence other than its home or parent economy:

- control over the structure and development of the tourism industry, or particular subsectors of the industry
- control over tourist markets and tourist flows
- prices obtained for host economy tourism products
- the destination of factor and input payments
- competition with locally-owned enterprises and the demonstration effects of production techniques.

Structure and development control

Very often MNEs are induced by the government of a host economy to set up an operation because local enterprise does not exist or possess the appropriate resources. Particularly in less developed countries (LDCs) this has tended to mean that the structure of sectors of tourism is controlled from outside, unless governments impose conditions on development. For example, a foreign-owned airline developing, under contract, services to and in a small country, may prevent other airlines from starting services, and impose a monopoly which may or may not be advantageous to the host economy. Even without inducements, a MNE may monopolise sufficiently in a host economy to prohibit both the entry of other MNEs and the development of local enterprises.

Some states have signed exclusive contracts with developers such as Club Mediterranee or United States hotel chains which not only restrict competition but also the host's autonomy in deciding the style of development. Developers may dictate the form of other sectors of tourism (Pearce 1989), by, for example, insisting on new airport construction, ground transportation and structure of ground handling.

If MNEs develop a monopolistic position in a host economy, they are able to exert pressure on governments to tailor future tourism to their own needs, including demands on hosts to spend on infrastructure. This has been noted in Spain (Sinclair and Sutcliffe 1988) as a transfer of benefits to inbound tourists from local residents who, through taxation, finance the infrastructure.

Despite the above problems, many countries still welcome foreign MNEs in tourism if the alternative is no development. Increasingly, governments have also become more sophisticated in negotiating with MNEs in early stages of development. As global tourism grows, and the number of MNEs seeking foreign operations increases, host governments acquire greater bargaining power against them.

Control over tourist markets and flows

The level of commitment which a MNE has to a host economy depends on the relative profitability to be gained from that economy compared with others. That profitability may emanate directly from the subsidiary's operations or, specifically in the case of international tourism, may reflect market conditions in economies at the other end of tourist flows. For example, Japanese tour operators pulled out of Canada in the early 1980s because of better profitability elsewhere, and at a similar time British hotel chains and tour operators scaled down subsidiaries in Malta primarily because British tourists were unwilling to go there. Tourist-generating markets may also, though less equally, be dependent on foreign MNEs to supply travel needs in small but significant generating countries such as Middle Eastern emirates.

A more subtle problem is that of multinational travel and tourism enterprises controlling *specific flows of tourists* between generators and destinations. An airline, for example, with associated hotel operations, seeks to maximise yields on its routes by selling into the most profitable market segments providing consistent load factors. Thus a particular Bahamaian resort area might consistently depend on middle-class New Yorkers, and a Thai resort on Japanese honeymooners. First, such specific dependence is risky, leaving the destination exposed to changes in individual market conditions. Secondly, the destination's NTO may no longer control market targeting. It may wish to attract few, high-spending, 'elite' tourists, but the commercial MNE may maximise profits from selling to mass-market tourists who bring home-preferred tastes with them (thus incurring imports) and little spending money (Lundgren 1972 and many later writers). At the extreme, such market concentration, together with economies of scale derived from mass markets and standardisation, can lead to *tourism enclave developments*. These may almost be independent of host economies, as well as physically and culturally separate.

Prices of tourism products

Discounts for quantity and/or regular purchases are common for many products. In addition, many tourism enterprises work with seasonal price differentials—usually expressed as off-season discounts—to regulate demand to match supply. Tour operators, general sales agents and other travel and tourism distributors with bargaining power make use of this to negotiate bulk rates with suppliers, which enables them to compete on price in generating markets (Cleverdon 1979). This happens in all mass tourism markets; for example, German and British tour operators are renowned for negotiating extremely cheap prices with Spanish and Greek hoteliers and tourism attractions. Multinational enterprise simply formalises and internalises the negotiations. Prices are set in relation to the MNE's marketplace (that is, in generating areas) and costing of component services provided by subsidiaries may well reflect group accounting and profit needs rather than those of each subsidiary.

Multinational operation thus leads to *transfer pricing* (Sinclair and Sutcliffe 1988). This is a method of artificially setting prices for each component of a multinational product, such as an IT, in such a way as to maximise corporate benefit. It is most often used in minimising tax liability, which in turn leads to government moves to regulate it—as in the United States in 1990. Transfer pricing and its associated flexible rescheduling of foreign exchange payments to take advantage of exchange rate variations can be a major loss to host economies.

Consider the following example:

A tour operator based in and selling in country A owns an airline registered in country B and destination facilities including accommodations in country C. It sells an IT at $1000 in country A, and does not buy nor sell components outside, but sets accounting prices internally between subsidiaries. Table 11.1 shows its tax-minimising procedure.

Table 11.1   Transfer pricing by a tour operator

Country	Tax rate	True 'arm's length cost price X	Contribution to selling price Y	'True' net profit Y-X	'True'tax liability
A HQ Office	40%	180	200	20	8
B Air travel	20%	360	400	40	8
C Destination	60%	360	400	40	24
		900	1000	100	40

		Transfer price (declared costs) Z	Declared profit Y-Z	Tax paid
A		200	0	0
B		300	100	20
C		400	0	0
		900	100	20

The MNE overvalues cost prices in economies with high tax rates, to reduce declared profit and therefore tax paid; vice versa in low-tax economies. It may do this by, for example, upvaluing destination assets in C, writing down aircraft in B, and reallocating overheads or inter-subsidiary transactions. The result reduces overall tax liability by 2% of gross revenue, or from 40% of profits to 20%. Non trading profits can be further enhanced by ensuring good timing of any foreign exchange payments to take advantage of favourable rates.

Destination of payments

Positive economic benefits to any country from travel and tourism are limited by the degree to which revenues leak from the economy. Leakages fall into two main groups:

- payments for imported goods and services
- payments to offshore factors of production.

There has been no solid evidence that a MNE subsidiary in a host economy has a higher propensity to import goods and services to run its operation than any comparable locally-owned enterprise. In fact many MNEs, anxious to protect their image in host economies, may deliberately source inputs locally where possible, as a matter of policy. It is, however, inevitable that tourism MNEs in particular will *not* always be comparable with local enterprises, as they must reflect connections with their home economies.

First, as noted above, subsidiaries in destinations often need goods and services required by tourists with 'home town tastes'. American-owned hotel chains normally stock American beer and cigarettes; Japanese-owned establishments catering for their own nationals often import foodstuffs and furnishings from Japan. Secondly, where representation of the home country's image is important or global standardisation needed, subsidiaries may have to reflect this in purchasing. Air France and Meridien Hotels worldwide promote their French image through displayed effects and consumables, as Royal Viking Line do their Norwegian background (despite a Florida base).

Payments to offshore factors of production pose a rather more serious leakage. Where LDCs induce enterprises from elsewhere because they do not possess the necessary resources themselves, then the leakage of factor rewards is inevitable (Dieke 1989). The only immobile factors of production in tourism are land and intrinsic attractions—even these may pass into foreign ownership. MNEs may provide other factor inputs from the most efficient sources to suit their production. Equity and loan capital will therefore be sourced, all else being equal, from low interest rate capital markets, assuming the host economy does not restrict capital flows; interest payments then represent a leakage. Skilled labour may be imported, especially for management, and allow little opportunity for local employees to gain responsible positions (Mill and Morrison 1985). The result is a leakage of the repatriated part of (probably the highest) wages.

Capital equipment imports tend to be no higher for MNE subsidiaries than for locally-owned enterprises. Ground passenger transportation equipment (for tour buses, taxis, rail systems, car rental and so on) is just as likely to be sourced from Japan, Germany or the United States by a local operator as by a MNE from one of those countries. Three quarters of the world's air seat/kilometres are flown by United States-built aircraft, almost regardless of the operator.

Perhaps the major leakage attributed to MNE operations is that of profits and fees. Whether MNEs own equity or operate on a participatory management contract or similar turnkey system, the rewards to entrepreneurial skill are generally a leakage. Although there is little evidence that MNEs earn supernormal profits in relation to their home economies, monopolistic positions may allow *relative* supernormal profits to be earned in host economies. Transfer pricing can effectively remove 'true' profits without there even seeming to be a leakage.

The aggregate effect of payment leakages, combined particularly with MNEs operating at both ends of a tourist flow, can reduce substantially the contribution of tourism to a host economy's GDP. It has been shown, for example, that only 31–33% of a tourist's total expenditure may go to, and remain in, the destination when the tourist buys an IT from an integrated multinational outbound operator (Bull 1990). Where essentially the same products are supplied individually and locally, destination-kept revenue may exceed 50%.

Production techniques and local competition

Whilst many tour operators and airlines extend multinational operation primarily to integrate production vertically for home markets, other MNEs in travel and tourism may extend horizontally across national frontiers to obtain economies of scale, and because they can employ superior production techniques to those of local enterprises. They may therefore earn higher profits (Root 1978).

In relation to hotel chains, production advantages cited are:

- logistical skills and experience in the industry
- access to sophisticated technology—of especial importance to luxury or international hotels
- wider and cheaper sourcing of staff and physical inputs than locals may obtain
- staff planning and training expertise, giving superior techniques of producing and delivering services. (Dunning and McQueen 1982).

To these can nowadays be added global CRS and accounting systems. The low transactions costs involved for a MNE transferring these techniques internationally are likely to provide competitive advantages against local enterprises, especially in LDCs. Exactly the same principles apply in travel agencies, car rental and other similar sectors.

The end benefit to a host country should be production technology transfer through demonstration effects. It is notable that benefits accrue most rapidly in countries such as Thailand and Tunisia, where superior production techniques are emulated and assimilated most quickly by local enterprise. Some governments now stipulate transfer of tourism skills and technology as a condition of multinational investment.

■ Effects on parent economies and tourism flows

Whilst the effect of tourism MNEs on host economies has received considerable attention, that on parent economies is less well documented.

At a microeconomic level, MNEs may change the structure and profitability of their industry sector in the parent economy, in several ways:

- a parent economy may be too small on its own to support an efficient travel and tourism marketplace in which economies of scale can be gained; Singapore Airlines and the Wagon-Lits Company could not exist as they do in their domestic markets alone.
- MNEs direct investment to those destinations which provide the highest marginal returns, therefore raising the average returns earned in the industry for the parent economy.
- by providing mass or integrated production of outbound tourism products to consumers, they generally reduce price levels.
- MNEs mainly providing outbound travel and tourism products may create monopolistic advantages for themselves in home markets; if the sector is already oligopolistic in nature, 'bunching' to protect trading positions may occur (Flowers 1976). (For example, very often a Sheraton hotel development in a destination means a Hilton or Holiday Inn may follow).

In macroeconomic terms, the influences of MNEs in travel and tourism are bound up with tourist flows. Many MNEs such as European tour operators have been responsible for stimulating outbound travel from their parent countries which might not otherwise have taken place (Holloway 1989). The resulting higher propensity to travel internationally creates a balance of payments outflow. On the other hand, multinational operation may save the loss of foreign exchange from outbound tourists who intended to travel anyway. If an American business tourist selects a United States-owned hotel in a foreign destination by preference, there is almost a form of import substitution. This is an additional benefit to that of the straight 'export sale' of goods and services supplied in that establishment to non-United States tourists.

By their existence, multinational travel and tourism enterprises have changed the flows of tourists as well as responding to demand. They have caused governments to alter fiscal arrangements and spending on tourism infrastructure, and forced the reappraisal of international tourism's value in many places.

Study questions

1 Summarize the main forms of foreign involvement which MNEs may take.
2 What immediate advantages might a financially well-backed tourism business based in France have, if it decided to operate in the destination businesses of West African countries?
3 Identify any significant differences between the reasons for multinational operation of airlines or hotels and those for multinational manufacturing enterprises.
4 Explain the reasons why non-investment management arrangements are becoming increasingly popular in multinational hotel operation.
5 Identify the advantages and disadvantages to a host economy of attracting MNEs to aid tourism development.
6 Explain in your own words what is meant by transfer pricing, as practiced by MNEs in tourism.
7 To what extent have MNEs caused changes in patterns of tourism flows?
8 Pick any three or four major tourism destinations. Consider whether in these destinations there has been 'bunching' of competitive hotel- or airline-operating MNEs from abroad.

The economic roles of government

■ Macroeconomic management

Few government authorities would nowadays deny their responsibility to provide economic management and play an integral role in many areas of economic activity. In contrast to the days of *laissez-faire*, *some* role is accepted—the scope of that role depending on the nature of the economic system and associated political doctrine.

There are three major roles which governments may play in the economy:

- taking measures to promote socio-economic well being, including improvement in standards of living, maintaining employment, and welfare equity.
- levying the economy in order to supply non commercial social provisions (such as justice and diplomacy).
- owning the means of production for specific goods and services, and managing them as enterprises.

These roles entail fiscal and monetary policy, regulation, planning and direct commercial management. With the exception of monetary policy, these could be carried out by any level of government from national (or supranational bloc) to local. The importance of the third role depends on the politico-economic system. In Marxian economies, governments engage heavily in what is termed the collective provision of goods and services (Samuelson 1989), but in mixed market economies government involvement may be minor.

All these economic activities are likely to have some effect on every industry, either directly (if that industry is the target of a specific policy, such as monetary policy and the banking sector) or indirectly (by changing demand, general costs, factor payment allocation and so on).

■ Sectoral economic management in tourism

As with other sectors, government policies may affect travel and tourism both directly and indirectly (Figure 12.1).

Figure 12.1   Government economic policy and tourism

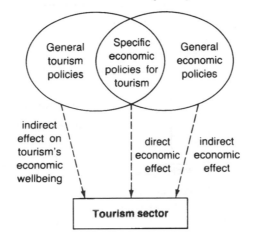

General economic policies, and those which may be directed at other sectors of the economy, may have substantial indirect effects on tourism. For example, business expenditure or 'fringe benefits' taxes may reduce demand for business travel and hospitality services through reduced tax deductibility; measures to control interest rates alter the marginal profitability of travel and tourism ventures. The directness of effects and their degree of influence are not necessarily correlated, as economy-wide policies may in the end have more pervasive influences throughout every channel of economic activity.

A government's general tourism policies are likely to reflect a range of objectives: economic, environmental, social/educational/diplomatic and so on (Ferguson 1988). Almost always, the non economic policies have considerable economic implications for tourism, particularly if equity or normative judgments are involved. Increasingly, policies are likely to be *composite*, addressing economic as well as non economic issues.

It is the intention of this chapter to examine some of the direct effects of government activity on tourism, rather than the indirect ones—which are better examined through texts on the general macroeconomic and micro-economic roles of government. The general goal for economic policy in tourism is likely to be the maximisation of tourism's contribution to national economic well being (OECD 1967). Contributory goals include:

- optimising contributions (usually inflows) to the balance of payments
- providing a focus for regional development or regional economic balance

- providing employment
- redistributing and improving incomes
- contributing to social (economic) welfare
- maximising opportunities for fiscal revenue.

These goals translate into the roles outlined in Figure 12.2.

Figure 12.2 The roles of government in tourism

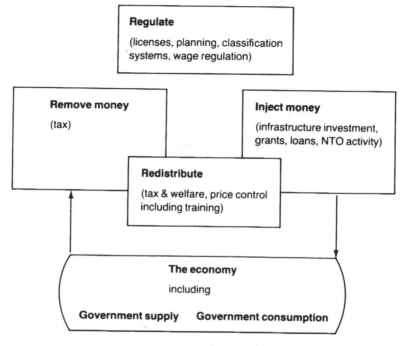

A government may remove money from an economy by taxation and borrowing (although the latter will be ignored here, as it does not relate specifically and directly to tourism). It may inject money through government expenditure, both for consumption and investment. It may combine removal and injection for the purposes of redistribution—for example, by levying employers to provide industry-wide industrial training programmes. A government may regulate the suppliers in travel and tourism, imposing controls on such things as output and prices. Finally, it may itself act as producer, and consumer, in many areas of travel and tourism activity.

◼ Tourism taxation

Many governments use tourism as a source of tax revenue, sometimes to fund expenditure within the sector and sometimes to include in general revenue. As travel and tourism is still regarded by most policy makers as a non essential activity, any indirect taxation on tourism services is likely to be progressive, with respect to consumers' incomes. Like other indirect taxes, those on tourism products may be *ad valorem* (a percentage of price), or *specific* (set amounts). They can be divided into three types:

- taxes on commercial tourism products
- taxes imposed on consumers in the act of being tourists
- user pays charges.

Taxes on commercial tourism products are straightforward examples of consumption (sales, value-added or purchase) taxes. They are normally levied on producers, who must then decide if it is possible to pass the incidence of taxation on to the consuming tourist. This depends on the price elasticity of demand facing each producer (see Chapter 6). Those in a highly competitive market are unable to raise prices and maintain demand, and thus are likely to absorb taxes. Where monopolistic or collusive practices prevail, lower price elasticity of demand means the incidence of such taxation falls more directly on tourists.

Favourite targets for this type of taxation are accommodation, meals, car rentals and fuel excise. Taxes on accommodations—room sales taxes—are imposed in most parts of the United States and in many other destinations. Like sales tax on eat-in meals and car rentals, or VAT/TVA in Europe, they are mostly *ad valorem* at rates ranging up to over 20%, and there is a considerable literature on their incidence (for example Mak 1988, Spengler and Uysal 1989, Hiemstra and Ismail 1992). The hypothesis has been advanced that taxes on fixed costs (such as land taxes) do not influence the equilibrium level of the tourism market in the same way that variable (for example, lodging) taxes do (Fish 1982); but this is only true in a short-run situation—say one season. In the longer run the effects of *any* consumption tax must be taken into consideration by suppliers in both short-run operation and long-run planning. This applies both to *ad valorem* taxes, as noted above, and to specific taxes such as fixed excise duties on fuel or licences and levy fees to operate gaming machines and casinos. Levy fees are a major revenue source for many governments, and in Monaco, for example, they provide almost all of the revenue in a state with no income tax.

A normative 'ideal' for tourism taxation is that the burden of providing services in location X, primarily for tourists from location Y, should fall on those visitors. This is sometimes known as *tax exportation*, from X to Y (Fujii, Khaled and Mak 1985), and avoids the 'immiserising' effect of taxing residents of X for the services (Clarke and Ng 1993). Whilst this depends, for consumption taxes, on demand elasticities, many governments impose specific taxes directly on tourists regardless of the bundle of goods and services purchased. These are generally levied on international tourists and collected at gateways.

First, some countries impose exit or travel taxes on their residents seeking to travel internationally. These taxes are primarily designed to deter foreign travel and consequent foreign exchange outflows, and hence may be relatively high—up to US$300 per person per trip. (The *opposite* case—of tax deductibility to *promote* outbound travel—is sometimes used by countries with an embarrassingly large balance of payments surplus; for example, Japan introduced this type of policy in 1993.)

Secondly, a few countries such as Paraguay and Venezuela impose an arrival tax on tourists. Whilst this is more overt, it is probably no more onerous than the hidden taxation in many countries' high prices of visas and other documentation, which often greatly exceed administrative costs of supply. The resulting monopolistic economic rent is a straight revenue-raiser.

Third is the most popular revenue-raiser, in the form of a departure tax, on both residents commencing a trip and returning tourists leaving a destination. In 1994, 110 of the world's 180 or so sovereign states levied some form of this tax. Some are nominally or effectively user charges for airport terminals (Airport or Civil Aviation Tax), although other states require airlines to include these in airfares. Others are general revenue Departure or Embarcation Taxes—the Philippines has both an airport and a departure tax.

Other than exit taxes, these imposts are usually too small to be deterrents to tourism consumption or to cause a shift in demand to another destination product. In Lancasterian demand terms the price increase caused by tax is below the perceptual threshold of substitution. Unfortunately, some tourists, such as Colombians going to Venezuela, would suffer *all* of the above taxes.

As was seen in Chapter 9, user pays charges are becoming increasingly accepted. There is no clear distinction between these charges as the price of a tourism facility purchased and as a tax on the use of that facility. In principle, the 'price' approach covers costs associated with supplying the facility, whilst the remaining economic rent may be regarded as tax. However, the distinction depends on accounting procedures used, especially in the allocation of overhead costs. Of a $20 entrance fee for a vehicle to a national park, for example, $8 may be assessed as relating to the direct costs of managing that park, and the remaining $12 is effectively tax. If the national parks authority has a large central bureaucracy, a further $5 or $6 may be attributed to central overhead costs, halving the nominal 'tax'. In general, authorities are moving increasingly both to identify and internalise all management costs into user charges, and to levy a tax surcharge if they wish to ration or deter use of a location by tourists.

■ Government spending on tourism

There is only rarely a link between taxation of tourism and government expenditure on the sector. Despite the presence of occasional purpose-named taxes (such as the Central African Republic's Tourist Development Tax), the principle of directly levying to fund the same sector applies only to certain aspects of tourism operation such as training, which will be discussed under redistribution below.

The bulk of government spending on tourism occurs in three areas:

- infrastructure investment and maintenance
- facilitation of tourism development
- undertaking tourism marketing (mostly through NTOs).

Infrastructure investment and maintenance

In most countries, the government is responsible for providing economic infrastructure. In relation to travel and tourism, infrastructure involves fixed passenger transportation investment, destination services such as power, water, sewerage, cleansing and health, fixed communications investment, and so on. A completely free market economy might see all these goods and services supplied by private enterprise, but—if only to avoid waste and duplication—governments usually have a significant interest in infrastructure.

Very little infrastructure is solely for tourism use unless it is part of enclave development. Roads, airports and terminals are likely to have multiple users in most places, and services generally supply residents as well as visitors. However, it may be possible to identify tourism as a *major* call on, say, infrastructure investment, and as a *marginal* cause of increased maintenance costs. If tourism is sufficiently identifiable and separable as an infrastructure user, it may be possible to avoid 'subsidising' tourists by levying user-pays charges. For example, where tolls are charged on highways, bridges and parking, a free pass may be issued to local residents.

Where large-scale investment in tourism-related infrastructure takes place, investment and maintenance costs can sometimes be recouped from rates and taxes charged to commercial enterprises whose development is then possible. Between 1965 and 1980, the French government spent some FFR1500 m on tourism infrastructure for Languedoc-Roussillon in south-west France. About one third of this sum was recouped through selling serviced blocks of land to private developers at prices representing infra-structure improvements, by levying land rates and taxes, and obtaining further revenues which would not otherwise have been collected.

International organisations have for many years been major suppliers of capital for tourism infrastructure investment (Pearce 1989). The World Bank, Inter-American Development Bank and Arab Development Bank are import-ant examples. Although these organisations usually provide capital with which governments then undertake infrastructure investment, they occasionally take a more direct role in investment themselves—perhaps where transnational infrastructure co-operation is required.

Facilitation of tourism development

Where national and regional authorities offer a policy of supporting the development of tourism as an income contributing sector of the economy, this normally entails some form of government expenditure to help with the commercial provision of services. This is especially important in tourism destinations which are in a developmental stage. Not only may government provide the funds required to ensure the viability of marginal projects, but overt political support can be a psychological reinforcer of decisions to invest (Bodlender and Ward 1987).

Table 12.1 lists the main methods by which governments use their spending to facilitate development:

Table 12.1 Public spending methods in tourism development

Direct expenditure
    grants and subsidies
    long-term low-interest loans
    state participation in equity
    interest rebates
    financing research assistance
    financing vocational training
Reduction of commercial liability
    tax exemption or reduction
    duty-free importation of materials
    preferential terms for sale or concession of state land
Guarantees
    surety bonds on commercial borrowing
    guaranteed work permits to foreign workers

Source: adapted from WTO 1983

Public spending in tourism development affects commercial enterprises in two main ways. First, it may reduce the capital requirement, or the cost of capital, such that the marginal productivity of an investment proposal is improved to a viable level. Secondly, it may reduce the operating costs of tourism suppliers, and hence improve profitability and long-term stability of their enterprises. Governments therefore attempt to direct spending into those areas where the direct multiplier effects on employment and business activity are highest. The majority of facilitation expenditure goes to hospitality, tourism attractions and capital-intensive transportation, with very little injection of expenditure into travel agency, tour operation and other less capital-intensive sectors.

Most public spending programmes on facilitation are part of tourism development plans. They may range from small ongoing commitments (such as providing government-subsidised research data through spending on regional or national tourist offices), to large multi-million dollar assistance

Figure 12.3   The impact of government grants and loans on a tourism market

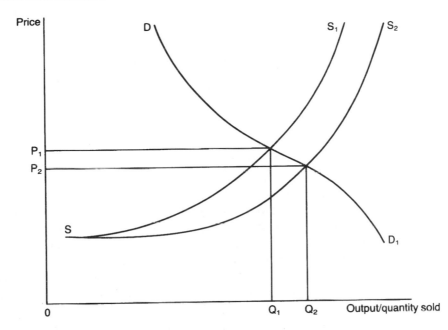

programmes such as Canada's TIDSA (Travel Industry Development Subsidiary Agreement). Additionally, many *ad hoc* agreements such as tax exemptions and the release of cheap government land for resort development are negotiated as the 'price' a government must pay to induce a specific developer.

There are two major objections to using public expenditure in commercial tourism support. The first is that the injections may distort markets. In pursuing tourism developments which offer high employment, for example, subsidies or guarantees may support 'lame duck' enterprises which would not continue to trade in a free market. Whilst it may be argued that the net welfare benefit of extra employment may exceed the disbenefits of economic inefficiency, there is often no evidence as to what opportunity cost uses there might have been for the expenditure which could offer greater welfare. Markets may also be distorted if one type of enterprise gets a greater share of funds; in Canada, for example, it was demonstrated that larger enterprises, with more time and skills available to submit proposals for grants, received a disproportionate share of funding (Montgomery and Murphy 1983).

The second objection is that, as with uncharged use of infrastructure, a proportion of the benefits generated go to tourists rather than suppliers. This is demonstrated in Figure 12.3, where the impact of public facilitation expenditure is to shift the supply of tourism facilities from S—S_1 to S—S_2. The result is a shift, depending on elasticities of supply and demand, of equilibrium in the market from Q_1 to Q_2, and of prices from P_1 to P_2. In other words, tourists benefit from lower prices for tourism facilities. In domestic tourism this may be unimportant unless public spending has been deliberately designed to benefit less-developed destination regions, and tourists originate from better-off regions. In international tourism, however, governments may once again be unintentionally subsidising inbound visitors from other countries.

Expenditure on NTO marketing

The third major area in which governments spend on tourism is likely to be on the marketing activities of tourist offices, defined, if they are country-wide, as National Tourism Administrations or National Tourist Organisations/ Offices (NTOs), or as regional tourist offices for domestic tourism. A few NTOs are non-government, co-operatively funded bodies, but the majority are either government departments, such as those of Spain and New Zealand, or semi-autonomous bodies with significant government funding, such as that of the United Kingdom. Governments become involved first because the individual suppliers of inbound and domestic tourism products are unlikely to be able completely to subordinate competition to co-operative marketing programmes—and they have a range of different interests. Secondly, a government may see a potential economic benefit nationally from tourism which transcends those of private market suppliers. Thirdly, a centralised marketing authority can gain economies of scale in operation.

Specific activities of each NTO vary (WTO 1980), but major expenditure areas are nearly always those of marketing:

- market and marketing research
- public relations
- advertising and other promotion
- product knowledge communication and distribution
- product development (possibly).

With the exception of services performed for and sold to tourism suppliers, these are cost-centred (rather than revenue-centred) activities.

NTOs choose whether to work by subvention to and through commercial suppliers, or to undertake their own centralised activities (Middleton 1988). If the former, they effectively reduce supply costs. Producers are therefore receiving the equivalent of an export subsidy, to make them artificially more competitive internationally, which is the same as any public tourism facilitation funding directed at international tourist attracting ventures. Centralised marketing, however, works to shift the international demand schedule for a destination's tourism upwards. Any difference in the price effects is likely to be less important to a government than an increased *quantity* or flow of tourists to a destination, and increased total tourism expenditure. These are the public objectives of NTO marketing programmes—that is, maximising tourist numbers or revenue. The internal objective may be one of satisficing, such as performing within budget, or achieving prestige.

■ Redistribution policies

Governments use a combination of taxation and expenditure to redistribute resources, incomes and economic benefits. This normally relates to the whole economy rather than any one sector, but has specific importance in particular areas such as public health. Taxation/ expenditure or *single-purpose levies* may be accompanied by price controls, monetary policy measures or other regulation.

In tourism there are only a few examples of redistribution policies. These concern:

- regional development
- social tourism
- price control in factor markets
- levies for reasons such as training.

As economic development and levels of income vary regionally in all but the smallest economies, a common policy goal is spatial redistribution. For those parts of travel and tourism in which resources are mobile (that is, other than fixed unique attractions) it is possible to develop fiscal and planning policies to aid economic redistribution. Several countries attempt to redirect flows of both generated and destination travel by designating and controlling airport development and use regionally. Restricting charter traffic to certain airports, for example, can favour the development of mass tourism in their area. Decentralisation and relocation of tourism activity is generally a part of broader regional economic policy. In countries such as Malaysia, Italy, Thailand and the United Kingdom, policies of this type have involved regionally-variable taxation and development grants, sometimes with the former funding the latter.

Social tourism has already been mentioned, as a system by which the state intervenes to provide tourism as a social welfare benefit to low income consumers. In some Eastern European countries this was in the past funded by a direct income tax contribution from all taxpayers. This directly provided a redistribution of income—except that unlike a general taxation-welfare payment system the benefit is tied directly to the receipt and consumption of a tourism product. (In some countries, such as Germany, social tourism is funded through labour unions or insurance schemes, which in turn receive taxation allowances for this activity.)

Levies on and control of elements of factor markets, especially labour, can have important redistributive effects, although these may not be their main rationale. In any industry with a diversity of types of producer and types of activity, governments may intervene to control restrictive trade practices, or to protect individuals and (subjectively judged) economic wellbeing. Labour markets in hospitality are frequently the subject of government intervention to fix minimum wages and conditions. In most countries the industry is fragmented, jobs are varied, and many positions unskilled, seasonal, part time and ill defined. Wages have been found on average to be 20% lower than for other sectors (OECD 1988). Labour market controls force a redistribution of incomes towards those whose continued employment would otherwise be at very low wages, but in doing so reduce the willingness of employers to keep workers (Lipsey 1983); they may further cause a shift of the capital-labour ratio towards higher use of capital. Where governments control capital markets directly, they may equally use variable interest rate controls.

Vocational training for a tourism labour force may also be income redistributive if it is financed by an industry levy. There is no guarantee that the efficiency benefits of training will return to, say, a hotel which is too small to have its own training and pays a levy. Workers may already be trained, or on completion of training may move elsewhere. It has been suggested that it is more equitable for training to be controlled by private enterprise and professional associations, as is generally the case in Switzerland (Zegg 1987). They may impose the *need* for training, and provided they do not force up the price of labour by artificially restricting apprenticeship supply, employers' expenditure on training should be reflected in their own businesses through superior production functions and profitability.

■ Regulation in travel and tourism sectors

The policies noted above merge into those which directly regulate both producers and consumers in travel and tourism. Regulations may be imposed by government bodies for a variety of reasons such as consumer protection, 'orderly markets' or as part of macroeconomic policy. They generally cover such questions as:

- *who* may supply a good or service
- what *quantity* of products or money may be traded
- what *prices* may be set
- under what *conditions* may production and exchange take place.

Government authorities frequently combine economic regulation with other controls, but only the former will be discussed here.

Economic controls on tourists

Most direct economic controls on tourists themselves are imposed as part of balance of payments policy. There is rarely a need to regulate domestic tourism, which merely shifts income within an economy. Those countries which see international tourism as an important contributor to balance of payments flows may impose foreign exchange restrictions in addition to the use of taxation and complex documentary requirements.

Effective demand for foreign tourism can be restricted in generating countries by exchange control regulations limiting the amounts of both domestic currency and foreign exchange which may be personally exported. Although during the 1980s most major generating countries had non restrictive controls or no limits, this is not always the case. Of course, tourists and suppliers attempt to circumvent restrictions. VFR traffic increases as tourists attempt to maximise trips without needing large amounts of exchange for accommodation. If regulations apply to a significant generating market, suppliers may attempt to integrate foreign tourism products and sell ITs in the home currency. The United Kingdom's 'V-form travel allowance' in the 1960s and 1970s increased tour operators' markets, as they were able to package overseas ITs with only a small component of foreign exchange required (Holloway 1989), and sell a product of which tourists were unable to purchase the separate components independently.

Countries may effectively restrict foreign business tourism by controlling its tax deductibility. If a trip is tax deductible, the cost to the purchasing enterprise is the price less the marginal corporate tax rate. To reduce non essential business travel (both domestic and foreign, but particularly the latter) governments limit deductibility. The United States government, for example, normally restricts deductibility to the daily travel allowances provided for government employees. This can limit consumption of incentive travel, or convention tourism to expensive destinations.

Destinations may also impose regulations on tourists in the form of compulsory currency exchange. In 1994 this applied to some 17 countries. A visitor to Egypt or Tanzania, for example, must exchange a minimum daily amount of convertible currency into local units, and on leaving the country may reconvert only a proportion of that exchanged. As local currency export is prohibited, this forces a minimum level of expenditure (or charity!) per tourist per day. Normally these levels are not substantial unless a destination authority wishes specifically to discourage low-spending, backpacker market segments.

Consumer protection

Consumer protection policies can easily have marketplace consequences, and there are two major examples in travel and tourism. Purchasers of travel must normally pay in advance of receiving the product, and therefore face the risk of losing at least a deposit, or possibly a large full payment, if suppliers or their agents fail in the interim. Many governments have introduced *licensing and bonding* arrangements to protect consumers. These apply to any suppliers who may take payments in advance, and therefore principally apply to travel agents. Together with regulations set by IATA for appointments to sell IATA tickets, such controls make a considerable barrier to entry, and ensure that travel markets are by no means perfectly contestable.

To obtain a licence, most regulated systems require agents and others to hold bonds, as insurance for clients' money. In turn the conditions for acquiring bond coverage may include size, trading reputation, staff qualifications, premises and physical assets. Thus it may be difficult for a new entrant to become a licenced travel agent or tour operator. Established enterprises support such schemes because they control supply and competition.

Licensing may be used, with varying degrees of effectiveness, to control other suppliers, mostly of services, in travel and tourism. Official licensing of, for example, tour guides, taxi operators and currency exchange dealers restricts entry and can easily be policed. On the other hand, licensing of street market souvenir traders in destinations such as Hong Kong fails dismally to prevent unlicensed selling from carts which vanish in a trice at the appearance of police.

A second example of consumer protection's economic effects is that of official accommodation classification systems. For an untried search commodity such as tourist accommodation, a simple classification system which provides an outline idea of physical product facilities is invaluable to intending consumers. Many countries have introduced official classification systems rather than rely on those produced by the industry or by independent guides and associations. Typically, systems classify accommodation into six or fewer categories. Classification does not itself form a barrier to entry—unless the requirements for a minimum rating impose unusually onerous conditions on investment in facilities. Control does become effective in situations where some countries (such as Spain up to the 1970s) accompany their classification systems with price controls linked to ratings.

Each establishment can then only charge rates permitted within a fixed band for its rating, and the rates may or may not reflect prices which would be set in a free market. For example, a 'three star' hotel in a popular location which may under free market conditions be able to charge 'four star' prices, may not be allowed to do so unless it upgrades. More interestingly, there have been cases where establishments have sought *downgrading*, in order to be able to sell at discounted rates. This situation is demonstrated in Figure 12.4. Assume some hotels or motels operate with relatively elastic demand $D–D_1$, and in a free market might achieve equilibrium at price $0–P_E$, selling quantity $0–Q_E$ of accommodation. If the government classifies them and sets a price band between P_L and P_H, then the best the suppliers can achieve for themselves is price $0–P_L$ and sales quantity $0–Q_L$—a considerably lower occupancy rate than equilibrium. Hoteliers may then seek a lower grading in order legally to be able to sell at price P_E. In this instance, a consumer protection policy has actually worked against consumers, forcing prices to be higher than they would be in a free market.

Figure 12.4 Price control in accommodation

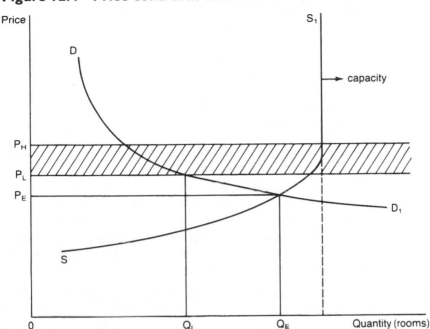

Orderly markets

Governments regulate prices and quantities produced or offered for sale in many markets. The reasons are varied, but are commonly concerned with 'orderly marketing' or the protection of existing suppliers. In many cases these policies are exactly the reverse of anti trust legislation designed to remove restrictive trade practices and promote competition. Anti trust legislation has loosely been accepted as part of *deregulation* policies, and orderly marketing as *regulatory*.

One of the major sectoral targets for regulatory policies is passenger transportation. The principles of bilateral air agreements (outlined in Chapter 10) generally regulate international air carriage, by controlling which airlines shall operate routes, and fixing supply quotas in terms of seats flown per time period. If chosen airlines then agree to fix fares collusively, as often happens, competition is eliminated, except in peripheral services and promotion.

In most countries there is similar regulation of domestic air, ground and water public transportation. The economic arguments in favour of regulation include stability of fares and services, guaranteed trading for operators, and the possible prevention of monopolisation as a result of competition forcing closures (Walther 1984). Contra-arguments are that regulation prevents suppliers from achieving cost efficiency, competition and the flexibility of altering service patterns, all of which contribute to lower market prices but enhanced profitability for the best suppliers.

The most celebrated removal of regulation was that relating to domestic United States air services. Between 1978 and 1985, controls set by the United States Civil Aeronautics Board were progressively dismantled. With new entrants to the industry and free market pricing, competition increased swiftly, but led in consequence to closures and takeovers as less efficient or well-backed operators could not compete. Exactly the same has happened in countries where bus travel has been deregulated, and is beginning to happen following the deregulation of intra-European air services.

There are three main impacts of such deregulation on travel and tourism:

- lower fares and increased promotion stimulate discretionary demand for travel
- carriers integrate, or make trading agreements, with suppliers of other tourism services such as accommodation to enhance their competitive position, which involves these other sectors in the deregulated markets
- later closures and takeovers lead to consolidation of transport on profitable routes and service reduction on unprofitable ones, thus increasing the market share of already popular destinations.

Deregulation in the United States has led to the establishment of some strong carriers with 'hub and spoke' route networks, which dominate services to and from those hubs (see also Brueckner *et al.* 1992). It has been shown that unfortunately such individual airline market power can lead to higher fares through monopolisation (Borenstein 1989).

Market deregulation in travel and tourism thus tends to concentrate the sector, in terms both of ownership and flows to particular destinations.

■ Government as supplier and consumer

In addition to regulation and other 'external' impacts which governments may have on a sector of the economy, national and local authorities themselves are significant suppliers and consumers of travel and tourism products.

Major areas of public ownership are in passenger carriage and tourism attractions, although in collectivist and less-developed economies government ownership may extend to almost every area. In air travel, 80 of the world's 155 or so IATA airlines (including both tariff co-ordinating and trade association only members) are government owned or have a majority government stock holding, although the proportion of state owned non IATA airlines is much lower. Most rail, and many bus and ferry, services are publicly owned or controlled. Even where carriers are privately owned, many terminals such as airports, bus terminals and seaports are publicly operated. Privatisation, following the models adopted in the 1980s in the United States and United Kingdom, requires a large enough capital market to supply private equity capital unless governments are prepared to allow foreign buyouts. (This latter is of course the way in which Eastern European businesses are being developed.)

Through public corporations, trusts or direct management, national and local governments own very many tourism attractions, especially where they are based on 'national heritage' resources or involve community recreation.

Roles and activities of government-owned suppliers reflect political as well as economic requirements. Enterprises with professional management may attempt to maximise profits or satisfice, but may be constrained in doing so. For example, many enterprises are required to buy domestically-produced equipment for their operations, although imported capital goods may be more suitable. Airlines are often required to service international routes for diplomatic rather than economic reasons, and domestic rail or air networks may be forced to supply services to isolated areas to meet social needs. Governments frequently direct attractions' managers to fulfil a primarily educational or conservation role (in, for example, art galleries or museum collections) to which tourism's needs are secondary.

A sensible analysis of the role of the government as tourism supplier should distinguish between those activities which are *primarily* undertaken for commercial tourism ends, and those which have some other objective. For example, it is possible to identify and distinguish in commercial terms the role of government owned theatres and cultural attractions in tourism markets, from their role in providing a local social and educational need; this has been done in Canada and the United States (Tighe 1986, Hughes 1987). It is then possible to see whether government can be as effective as private enterprise in commercial tourism supply.

Finally, governments play a role in tourism through consumption of services. The market share of tourists travelling on government business ranges from an average of 3% of tourists in Europe to 12% in Africa (WTO 1993); of domestic tourists in specific countries it may be markedly higher. Government demand for tourism has some notable features:

- daily allowances for each grade of staff will, all else being equal, determine expenditure levels on food and lodging
- tourism largely emanates from, and flows to, administrative centres; if these centres have administration as their major function (such as Washington, USA, Canberra, Australia or Brasilia, Brazil), then much of their tourism plant must be geared to government tourism needs
- governments may limit their employees' choice of suppliers by, for example, contracting for all air trips to made on a state owned airline
- in some countries government owned tourism services must be supplied free of charge to government officials, or at preferential rates which do not reflect true costs.

Because of a variety of control and accounting procedures, it is difficult to estimate the true impact of government consumption on travel and tourism markets. It is likely to be greater than many national authorities would admit.

Study questions

1 What are the published goals of tourism policy in your state? How do they contribute to the economy?

2 Identify and classify the main types of taxes imposed on tourism.

3 In some countries there are moves to privatize expenditure on tourism-related infrastructure. Assess the probable benefits and costs to an economy of doing this.

4 Examine the main reasons for government expenditure on facilitation and promotion of tourism.

5 Would you agree that exchange control is the fairest and most effective way of controlling outbound (foreign) tourist spending? Explain your answer.

6 Licensing and classification systems are regarded as important in consumer protection. Examine what impact improved information technology in tourism marketplaces might have in reducing the need for these systems.

7 Does deregulation of transportation stimulate tourism?

CHAPTER

13

Tourism investment

■ Principles of investment

Investment is defined by economists as the allocation of resources to fixed capital formation: that is, to enable further production to take place. In macroeconomic terms, investment is that part of an economy's production which is not consumed, and is financed by the share of income which is not spent on consumption. In microeconomic terms, investment relates to the allocation by an enterprise of whatever resources are needed as *productive assets*. There is a need for investment in three areas:

- new fixed assets, such as buildings, plant, equipment and fixtures
- refurbishment or replacement of fixed assets which have reached the end of their useful life in current form
- working capital, to provide a fund from which to pay recurrent costs of production.

The growth and development of any industry depends on its ability to generate a return on investment, and therefore to be able to fund that investment through capital markets and internal earnings. Returns are measured primarily through the factor rewards (interest and dividends) earned by investment, but also by capital growth and other benefits. It is important to distinguish between the meaning of investment in economics and the use of the term in popular business finance, where it may relate only to aspects of the capital market to which saving may be directed, or using savings to buy an existing asset—which to an economist is a simple transfer of ownership.

The principal factor determining the amount of new investment which takes place is the *profitability* which can be gained. This is the difference between the net revenue or yield which can be expected from the investment, and the cost of capital employed. Net revenue consists, in commercial enterprises, of expected sales less expected costs, so is dependent in tourism on expectations of tourist numbers, their patterns of demand and expenditure, and some assumptions of what will happen to costs of goods and services required. In a non commercial venture net revenue may include valuations of expected social benefits and costs of an investment project. The cost of capital is the average rate of interest needed. Capital may come from several sources (Jones 1979):

- *internal finance*: retained profits or surpluses; provision for depreciation; provision for taxation
- *external finance*: equity (and investment grants); long-term loan capital; short term finance (bank credit, hire purchase, trade credit and so on).

Whilst borrowed finance carries a direct rate of interest, equity requires dividends in line with the risk class for the type of investment proposed, and on internal finance there is an opportunity cost of capital which could otherwise be employed elsewhere.

Several ways are used to evaluate investment projects. The principal ones are shown in Table 13.1. Most sophisticated investment appraisers use some form of discounting on future costs and revenues to bring them back to present values, and if possible incorporate a statistical risk analysis, but it has been shown that enterprises vary their evaluation methods and even change their own decision rules for going ahead with investment (Schall *et al.* 1978). In any event, an enterprise's decision about an investment depends largely on expectations in marketplaces and of the economy.

Table 13.1 Investment project valuation methods

Type	Uses discounting	Method rule
Payback	No	Time period for repaying investment
Discounted payback	Yes	Time period for repaying investment
Average accounting return	No	Average % return on investment
Internal rate of return*	Yes	Rate of return making discounted income equal investment cost
Net present value	Yes	Value of discounted revenue's surplus on investment cost
Profitability index	Yes	Ratio of discounted revenue to investment cost

(*more or less equivalent to Marginal Efficiency of Capital)

Source: Ross, Westerfield and Jaffe 1993

Most of the above techniques make the assumption that investment decisions are 'black or white'—that is, a business will or will not go ahead with the investment. Modern theory suggests, however, that investment decisions may be made within an elastic time frame (Dixit and Pindyck 1994). That elastic time frame incorporates a period of accounting for *uncertainty*. At the beginning of the period, the investment may appear profitable, but may be subject to a great number of risks. Over time, risky unknown values—of costs or price levels, say—become known values, and the level of profitability becomes more certain. If a business decides to go ahead with its investment earlier rather than later, it requires a higher predicted level of profitability to compensate for the uncertainties involved. If the business holds off until later, it is similar to buying an option on an asset rather than buying the asset itself; hence, this theory is termed the *real options theory* of investment. The value to a business (the option price) of holding off from an investment project until uncertainties diminish explains why many businesses seem to be slow in taking up investment opportunities.

Replacement investment tends to be cyclical, and depends on depreciation provisions—largely determined by taxation rules—as well as advances in production technology and the extent to which competitiveness requires asset replacements. Car rental companies, for example, replace vehicles frequently as much for promotional reasons as to meet technical needs. There is therefore a tendency for replacement investment to increase in proportion, following the life span of assets acquired during a boom in new investment.

When GDP is increasing and expectations are high, the level of investment will increase, if all else stays the same. This investment in turn will generate further increased income and expenditure—through Keynesian multiplier effects—with increased income providing a fresh supply of capital for yet further investment: the *accelerator* principle.

■ Investment in travel and tourism

In most countries, and most sectors of travel and tourism, investment depends on the same commercial principles as any other industry. Suppliers anticipate profitable returns from selling products either to tourists or in some supporting sector, and set their own decision rules and methods on evaluating projects. Tourism, however, brings out some other reasons for investment which are often linked to the general objectives of enterprises in the sector.

First, governments often undertake investment in tourism projects for non commercial social end benefits. Investment in transport infrastructure, tourist information centres, national parks' amenities or interpretation centres, training establishments and the like may be justifiable on the basis of cost-benefit analysis rather than pure commercial profitability (Curry 1989). The methods of project appraisal and use of benefit expectations are in other respects the same as those of commercial investment appraisals (WTO 1983b).

Secondly, a great deal of fixed capital formation in tourism destination areas is *property driven*. Entrepreneurs who are primarily property developers construct new buildings such as hotels, resorts, trade and convention centres as alternatives to offices, factories or warehousing. Their investment motivation is a profitable rate of return from rental income, but more importantly a significant growth in capital value of the property—compared with investment in assets which tend to depreciate in value. Tourism is then merely a tenanting user of property, and returns must compete with those obtainable from alternative tenants. Investing developers may therefore be organisations with no active interest in tourism at all, such as banks, finance trusts, insurance, construction and manufacturing corporations. The separation of property investment from investment in tourism service production (operations) is especially notable in the United States, where accounting principles make it advantageous for owners and operators of tourism plant to be separated (Slattery 1990).

Thirdly, some investments are made for 'lifestyle' reasons. For example, individuals seeking a pleasant lifestyle or tax loss may invest in a yacht for wet chartering, or develop a dude ranch or other leisure attraction. Tourism may be needed to subsidise an existing lifestyle: cash-strapped owners of stately homes and chateaux in Britain and Europe may invest in tourism facilities for this reason.

Special considerations in tourism investment

It is possible to identify a number of special features that influence investment in tourism rather more than in other sectors. On the whole, they add to the potential profitability of a project rather than making it less feasible. Six main features may be important in tipping the balance in considering a marginal project.

1 Many investment projects are designed to provide *joint use*, between tourists and other consumers, of products that result. In destination cities, for example, city buses may be required for excursion tours and general tourist travel, but may also serve local commuter and other resident travel needs. Any investment in new equipment will then yield joint cash flows and returns from both sets of consumers. Whilst this double income may mean the viability of purchasing assets which could not be justified to serve one market alone, it may also place constraints on the type of assets acquired, and demands that they be useable compatibly: it is inconceivable to an international tourist that London buses should not be double-decked and red, yet such vehicles may not always be suitable for residential services.

Similarly, convention centres have been built in locations as diverse as Las Vegas USA, Djakarta Indonesia and Bournemouth England, which to be viable provide joint use as entertainment or sporting centres for (mostly) local residents. Their convertibility may be less than perfect, which may damage their economic viability in either or both markets.

2 Tourism provides an opportunity for many short term projects with quick payback periods. Because tourists travel *to* the production 'plant', consume

mostly services, and frequently demand new, location non specific attractions, it is possible to develop projects which offer very quick returns. This will be examined more fully in the next section—tourism 'events'.

3 Where producers invest in tourism property, they may take into consideration future substitute uses of that property, which increase the end value of the assets. A new city centre hotel tower with an income producing life, in tourism use, of x years could then perhaps have a further useful life if converted to offices or apartments. By comparison, any investment in assets restricted to one type of use, such as dedicated manufacturing machinery, can only possess an end value or second hand value related to the economic well being of that industry.

4 In similar fashion, transportation equipment purchased as travel and tourism assets can be used in other sectors. Car rental companies sell off cars normally at anything between 9 and 24 months to fleet, taxi or individual purchasers, who may pay reasonably high second hand prices if they respect the rental company's care and maintenance practices. Major bus operators in some countries purchase new vehicles for tourist excursion use, transfer them after some time to regular bus line operation, and finally commission them for school transport or similar use. Within tourism, vehicles may be easily switchable; an airline which purchases aircraft to service a particular route may at a later stage switch aircraft to use on a different route which hitherto had not been considered as an investment opportunity. This is likely to happen where a carrier uses agents to provide services at on-line stations rather than operating them itself as a fixed route network. Investment decision making is then related to aircraft as individual assets rather than to routes as income-producing projects.

5 Many destination based ventures are *mixed use* ventures involving some investment for tourism purposes and some for non tourism reasons. Unlike joint use projects (see 1 above), these possess separate elements of

Figure 13.1 Elements of investment in the Crumbles Harbour Village project, Eastbourne, England

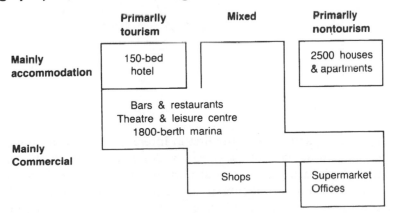

investment which are complementary in nature but separate in use. This sort of investment is typified by marina projects in the Mediterranean area, California, and in many other destinations such as Crumbles Harbour Village in Eastbourne, England (see Figure 13.1).

   This investment project of some UK£500 m (US$750 m) requires each element of a mixed-use venture to complement and enhance the expected yields of the others. Typically, residential investment projects may yield higher returns which subsidise tourism elements, in financial terms, but the tourist attractiveness of the whole improves the marketability of residential units.

6 Despite the existence of some projects—'events'—which provide a fast payback, much investment in travel and tourism plant depends on a long-term stream of returns for its viability—that is, investments are multi-point output or continuous output ventures. A characteristic of much tourism activity is its seasonality, hence the irregular nature of periodic income values. This is one feature of tourism investment which tends to depress rather than enhance expected profitability. Seasonality implies a need for good cash management, which requires either:

- short-term credit to cover low season costs, or
- savings from high season cash flows in short-term deposits or securities, to be withdrawn to cover low season costs (see Figure 13.2).

Figure 13.2   Seasonal cash flow management

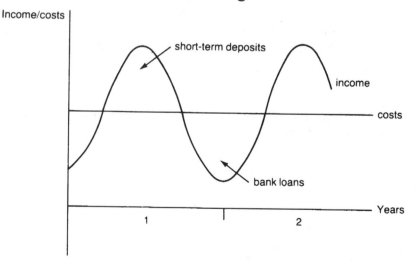

Both of these incur a cost—the first in interest payable, and the second in the opportunity cost of use of funds. An investment which generates $x per year in a highly seasonal pattern of income is therefore less profitable than one producing $x at a constant rate. Virtually all travel and tourism investments producing for the vacation market are seasonal to some extent. If seasonality is inescapable, astute entrepreneurs can assuage cash flow problems by using assets in contra-cyclical production. Some Colorado winter ski resorts are used highly successfully as fitness, climbing and grass skiing centres in summer; cruise lines reposition vessels from summer cruising grounds around Scandinavia to the Caribbean in winter.

■ Investment in tourism 'events'

One area of tourism product development which has grown considerably during the 1980s and 1990s is that of tourism events. These are tourist attractions of fixed duration. They may range from small, local festivals to major international activities or *hallmark events* (Hall 1992). Investment in events of fixed duration is related to different factors from investment in permanent tourism plant. Some events need mostly working capital only, using otherwise fixed facilities, such as major sporting events and dance festivals. Others require more significant fixed capital formation, but still have a short payback period—such as biennial expositions. Although it may take some time to recover land costs from site redevelopment after expositions such as Vancouver in 1986 and Brisbane in 1988, the major yields come from tourism during the opening time of the event—which may only be some six months. Such tourism investment projects are therefore very attractive to entrepreneurs who appraise on the basis of fast payback, compared with longer-term investment in, say, natural resources or manufacturing—especially where an economy's long-term future is adjudged risky.

Many large hallmark or 'mega' events require both public and private investment. Whilst the payback for many commercial operators may come from revenues earned during the life of the event itself, investment in public—and many private—facilities may only be warranted if those facilities have a complementary long-term use after the event. For example, the total public and private investment necessary to stage the Olympic Games may nowadays exceed US$5 billion, of which only a modest percentage will be recouped during the three-week Games period. Hot-dog-stand operators and souvenir sellers recoup their investment in inventory, fittings and equipment within the three weeks, but investment in sports venues, hotels, transport and communications infrastructure and so on must inevitably rely on long-term post-Games revenues. Overestimation of these revenues has left hoteliers and taxpayers with long-term losses in destinations such as Seoul and Barcelona (the total value of investment linked to the 1992 Olympics in Barcelona was US$6.7 billion). It is partly the economic scale, as well as the social scale, of such events that causes the need for them to be integrated into general public policy and planning (Roche 1994).

■ Feasibility studies and investment models

Individual new investment decisions in travel and tourism depend heavily on feasibility studies. A feasibility study includes economic, marketing, financial and operational variables in assessing whether an individual project is likely to be viable. Such studies are well developed in analysing property-based investments such as new hotels, motels or resorts (Beals and Troy 1982). They usually relate to the development of a specific venture in a specific location, which demands more detailed analysis than a more general appraisal of investment potential.

With respect to a resort or hotel, Figure 13.3 provides an example of the stages of a feasibility study:

Figure 13.3   Feasibility study for a hotel

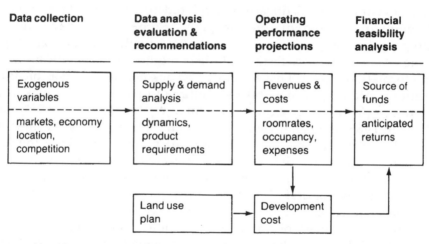

Source: adapted from Horwath International

Feasibility studies provide the methodology to incorporate expectations, parameters and projections in a multivariate analysis. They normally incorporate Bayesian methods of assessing risk through probabilities of different outcomes, and may include a sensitivity analysis to identify which variables may be the most important in influencing profitability. Risk levels are an important determinant of investment decisions. The tourism industry is often perceived as a 'high risk class' for investment, which must be compensated for by anticipated higher returns.

In considering investment in fixed facilities to which tourists must travel to consume services, location and site selection are important variables. The location of a motel, roadhouse, attraction, souvenir shop or travel agency outlet cannot be 'footloose' as a headquarters office or taxi maintenance facility could be. Location theory and regional economics have not contributed greatly to the analysis of individual investment decisions, but retail location strategy has been used for tourism investments (Gearing and Var 1977, Smith 1989). Hedonic valuation (Corgel and deRoos 1992) and other investment decision rules (see, for example, Kimes 1987) may be helpful.

Since the methodology of appraising investment in tourism can involve such a large number of variables, feasibility studies can sometimes turn into full scale investment models. These may be based on programming approaches (for example, Powers and Powers 1977), especially where there is government involvement, the need to consider social as well as commercial returns, and where calculating shadow prices of investment activity may be important. An integrated resort development, for example, can involve state investment in infrastructure (which may have opportunity costs), private investment in operational superstructure, and a government interest in maximising social returns. Complex, programming-type models are needed to encompass all of these areas (see, for example, Stanton and Aislabie 1992).

A difficulty arises if governments and commercial enterprises have different objectives from tourism investment. If, for example, governments want more international tourists, and more tourist expenditure, they may encourage investment in more hotels and infrastructure. Commercial businesses, however, may feel that this is the last thing they want if hotel occupancy rates are only around 55-60% and properties are overvalued.

More general economic modelling can be used to assess the regional or national viability of large scale tourism development. Very little empirical research has been conducted to use models in assessing aggregate sectoral investment in tourism. In many economies—certainly in less-developed countries—the major concern is to appraise what amount of limited scarce resources should be invested in tourism compared with investment in other sectors (Gearing, Swart and Var 1973). The variable to be determined by models is then neither the viability of an individual investment project nor total investment in the economy, but the relative share which is appropriate to tourism: that is, I_t/I where I_t is investment in tourism and I is total investment in the economy. Investment functions based on the marginal efficiency of capital, accelerator principles or programming models can then determine the optimal value of I_t/I. One major problem for small and less-developed economies is that both the sources of capital and the consuming markets are likely to be external to the economy, so that the economy determines neither the financial values nor the availability or desirability of investment itself.

■ Sources of capital

A significant feature of tourism industries around the world, which has been noted here, is their fragmentation. On the one hand this means a plethora of small enterprises, from individual souvenir hawkers and taxi operators to small shops, travel agencies and intermediaries. On the other hand there is the increasing separation of *ownership* of fixed capital such as resorts, airports and major attractions, from their *operation*. This results in a great variety of sources of capital for small investments, and the development of specialist financing for the owner enterprises of fixed assets. As many of the latter involve property investment, they attract trust-type funds, some of full trustee status, from insurance companies, superannuation funds and the like. Large manufacturing corporations such as Matsushita or ITT use retained earnings to diversify directly into tourism ventures. Activity by these enterprises, combined with lending by large banks and organisations such as the IBRD, contributes to the increasing internationalism of tourism investment. They have access to those capital markets with the lowest rates of interest (such as Japan and Switzerland in the 1980s and 1990s); they also have familiarity and experience in those markets, which means that transactions costs of capital acquisition are low.

During the 1990s there has been a move in tourism enterprises to reduce levels of *gearing*—that is, the ratio between debt and equity capital in a business. High debt levels, together with high interest rates, contributed to corporate problems and failures in such companies as PanAm (United States), Queens Moat Houses (United Kingdom) and Qintex (Australia). The impact of such events reduces business confidence, forces businesses to be more reliant on their own equity, and depresses the overall level of investment.

Investment by publicly owned enterprises in travel and tourism is usually funded either by direct government subvention, in which case public sector accounting rates of interest rather than commercial ones determine viability, or by public bond issue. Again, the cost of capital may be cheaper than commercial market rates because of the lower risk level attached to government-backed borrowing. In those countries with both a private and a state owned airline, for example, the state may enjoy a lower cost of capital to finance investment in new aircraft.

As has been seen, governments direct grants, loans and other subsidies towards specific sectors of tourism to enable investment and growth in those areas. Such aid in theory either reduces the cost of the investment, reduces the cost of capital, or reduces the risk. In practice, research has found that risk reduction is the most important aspect of government incentives (Wanhill 1986). Incentives are usually insufficient to attract international capital to investments in a country where returns are not competitive, but may induce a domestic enterprise, especially a highly leveraged one, to take on a project.

■ Factors influencing travel and tourism's yields and future

Development of travel and tourism globally depends heavily on the expected future profits (and social benefits) which enterprises and governments forecast from their investments. Whilst a holistic view of tourism provides the fullest picture of trends, entrepreneurs tend to take a Paretian view, of isolating and analysing only the major factors likely to influence the viability of investing in travel and tourism. The volatility of tourism in general during the 1960s–1990s has been relatively low, with overall global growth of around 6% per annum; variations emanate mainly from seasonality and stochastic events such as terrorist activity or natural disasters. A number of specific factors, however, influence individual and regional tourism investment.

Short-term factors

Other than changes in market rates of interest, and anticipated changes in inflation, two major factors influence viability in the short term. The first is change in tourist flows, caused by altered circumstances in generators, destinations or links. This is principally locational change in the pattern of tourism demand. International tourism is highly susceptible to exchange rate variations which alter prices, both in generators and destinations. Equally, government fiscal and control policies, transport costs or poor weather for one or two seasons markedly change tourist flows. Specific locations thus gain or lose potential profitability.

The second short term factor is the high level of inter-dependence between suppliers of travel and tourism products. The viability of a roadhouse on a tourist travelled highway depends partly on the supply of sufficient camp grounds, lodging and attractions in destinations; that of a resort hotel in Hawaii or Majorca depends on air services, ground transfers, and retailing and tour operating in generating markets. With complementary products, any one may be the limiting factor, such as airport capacity, amenities or inter-island ferry travel (Sathiendrakumar and Tisdell 1989). Cross effects on viability are therefore substantial.

Stochastic shocks

Econometric and other techniques to predict the impact of the above short-term influences are becoming increasingly sophisticated, but cannot deal adequately with the effects of stochastic or periodic shocks on tourism. Researchers can estimate the effects that such shocks will cause, but cannot predict the occurrence nor severity of the events themselves. In tourism, these events tend to relate either to destinations, and therefore to products supplied, or their perception, or to travel links.

Air traffic control strikes (Europe), pilots' stoppages (Australia) and air terrorism are examples of stochastic events affecting travel in the 1980s. The Gulf War in 1991 adversely affected international travel worldwide, but boosted domestic tourism in many countries as a substitute for international trips. Substantial fuel price changes also have an impact (Steinnes 1988) on car and air travel. Political violence and natural disasters such as hurricanes or earthquakes may both reduce tourism demand and destroy tourism production plant in destinations (Lea and Small 1988). All of these events demonstrate lagged effects on the industry, with recovery times varying between two months and five years. Any investment depending on yields during these periods may only become profitable afterwards, or if it involves significant holding costs, may never be profitable.

Long term factors

What of the long term future development of travel and tourism? Entrepreneurs investing in significant destination facilities or attractions, or in capital-intensive transport assets, need to identify potential changes in trends, and significant new opportunities. For example, tourists' tastes and comfort requirements can change over a number of years. This stimulates the need for shorter cycles of replacement investment, to upgrade facilities to currently accepted standards; hotel chains such as Sheraton budget to refurbish properties in as little as three years after new opening. Not only are tourist needs influenced by fashion and the search for 'new experiences', but the relative importance of tourist-generating markets changes, through economic and social variables. Long term investment must cater for the cultural requirements of future markets which may currently be insignificant.

Environmental changes, including such things as shifts in climatic patterns, have the ability to affect destinations, by directly changing some attributes of the tourism product itself and by altering locational advantages of different types of destination (Craig-Smith and Bull 1990). Techniques of prediction are only in their infancy but may in time allow appropriate risk analysis to be built into investment appraisal.

Perhaps one of the most important variables affecting travel and tourism is technological change. Industrial technology was the pre-requisite for tourism demand in the 19th century, providing production methods in manufacturing which could stop for public holidays, and steam power for mass transport by rail and sea. In the twentieth century transport technology for air, road and off road vehicles has allowed the spread of mass tourism to widespread destinations, rather than being limited to those reachable by rail or ship. Suppliers of tourism attractions have quickly adopted technical advances in such areas as gaming machines, theme park rides or exhibits (Stipanuk 1993), and synthetic tourist experiences which may for example simulate wilderness or subaquatic environments, saving the originals. Information technology is making travel and tourism markets more efficient and competitive, as more perfect information is available to consumers, and more competitive distribution to producers. It seems inevitable that advances in technology will continue to have major impacts on the economics of travel and tourism.

Study questions

1 Identify three main types of investment need.
2 Investment in travel and tourism is not always directly linked to anticipated commercial returns. Give three main noncommercial reasons for investment, and find supporting examples.
3 What is meant by 'property-driven' tourism investment, and why is its viability not totally bound up with growth in tourism demand?
4 How should the optimal share of total investment in an economy going to travel and tourism projects be assessed?
5 Identify the main sources of capital used in tourism investment in your country, and suggest reasons for the particular mix found.
6 Summarize the main factors likely to influence long-term yields on tourism investment.

CLUB MEDITERRANEE

One of the world's best-known multinational enterprises in tourism is Club Mediterranee, operating now in most countries as 'Club Med'. The business is incorporated as a limited liability company in France as Club Mediterranee S.A. Its main business is the development, construction and operation of holiday villages, together with packaging ITs to those villages and selling in several generating markets. Club Med operates over 80 holiday villages in 31 countries, as well as two large sail/ motor cruise liners, smaller 'villa' hotels, escorted tours, tour buses and boats.

The organization has developed, from the 1950s, to the stage where it employs 30 000 people and is a powerful influence in tourism, particularly in less-developed countries and those regions in which it is a major economic player.

Demand

Club Med sells to between 1 and 1.3 million people each year. About one-third of consumers are residents of France; the other major generating markets for the Club's products are Italy, Japan, Germany and the United States. The fastest-growing markets are those of Eastern Asia, such as Japan, Malaysia and South Korea. Club Med's long-term image as a supplier of relatively expensive, fully-inclusive activity holidays has in the past associated it with younger age groups. In the 1980s and 1990s however, customer loyalty and selective market targeting have led to a greater demand from older consumers (clients' mean age is 38), and families with small children. Demand is not highly price-elastic, which is partly due to the higher-income status of many consumers, and partly to Club Med's products being sufficiently differentiated from any others to create a degree of monopoly.

Club Med's product

The standard product offered is an all-inclusive holiday. It technically includes club membership (and so there is a subscription fee), and incorporates accommodation, all meals with table beverages, sports and recreation activities and entertainment. Products packaged as ITs include scheduled or charter transportation and local transfers. Club Med acts as a tour operator, purchasing seats *en bloc* from carriers, but does not own or operate any of its own international carriages.

A typical holiday village may consist of 300-400 twin-bedded bungalows or hotel rooms in a beachfront location, with three or four restaurants.

Tennis, watersports, swimming pools, craft activities, 'children's clubs' and a nightclub may be provided at an inclusive price. In many villages, golf and excursions are extra-priced options. For extras such as bar beverages, Club Med was one of the first operators to feature prepurchased (and non-refundable) beads as a means of payment, although since American Express became a shareholder in the company, Amex card payments have become more accepted. During 1990-93, Club Med's average occupancy rate was around 65-72%. A feature of the product is that staff (known as 'gentils organisateurs', or kind hosts) mingle freely with guests (known as 'gentils membres' or kind members). The standard guest to staff ratio is 5:1.

Investment and development

Club Med usually researches and selects its own development sites. In this, the company is mostly a development leader rather than a follower, and frequently is a monopoly provider (in, for example, San Salvador in the Bahamas or Les Almadies in Senegal). Occasionally, the company develops a property as the result of government invitation, as in Bali, Indonesia. Holiday villages are designed to be tourist self sufficient, so that visitors need never leave the grounds if they do not wish to.

Club Med acts as a management company at most of its properties. The *owners* of the land and buildings may be governments, banks, local companies or any property investors, with whom Club Med hold a management contract. Where there is a disagreement between owners and managers, or where destination trade is uneconomic, the company may cease acting as managers. (This happened, for example, in Hawaii in the late 1970s). In common with major hotel management companies, Club Med sets guidelines for operational methods, standards, product content and style, and it controls marketing and pricing.

In many locations, Club Med contracts with local or regional government bodies that it will undertake to purchase a certain amount of materials locally, hire a certain percentage of local labour, and contribute to local infrastructure. Increasingly, this form of undertaking may be a prerequisite to gain a development permit.

Discussion question

In the light of the impacts which a multinational enterprise in tourism may have on a host economy, what benefits does it seem Club Med brings, and what economic problems may it cause, to

(a) a developed host economy (such as Italy or the United States), and
(b) a less-developed economy?

LOCAL GOVERNMENT AND TOURISM

Although the major share of government economic activity in tourism is that of national governments, local government bodies also play a significant role. The Borough of Southend-on-Sea in the United Kingdom is the local government organization with responsibilities for a range of municipal services and undertakings provided in its metropolitan area spread along beachfront some 60 kilometres east of London. (The population is some 160 000, and the scale of operation would be equivalent to that of a city authority in, say, the United States.)

The town was a major tourism and excursion destination, especially for Londoners, in the last century. It has declined in touristic importance as generating markets have sought to visit perhaps more glamorous, more distant destinations. Nevertheless, it still attracts some 2 million visitors during the main summer season—mostly excursionists. Attractions include: 12 miles of beachfront; a 'Golden Mile' of amusement arcades, pubs and restaurants; the 2-kilometre long pleasure pier; shopping, convention, entertainment and recreational facilities.

Borough-owned tourism facilities

The Borough owns:

- the Cliffs Pavilion: a 1600 seat entertainment and convention centre
- the pleasure pier: an historic attraction, the first part of which was opened in 1829
- several hectares of parks and gardens
- an art gallery and three museums
- a campsite and caravan site (privately operated on contract)
- part owner of the local airport.

Many of the facilities are provided jointly for tourists and residents. The proportion of use by each is not easy to determine in most cases; however, if a facility is provided primarily for local residents, it may have a value as a tourist amenity, but the *marginal cost* of provision for tourist users would be negligible.

Recreation and tourism within the town budget

The Borough's budget (general fund) for 1993-94 was UK£18.4 m. This was funded principally from local taxation (community charge) and subvention from central government tax revenues. The two main areas of expenditure with tourism interest were:

- Entertainments and tourism   £2.4 m
- Recreation   £4.0 m.

Entertainments and tourism

Total budget: £4.2 m, of which £1.8 m came mostly from entrance fees and charges

Major tourism-related items:

- Operation of Cliffs Pavilion   £0.75 m
- Operation of gallery and museums   £0.48 m
- Tourism & other marketing   £0.58 m

Activities included operation of the Cliffs Pavilion, art gallery and museums, a financial contribution to the English Tourist Board, operating two tourist information centres, promotion, and staging special events such as an annual air show. (Additionally, the Borough spent £4 m from its capital works fund on investing in the refurbishment of the Cliffs Pavilion during 1991 through 1994.)

Recreation

Total budget: £4.0m

Major tourism-related items:

- Maintenance of parks and gardens   £2.4m
- Operation of the pier   £0.4m net

The pier attracts about 300 000 paying visitors a year, so the above figure is the net cost of operation, including entertainments such as a jazz festival and band concerts. One of the three stated objectives in the Recreation Division is 'to maintain, develop and promote foreshore and visitor attractions.' This includes providing patrol boats, moorings, slipways and beach cleaning.

Other related activities

The Borough is involved in other activities which impinge on tourism, such as:

- providing carparking and a central bus depot
- providing 34 public toilets
- licencing taxis
- promoting conservation, including heritage planning for 12 conservation areas and 150 heritage-listed buildings.

Some of these activities, such as carparking, are revenue-generating, but the bulk involve a net cost to the authority.

Economic benefits

It is very difficult to assess the total economic benefits brought to Southend by tourism. There is only a limited accommodations sector, and the bulk of visitation is by day excursion. As seen above, the bulk of local government-owned facilities do not generate sufficient income to cover all costs. A number of businesses, such as amusement arcades and some food and beverage outlets, rely on visitors for revenue, which generates employment and local taxation revenues. Other businesses, such as shops and entertainment, obtain *marginal* revenues from tourists which in some circumstances may 'make the difference' in keeping the businesses trading. Again, there will be indirect and induced impacts from these.

Discussion question

Compare the economic roles of local government in tourism at Southend-on-Sea with those in a local area with which you are personally familiar. What differences in roles are there, and why do you think they exist?

Abbreviations

ABTA	Association of British Travel Agents
AHMA	American Hotels and Motels Association
AIO	activities, interests and opinions
C	consumption
CRS	computerised reservation system
FC	fixed costs
GDP	gross domestic product
GNP	gross national product
HKTA	Hong Kong Tourist Association
I	investment inflow
IATA	International Air Transport Association
IT	inclusive tour
ITC/CIT	inclusive tour by charter
LDC	less-developed country
MAPC	minimum acceptable profit constraint
MC	marginal cost
MNE	multinational enterprise
MPC	marginal propensity to consume
MPI	marginal propensity to invest
MPS	marginal propensity to save
MR	marginal revenue
MTR	marginal tax rate
NEW	net economic welfare
NIMA	non-investment management arrangement
NTO	National tourism organisation/office
NUC	neutral units of currency
O	outflow
OECD	Organisation for Economic Co-operation and Development
OSZ/FW	(Austrian National Tourism Office)
per pax	per passenger
PLC	Proprietary Limited Company
ps/km	passenger seat kilometres
RTO	Regional (or state) Tourism office
S	savings
SFC/SVC	semi-fixed costs
T	taxation
TIC	tourist information centre
TIM	tourism income multiplier
VAT/TVA	value-added tax

Bibliography

American Hotel and Motel Association 1986, *Uniform System of Accounts and Expense Dictionary for Small Hotels and Motels* Educational Institute of AHMA, E. Lancing, Mich. 3rd edn

Aislabie, Colin 1988, 'Economics and Tourism: Major Issues in the Literature' in: Tisdall, Aislabie & Stanton, *Economics of Tourism: Case Study & Analysis*, Univ. of Newcastle, Australia

Archer, Brian H. 1977, *Tourism Multipliers: The State of the Art* University of Wales Press, Bangor, UK

Archer, Brian H. 1987, 'Demand Forecasting and Estimation' in: Ritchie, J. R. Brent, & Goeldner, C.R., *Travel, Tourism & Hospitality Research* Wiley, New York, pp 77–86

Archer, Brian H. 1989, 'Tourism and Island Economies: Impact Analyses', in: Cooper, C. P. (ed) *Progress in Tourlsm, Recreation and Hospitality Management* Belhaven Press, London

Archer, Brian H. & Fletcher, J. 1990, *Multiplier Analysis in Tourism*, Cahiers du Tourisme C103, C.H.E.T., Aix-en-Provence, France

Arrow, Kenneth J. 1951, *Social Choice and Individual Values* Wiley, New York

Australia, Commonwealth of, 1989 *Some Economic Implications of Tourism Expansion* Discussion Paper No. 2, (March) Industries Assistance Commission, Canberra, Australia

Baretje, Rene 1982, Tourism's External Account and the Balance of Payments, *Annals of Tourism Research* vol. 9, pp. 57–67

BarOn, R. 1975, *Seasonality in Tourism—a Guide to the Analysis of Seasonality and Trends for Policy Making*, EIU, London, UK

Baum, C. 1993, 'Cruise Industry Sails Towards Larger Market Share', *Hotels*, March, pp. 54–56

Baumol, William J. 1977 *Economic Theory and Operations Analysis*, 4th edition, Prentice-Hall, Englewood Cliffs, NJ

Baumol, William J. & Oates, W. E. 1979, *Economics, Environmental Policy and the Quality of Life*, Prentice-Hall, Englewood Cliffs, NJ

Baumol, William J., Panzar, John C. & Willig, Robert D. 1982, *Contestable Markets and the Theory of Industry Structure*, Harcourt Brace Jovanovich, New York

Beals, P & Troy, D. A. 1982, 'Hotel Feasibility Analysis', *Cornell HRA Quarterly* vol. 23 no.1 pp. 10–17 & 23 no.3 pp. 58–64

Becker, G. S. 1965, 'A Theory of the Allocation of Time', *Economic Journal* vol. 75 no. 299 pp. 493–517

Becker, G.S. 1991, 'A Note on Restaurant Pricing and Other Examples of Social Influence on Price', *Journal of Political Economy*, vol. 99 no. 5, pp. 1109–1116

Bevan, D. L. & Soskice, D. W. 1976, 'Appraising Tourist Development in a Small Economy', in: Little, I. M. D. & Scott, M. F.G. *Using Shadow Prices*, Heinemann, London, pp. 205–229

Bitner, Mary J. and Booms, Bernard H. 1982, 'Trends in Travel and Tourism Marketing: The Changing Structure of Distribution Channels', *Journal of Travel Research* vol. 20 no. 4, Spring

Blaine, T.W. 1993, 'Input–Output Analysis: Applications to the Assessment of the Economic Impact of Tourism', in: Khan M., Olsen M. & Var T. (eds.), *Encyclopedia of Hospitality and Tourism*, Van Nostrand Reinhold, New York, pp. 663–670

Bodlender, J.A. & Ward, T.J. 1987, *An Examination of Tourism Investment Incentives*, WTO, Madrid

Borenstein, Severin 1989, 'Hubs and High Fares: Dominance and Market Power in the US Airline Industry', *Rand Journal of Economics* vol. 20 no.3, Autumn, pp. 344–365

Britton, S. G. 1980, 'Tourism & Economic Vulnerability in Small Pacific Island States: The Case of Fiji, in: Shand, R. J. (ed), *Island States of the Pacific and Indian Ocean*, ANU, Canberra, Australia

Brookshire, D., Thayer, M., Schulze, W. D & Arge, R. 1982, 'Valuing Public Goods: A Comparison of Survey and Hedonic Approaches', *American Economic Review* vol. 72 no. 1, March, pp. 165–177

Brueckner, J.K., Dyer, N.J. & Spiller, P.T. 1992, 'Fare Determination in Airline Hub-and-Spoke Networks', *Rand Journal of Economics*, vol 2 no. 3, pp. 309–333

Bryden, J. 1973, *Tourism and Development: A Case Study of the Commonwealth Caribbean*, Cambridge University Press, Cambridge, UK

Bull, A.O. 1985, *Commercial Operation of the Durundur Railway as a Tourist Attraction* ANGRMS Report, August, Brisbane, Australia

Bull, A.O. 1990, 'Australian Tourism: Effects of Foreign Investment', *Tourism Management*, vol. 11 no. 4 , pp. 325–331

Bull, A.O. 1994, 'Pricing a Motel's Location', *International Journal of Contemporary Hospitality Management*, vol. 6, no. 6

Burkart, A. J. and Medlik, S. 1981, *Tourism Past, Present and Future*, Heinemann London 2nd edn

Burns, M. 1988, *Some New Dimensions in the Economic Analysis of Tourism* Proceedings of the Frontiers of Australian Tourism Conference, Canberra

Byrnes, J.L.S. 1985, *Air Carrier Diversification*, UMI, Ann Arbor, USA

Bywater, Marion 1992, *The European Tour Operator Industry*, EIU Publications, London

Caves, R.E. 1971, 'International Corporations: The Industrial Economics of Foreign Investment', *Economica*, vol. 38, pp. 1–27

Chadwick, R.A. 1981, 'Some Notes on the Geography of Tourism: A Comment' *Canadian Geographer*, 25 , pp. 191–197

Chamberlin, Edward H. 1956, *The Theory of Monopolistic Competition*, Harvard University Press, Cambridge, Mass.

Chenery, H. B. 1961, 'Comparative Advantage and Development Policy', *American Economic Review*, vol. 51, March, pp. 18–51

Cheshire, P.C. & Stabler, M. J. 1976, 'Joint Consumption Benefits in Recreational Site Surplus: An Empirical Estimate', *Regional Studies*, vol. 10 no. 3, pp. 343–351

Civil Aviation Authority, UK 1984, *Deregulation of Air Transport:A Perspective on the Experience in the United States*, CAA Paper 84009, London, UK

Clarke, Harry R. & Ng, Yew-Kwang 1993, 'Tourism, Economic Welfare and Efficient Pricing', *Annals of Tourism Research*, vol. 20 no. 4, pp. 613–632

Clawson, Marion C. & Knetsch, J. L. 1966, *The Economics of Outdoor Recreation*, Johns Hopkins Press, Baltimore, Ohio

Cleverdon, Robert 1979, *The Economic and Social Impact of International Tourism on Developing Countries*, Special report no. 60, Economist Intelligence Unit, London

Cleverdon, Robert 1985, *International Business Travel*, Travel & Tourism Report no.2, Economist Intelligence Unit Special Report 189, London

Cohen, E. 1972, 'Towards a Sociology of International Tourism', *Social Research*, vol. 39 pp. 164–182

Corgel, J.B. & deRoos, J.A. 1992, 'Pure Price Changes of Lodging Properties', *Cornell H.R.A. Quarterly*, vol. 33 no. 2, pp. 70–77

Craig-Smith, S.J. & Bull, A.O. 1990, *Climatic Change and its Possible Effects on Tourism Activity in the South West Pacific*, Proceedings of the ANZAAS Conference, Hobart, Australia

Curry, Steve 1989, 'Cost–Benefit Analysis' in: Witt, S. F. & Moutinho, L. *Tourism Marketing and Management Handbook*, Prentice-Hall, Hemel Hempstead, UK pp. 83–87

De Kadt, E. 1979, *Tourism—Passport to Development*, Oxford University Press, New York

Defert, P. 1966, *La Localisation Touristique: Problemes Theoretiques et Pratiques*, Editions Gurten, Berne, Switzerland

Demas, W.G. 1965, *The Economics of Development in Small Countries with Special Reference to the Caribbean*, McGill University Press, Montreal, Canada

Dev, C.S. & Klein, S. 1993, 'Strategic Alliances in the Hotel Industry', *Cornell H.R.A. Quarterly*, vol. 34 no. 1, pp. 42–45

Diamond, Peter 1969, 'On the Economics of Tourism', *East Africa Economic Review*, vol. 1 no. 2, December

Dieke, Peter U.C. 1989, 'Fundamentals of Tourism Development: A Third World Perspective', *Hospitality Education & Research Journal* vol. 13 no. 2, pp. 7-22

Dixit, Avinash & Pindyck, Robert 1994, *Investment Under Uncertainty*, Princeton University Press, USA

Doering, I. R. 1976, 'A Re-examination of the Relative Importance of Tourism to State Economies', *Journal of Travel Research*, vol. 15 no.1, pp. 13–17

Doganis, Rigas 1985, *Flying Off Course: The Economics of International Airlines*, Allen & Unwin, London

Dunning, John H. 1979, 'Explaining Changing Patterns of International Production: In Defence of the Eclectic Theory', *Oxford Economic Papers*, vol. 41.4, pp. 269–295

Dunning, John H. & McQueen, Matthew 1981, *Transnational Corporations in International Tourism*, UN Center for Transnational Studies, New York

Dunning, John H. & McQueen, Matthew 1982, 'Multinational Corporations in the Hotel Industry', *Annals of Tourism Research*, vol. 9, pp. 69–90

Dwyer, L. & Forsyth, P. 1993, 'Assessing the Benefits and Costs of Inbound Tourism', *Annals of Tourism Research*, vol. 20 no. 4, pp. 751–768

Eadington, William R. & Redman, Milton 1991, 'Economics and Tourism', *Annals of Tourism Research*, vol. 18 no. 1, pp. 41–56

Edwards, Anthony (for E.I.U.) 1987, *Choosing Holiday Destinations*, Economist Publications, London, EIU T&T Report no. 5

Edwards, Steve F. 1987, *An Introduction to Coastal Zone Economics: Concepts, Methods and Case Studies*, Taylor and Francis, New York

Engel, J.F., Blackwell, R.D. & Miniard, P.W. 1987, *Consumer Behavior*, CBS Publishing, New York

Erbes, Robert 1973, *International Tourism and the Economy of Developing Countries*, June, OECD, Paris

Falvey, R.E., Fried, H.O. & Richards, B. 1992, 'An Hedonic Guide to New Orleans Restaurants', *Quarterly Review of Economics & Finance*, vol. 32 no. 1, pp. 123–133

Farver, Jo Ann M. 1984, 'Tourism and Employment in the Gambia', *Annals of Tourism Research*, vol. 11, pp. 249–265

Ferguson, J. 1988, 'The Tourism Industry—A Government Perspective' in: Blackwell, J (ed) *The Tourism and Hospitality Industry*, I.M.S. Sydney, Australia

Fish, Mary 1982, 'Taxing International Tourism in West Africa', *Annals of Tourism Research*, vol. 9, pp. 91–103

Flowers, E.B. 1976, 'Oligopolistic Reactions in European and Canadian Direct Investment in the U.S., *Journal of International Business Studies*, Fall, pp. 43–55

Forbes, Anne M. 1976, 'The Trinidad Hilton: A Cost-Benefit Study of a Luxury Hotel' in Little, I.M.D. & Scott, M.F.G., *Using Shadow Prices*, Heinemann, London, pp. 15–42

Forster, B. 1989, 'Valuing Outdoor Recreational Activity: a Methodological Survey', *Journal of Leisure Research*, vol. 21 no. 2, pp. 181–201

Frank, R.E., Massy, W.F. & Wind, Y. 1972, *Market Segmentation*, Prentice-Hall, Englewood Cliffs, NJ

Frechtling, Douglas C. 1987(a) 'Assessing the Impacts of Travel and Tourism—Measuring Economic Benefits', in Ritchie, J. R. Brent & Goeldner, C. R., *Travel Tourism & Hospitality Research*, Wiley, New York, pp. 333–352

Frechtling, Douglas C. 1987(b) 'Assessing the Impacts of Travel and Tourism—Measuring Economic Costs', in Ritchie, J. R. Brent & Goeldner, C. R., *Travel, Tourism & Hospitality Research*, Wiley, New York, pp. 333–352

Fritz, R.G., Brandon, C. & Xander, J. 1984, 'Combining Time Series and Econometric Forecast of Tourism Activity', *Annals of Tourism Research*, vol. 11, pp. 219–229

Fujii, E., Khaled, M. & Mak, J. 1985, 'The Exportability of Hotel Occupancy and Other Tourist Taxes', *National Tax Journal* vol. 38, pp. 169–177

Galbraith, J.K. 1967, *The New Industrial State*, Houghton Mifflin, Boston USA

Gearing, C.E. & Var, I. 1977, 'The Site Selection Problem in Touristic Feasibility Reports', *Tourist Review*, vol. 32 no. 2, pp. 9–16

Gearing, C. E., Swart, W. W. & Var, T. 1973, 'Determining the Optimal Investment Policy for the Tourism Sector of a Developing Country', *Management Science*, vol. 20 no. 4, December, pp. 487–497

Goodall, Brian 1988, 'How Tourists Choose Their Holidays', in Goodall B. & Ashworth G. (eds) *Marketing in the Tourism Industry*, Croom Helm, London, UK

Goodrich, Jonathan N. 1977, 'Benefit Bundle Analysis: An Empirical Study of International Travelers', *Journal of Travel Research*, vol. 2, pp. 6–9

Gray, H. Peter 1970, *International Travel: International Trade*, D C Heath, Lexington, USA

Gray, H. Peter 1982, 'The Contributions of Economics to Tourism', *Annals of Tourism Research*, vol. 9, pp. 105–125

Gray, H. Peter 1984, 'Tourism Theory and Practice: A Reply to Alberto Sessa', *Annals of Tourism Research*, vol. 11 pp. 286–289

Greene, Melvyn 1983, *Marketing Hotels into the '90s*, Heinemann, London

Greer, T. & Wall, G. 1979, 'Recreational Hinterlands: A Theoretical and Empirical Analysis', in: Wall C (ed) *Recreational Landuse in S Ontario*, Dept of Geography Pub. 14, University of Waterloo, Canada

Gregory, Aryear 1985, *The Travel Agent —Dealer in Dreams*, National Publishers, USA, 2nd edn

Gunn, C.A. 1989, *Tourism Planning*, Taylor and Francis, New York, 2nd edn

Hall, C. Michael, 1992, *Hallmark Tourist Events*, Belhaven Press, London

Hall, D.R. (ed) 1991, *Tourism and Economic Development in Eastern Europe and the Soviet Union*, Belhaven Press, London

Hanlon, J.P. 1984, 'Sixth Freedom Operations in International Air Transport'. *Tourism Management*, September, pp. 177–191

Hanlon, J.P. 1989, 'Hub Operations and Airline Competition', *Tourism Management*, vol. 10, June, pp. 111–124

Haulot, Arthur 1974, *Tourisme et Environnement: La Recherche d'un Equilibre*, Editions Marabout, Verviers, Belgium

Hawes, Douglas K. 1974, 'Time Budgets and Consumer Leisure-Time Behaviour', *Advances in Consumer Research*, vol. 4, pp. 224–228

Hawkins, C.J. 1973, *Theory of the Firm*, Macmillan, London

Henderson, James M. & Quandt, Richard E. 1971, *Microeconomic Theory: A Mathematical Approach*, McGraw Hill, Kogakusha, Tokyo, Japan

Herzberg, D. 1966, *Work and the Nature of Man*, World Publishing, New York

Hiemstra, S.J. & Ismail, J.A. 1992, 'Analysis of Room Taxes Levied on the Lodging Industry', *Journal of Travel Research*, vol. 31 no. 1, pp. 42–49

Hiemstra, S.J. & Ismail, J.A. 1993, 'Incidence of the Impacts of Room Taxes in the Lodging Industry', *Journal of Travel Research*, vol. 31 no. 4, pp. 22–26

Hobson, J.S.P. 1993, 'Analysis of the U.S. Cruise Line Industry', *Tourism Management*, vol. 14 no. 4, pp. 453–462

Holloway, J.C. 1989, *The Business of Tourism*, 3rd edn, Pitman, London

Holloway, J.C. & Plant, R.V. 1992, *Marketing for Tourism*, 2nd edn, Pitman, London

Hudson, J.E. 1969, *Les Liens Entre Compagnies et Hotels*, Institut du Transport Aerien, Paris, France

Hudson, J.E. 1972, *L'Integration Verticale dans L'Industrie des Voyages et des Loisirs* Institut du Transport Aerien, Paris, France

Hughes, H.L. 1987, 'Culture as a Tourist Resource—A Theoretical Consideration', *Tourism Management*, vol. 8, September, pp. 205–216

Hunt, J. 1993, 'Foreign Investment in Eastern Europe's Travel Industry', *Travel and Tourism Analyst*, No. 3, pp. 65–85

Hunziker, W. 1951, *Social Tourism: Its Nature and Problems*, Alliance Internationale de Tourisme, Geneva, Switzerland

IATA (Air Canada et al.) 1988, *Air Tariff–New Currency System*, November, Air Canada, BA, JAL, QANTAS & TWA

Jenkins, C.L. & Henry, B.M. 1982, 'Government Involvement in Tourism in Developing Countries', *Annals of Tourism Research*, vol. 9 no. 4, pp. 499–521

Jensen, R.C. & West, G.R. 1986, *Input–Output for Practitioners: Theory and Applications*, Australian Government Publications, Canberra

Johnson, Peter & Thomas, Barry 1992, *Tourism, Museums and the Local Economy*, Edward Elgar, Aldershot, UK

Jones, R.M. 1979, in: Devine, P.J., Lee N., Jones, R.M. & Tyson, W.J. (eds), An *Introduction to Industrial Economics*, 3rd edn, Allen & Unwin, London, pp. 269–299

Kaldor, Nicholas 1955, 'Alternative Theories of Distribution' *Review of Economic Studies*, vol. 23 no. 2

Kane, A.W. 1984, 'The Cruise Catalysts', in *Travel Research*, 15th Annual TTRA Conference, Philadelphia USA

Kaspar, C. 1986, *Die Fremdenverkehrslehre im Grundriss*, Ed. Haupt, Berne, Switzerland 3rd edn

Katona, George 1975, *Psychological Economics*, Elsevier Scientific, New York

Keown, Charles F. 1989, 'A Model of Tourists' Propensity to Buy: The Case of Japanese Visitors to Hawaii', *Journal of Travel Research*, vol. 27 no. 3, Winter, pp. 31–34

Kimes, S.E. 1987, *Location Analysis in the Lodging Industry*, PhD Thesis, Univ. of Texas at Austin, USA

Kirk, David 1989, 'Advances in Catering Technology', in: Cooper, C.P. (ed), *Progress in Tourism, Recreation and Hospitality Management Vol. 1*, Belhaven Press, London

Knickerbocker, F. T. 1973, *Oligopolistic Reaction and Multinational Enterprise*, Harvard University, GBSA Paper, Boston, USA

Kotler, P. 1965, 'Behavioural Models for Analysing Buyers', *Journal of Marketing*, vol. 29 October, pp. 37–45

Lancaster, Kelvin J. 1966, 'A New Approach to Consumer Theory', *Journal of Political Economy*, vol. 74 no. 2, April, pp. 132–157

Lane, Harold E. 1986, 'Marriages of Necessity: Airline and Hotel Liaisons'. *Cornell H. R. A. Quarterly*, vol 27 no. 1, May, pp. 73–79

Lea, John & Small, Jennifer 1988, *Cyclones, Riots & Coups: Tourist Industry Responses in the South Pacific*, Proceedings of the Frontiers of Australian Tourism Conference, Canberra, Australia

Lee, Daniel R. 1985, 'How They Started: The Growth of Four Hotel Giants', *Cornell H. R. A. Quarterly*, vol. 26 no. 1, May, pp. 22–32

Leiper, Neil 1993, 'Defining Tourism and Related Concepts: Tourist, Market, Industry, and Tourism System', in: Khan M.A., Olsen M.D. & Var T. (eds), *Encyclopedia of Hospitality & Tourism*, Van Nostrand Reinhold, New York, pp. 539–558

Leontief, W. 1966, *Input–Output Economics*, Oxford University Press, Oxford, UK

Lessig, V. Parker, & Tollefson, John O. 1972, 'Market Segment Identification, etc.' in: Engel, J. F., Fiorillo, H.F. & Cayley, M.A. (eds), *Market Segmentation*, Holt, Rinehart and Winston, New York

Lin, Tzong-Biau and Sung, Yun-Wing 1984, 'Tourism and Economic Diversification in Hong Kong', *Annals of Tourism Research*, vol. 11, pp. 231–247

Lipsey, Richard G. 1983, *An Introduction to Positive Economics*, Weidenfeld & Nicolson, New York, 6th edn

Littlejohn, David 1985, 'Towards an Economic Analysis of Trans-/Multinational Hotel Companies', *International Journal of Hospitality Management*, vol.4 no. 4, pp. 157–165

Little, I.M.D. & Mirlees, J.A. 1974, *Project Appraisal and Planning for Developing Countries*, Heinemann, London

Liu, Juanita & Var, Turgut 1982, 'Differential Multipliers for the Accommodation Sector', *International Journal of Tourism Management*, Sept, pp. 177–187

Loeb, Peter D. 1982, 'International Travel to the U.S.: An Econometric Evaluation', *Annals of Tourism Research*, vol. 9 no. 1, pp. 7–20

London Tourist Board 1989, *Annual Report for 1988*, L.T.B., London

Lundgren, J.O.J. 1972, 'The Development of Tourist Travel Systems—a Metropolitan Economic Hegemony *Par Excellence*', *Jahrbuch Fur Fremdenverkehr*, vol.20, pp. 86–120

MacDougall, G.D.A. 1960, 'The Benefits and Costs of Private Investment from Abroad: A Theoretical Approach', *Economic Record*, vol. 36, pp. 13–35

Mak, James 1988, 'Taxing Hotel Room Rentals in the U.S.', *Journal of Travel Research*, vol. 27 no. 1, Summer, pp. 10-15

Mak, James 1989, 'The Economic Contribution of Travel to State Economies', *Journal of Travel Research*, vol. 28 no. 2, Fall, pp. 3-5

Mak, James and Nishimura, E. 1979, 'The Economics of a Hotel Room Tax', *Journal of Travel Research*, vol. 17 no. 4, Spring, pp. 2–6

Martin, C.A. & Witt, Stephen F. 1989, 'Forecasting Tourism Demand: A Comparison of the Accuracy of Several Quantitative Methods', *International Journal of Forecasting*, vol. 5 no. 1, pp. 7–19

Mathieson, Alister and Wall, Geoffrey 1982, *Tourism: Economic, Physical and Social Impacts*, Longman, Harlow, UK

McIntosh, Robert W. & Goeldner, Charles C. 1990, *Tourism: Principles, Practices, Philosophies*, Wiley, New York, 6th edn

Mescon, T.S. & Vozikis, G.S. 1985, 'The Economic Impact of Tourism at the Port of Miami', *Annals of Tourism Research*, vol. 12, pp. 515–528

Middleton, Victor T. C. 1988, *Marketing in Travel and Tourism,* Heinemann, London

Mill, R.C. & Morrison, A.M. 1985, *The Tourism System,* Prentice Hall, Englewood Cliffs, NJ

Montgomery, G. & Murphy, P.E. 1983, 'Government Involvement in Tourism Development: A Case Study of TIDSA Implementation in British Colombia', in: Murphy, P.E., *Tourism in Canada,* Univ. of Victoria, Canada

Morison, J. & Powell, R. 1988, 'Using Input–Output Methods for Economic Impact Analysis of Tourism', in: *Proceedings of the Frontiers of Australian Tourism Conference,* BTR, Canberra, Australia, pp. 261–268

Moroney, J.R. & Walker, J.M. 1966, 'A Regional Test of the Heckscher-Ohlin Hypothesis', *Journal of Political Economy,* vol. 74, pp. 573–586

Murphy, P.E. 1985, *Tourism: a Community Approach,* Methuen, New York

Narodick, Kit G. 1972, 'What Motivates the Consumer's Choice of an Airline?', *Journal of Retailing,* vol. 48 no. 1, Spring, pp. 30–38 and 96

Nordhaus, W. & Tobin, J. 1972, 'Is Growth Obsolete?', in *50th Anniversary Colloquium, National Bureau of Economic Research,* Columbia, University Press

Norton, G.A. 1984, *Resource Economics,* Edward Arnold, London

Olsen, M.D. 1993, 'International Growth Strategies of Major U.S. Hotel Companies', *Travel and Tourism Analyst,* No. 3, pp. 51–64

Organisation for Economic Cooperation & Development 1967, *Tourism Development and Economic Growth,* OECD, Paris

Organisation for Economic Cooperation & Development 1981, *The Impact of Tourism on the Environment,* OECD, Paris

Organisation for Economic Cooperation & Development 1988, *Tourism Policy and International Tourism in OECD Member Countries,* OECD, Paris

Organisation for Economic Cooperation & Development 1993, *National Accounts,* OECD, Paris

Pannell, Kerr, Forster 1988, 'Hotel Management Contracts', in: *Tourism Trends,* PKF, Sydney, Australia

Paraskevopoulos, G. 1977, *An Econometric Analysis of International Tourism,* Centre of Planning & Econ. Research, Paper no. 31, Athens

Pearce, Douglas G. 1987, *Tourism Today: A Geographical Analysis,* Longman, Harlow, UK

Pearce, Douglas G. 1988, 'Tourist Time Budgets', *Annals of Tourism Research,* vol. 15, pp. 106–121

Pearce, Douglas G. 1989, *Tourism Development,* Wiley, New York/ Longman, UK, 2nd edn

Percival, Jeff 1987, 'Railways', in: Hodgson, A. (ed), *The Travel & Tourism Industry— Strategies for the Future,* Pergamon, Oxford, UK, pp. 20–36

Peters, Michael 1969, *International Tourism,* Hutchinson, London

Pigou, A.C. 1950, *The Economics of Welfare,* Macmillan, London, 3rd edn

Plog, S.C. 1972, *Why Destination Areas Rise and Fall in Popularity,* Proceedings of the Southern California Chapter, Travel Research Association, USA

Plog, S.C. 1987, 'Understanding Psychographics in Tourism Research', in: Ritchie J. Brent & Goeldner C. (eds), *Travel, Tourism & Hospitality Research,* Wiley, New York, pp. 203–213

Poole, M., Davis, G. and James, S. 1988, *Trends and Prospects for Australian International Air Transport,* Bureau of Transport & Communications, Canberra, Australia

Powers, Terry A. & Powers, Priscilla A. 1977, 'A Dynamic Programming Model for Optimizing Economic Returns to Tourist Resort Projects in Developing Countries', *Journal of Travel Research,* vol. 16 no. 2, pp. 16–21

Powers, Thomas F. 1992, 'The Advent of the Megachain: a Case of the Emperor's New Clothes', *Hospitality Research Journal*, vol. 15 no. 3, pp. 1–11

Prest, A.R. & Turvey, R. 1965, 'Cost–benefit analysis: A Survey', *Economic Journal*, vol. 75 no. 300 pp. 683–735

Relihan, W.J. 1989, 'The Yield-Management Approach to Hotel Room Pricing', *Cornell H.R.A. Quarterly*, vol. 30 no. 1, pp. 4–45

Renoux, Maurice 1973, 'Les methodes de Prevision de la Demande Touristique et Recreative', *Revue de Tourisme*, vol. 28. nos 1/2, pp. 21–26 & 66–70

Roche, M. 1994, 'Mega-Events and Urban Policy', *Annals of Tourism Research*, vol. 21 no. 1, pp. 1–19

Rogers, H. Anthea 1976, 'Price Formation in Hotels', *HCIMA Review*, No. 4, Spring, pp. 226-237

Root, F.R. 1978, *International Trade and Investment*, South-Western Publishing, Cincinnati, Ohio

Ross, S.A., Westerfield, R.W. & Jaffe, J.F. 1993, *Corporate Finance*, 3rd edn, Irwin, Homewood, Ill

Rothenberg, Jerome 1961, *The Measurement of Social Welfare*, Prentice-Hall, Englewood Cliffs, NJ

Rugg, Donald D. 1971, *The Demand for Foreign Travel*, PhD Thesis, University of California, USA

Sadler, P., Archer, B. & Owen, Christine 1973, *Regional Income Multipliers*, Occasional Paper in Economics no.1, University of Wales, Bangor, UK

Salmon, L. C. 1980, *Microeconomics*, Addison-Wesley, Reading, USA, 3rd edn

Samuelson, P.A. (with Nordhaus, W.D.) 1989, *Economics*, McGraw-Hill, New York, 13th edn

Sathiendrakumar, R. & Tisdell, Clem 1989, 'Tourism and the Economic Development of the Maldives', *Annals of Tourism Research*, vol. 16, no. 2, pp. 254–269

Schall, L., Sundem G. & Gerjsbeek, W.R. 1978, 'Survey and Analysis of Capital Budgeting Methods', *Journal of Finance*, vol. 33, March, pp.281–287

Schewe, C. and Calantone, R. 1978, Psychographic Segmentation of Tourists', *Journal of Travel Research*, vol.16, pp. 14–20

Schiffman, L.G. and Kanuk, L.L. 1987, *Consumer Behavior*, Prentice Hall, Englewood Cliffs, USA, 3rd edn

Sessa, A. 1983, *Elements of Tourism Economics*, Catal, Rome, Italy

Sessa, A. 1984, 'Comments on Peter Gray's "The Contributions of Economics to Tourism"', *Annals of Tourism Research*, vol. 11, pp. 283–286

Shaw, Stephen D. 1985, *Airline Marketing and Management*, Pitman, London, 2nd edn

Shaw, S.D. 1989, 'Asian Hotel Groups Fan Out', *Pacific Travel News*, October, pp. 8–9

Shaw, S.D., Muqbil, I., Thomas, G. & Jara M. 1988, 'Tour Guides: Shepherds or Shysters', *Pata Travel News*, July, pp. 6–10

Sheldon, Pauline J. 1986, 'The Tour Operator Industry: An Analysis', *Annals of Tourism Research*, vol. 13, pp. 349–365

Sheldon, Pauline J. 1993, 'Forecasting Tourism: Expenditure versus Arrivals', *Journal of Travel Research*, vol. 32.1, pp. 13–20

Simon, Herbert A, 1959, 'Theories of Decision Making in Economics', *American Economic Review*, vol. 49, June

Sinclair, Thea, Clewer, A. & Pack, A. 1990, 'Hedonic Prices and the Marketing of Package Holidays: the Case of Tourism Resorts in Malaga', in: Ashworth G. & Goodall B. (eds) *Marketing Tourism Places*, Routledge, London, pp. 85–103

Sinclair, Thea & Sutcliffe, Charles 1982, 'Keynesian Income Multipliers with 1st and 2nd Round Effects: An Application to Tourist Expenditure', *Oxford Bulletin of Economics & Statistics,* vol. 44 no. 4, pp. 321–338

Sinclair, Thea & Sutcliffe, Charles 1988, 'The Economic Effects on Destination Areas of Foreign Involvement In the Tourism Industry: A Spanish Application', in: Goodall & Ashworth, *Marketing in the Tourism Industry,* Croom Helm, London, pp. 111–132

Sinden, Jack 1977, 'Utility Analysis in Recreational Research' in: Mercer, D. (ed), *Leisure and Recreation in Australia,* Sorrett Publishing, Malvern, Vic, Australia, pp. 129–140

Sinden, John A. & Worrell, Albert C. 1979, *Unpriced Values,* Wiley, New York

Slattery, P. 1990, 'Models for Financing Tourism Facilities', *Travel and Tourism Analyst,* No. 4, pp. 50–63

Slattery, P. & Johnson, S.M. 1993, 'Hotel Chains in Europe', *Travel and Tourism Analyst,* No. 1, pp. 65–80

Smeral, Egon 1989, 'Economic Models of Tourism' in: Witt, S. F. & Moutinho, L. (eds) *Tourism Marketing and Management Handbook,* Prentice-Hall, Hemel Hempstead, UK, pp. 113–118

Smith, Stephen L.J. 1989, *Tourism Analysis: A Handbook,* Longman, Harlow, UK

Smith, Stephen L.J. 1994, 'The Tourism Product', *Annals of Tourism Research,* vol. 21.3, pp. 582–595

Smith, V.L. 1977, *Hosts and Guests: the Anthropology of Tourism,* University of Pennsylvania Press, Philadelphia, USA

Spengler, John O & Uysal, Muzaffer 1989, 'Considerations in the Hotel Taxation Process', *International J ournal of Hospitality Management,* vol. 8 no. 4, pp. 309–316

Stabler, Michael J. 1988, 'The Image of Destination Regions: Theoretical and Empirical Aspects' in: Goodall, B. & Ashworth, G. (eds) *Marketing in the Tourism Industry,* Croom Helm, London

Stanton, John & Aislabie, Colin 1992, 'Up-Market Integrated Resorts in Australia', *Annals of Tourism Research,* vol. 19 no. 3, pp. 435–449

Steinnes, Donald N. 1988, 'A Statistical Analysis of the Impact of Oil Price Shocks on Tourism', *Journal of Travel Research,* vol. 26 no. 2, Fall, pp. 39–42

Stipanuk, D.M. 1993, 'Tourism and Technology: Interactions and Implications', *Tourism Management,* vol. 14 no. 4, pp. 267-278

Summary, Rebecca 1987, 'Estimation of Tourism Demand by Multivariable Regression Analysis', *Tourism Management,* vol. 8 no. 4, December, pp. 317–322

Sussman, S. & Fletcher, J. 1994, 'Use of Spreadsheet in Forecasting', *Annals of Tourism Research,* vol. 21 no. 1, pp. 156–157

Taneja, Nawal K. 1988, *The International Airline Industry,* D. C. Heath, Lexington, USA

Tighe, A. J. 1986, 'The Arts–Tourism Partnership', *Journal of Travel Research,* vol. 24, no. 3, Winter, pp. 2–5

Toh, Rex S., Kelly, M.K. and Hu M.Y. 1986, 'An Approach to the Determination of Optimal Airline Fares', *Journal of Travel Research,* vol. 25 no. 1, Summer, pp. 26–38

Truong, T.P. & Hensher, D.A. 1985, 'Measurement of Travel Time Values and Opportunity Cost from a Discrete Choice Model', *Economic Journal,* vol. 95, pp. 438–451

Turner, L. 1976, 'The International Division of Leisure: Tourism and the Third World', *World Development.* vol. 4, pp. 253–260

Van Dijk, J.C., Hagens, J.S. & Windmeijer, F. 1991, *A Simulation Model of the Dutch Tourist Market,* Foundation for Economic Research report no. 255, Amsterdam

Van Dijk, J.C. & Van der Stelt-Scheele, D.D. 1993, 'Price Formation in Tourism Industry Branches', *Annals of Tourism Research,* vol. 20 no. 4, pp. 716–728

Van Doren, C.S. 1993, 'PanAm's Legacy to World Tourism', *Journal of Travel Research*, vol.32 no. 1, pp. 3–12

Van Dyke, Tom & Olsen, Michael D. 1989, 'A Comparison of Performance Variables of Highly Profitable Midpriced Hotels/ Motels with Marginally Profitable or Losing Operations', *Hospitality Education & Research Journal*, vol. 13 no. 1

Van Raaij, W. Fred 1986, 'Consumer Research on Tourism: Mental and Behavioral Constructs', *Annals of Tourism Research*, vol. 13, pp. 1–9

Var, Turgut & Lee, C-K. 1993, 'Tourism Forecasting: State of the Art Techniques', in: Khan M., Olsen M. & Var T. (eds.), *Encyclopedia of Hospitality and Tourism*, Van Nostrand Reinhold, New York, pp. 679–696

Var, Turgut & Quayson, Jojo 1985, 'The Multiplier Impact of Tourism in the Okanagan', *Annals of Tourism Research*, vol. 12, pp. 497–514

Vlitos-Rowe, Irene 1993, 'The European Market for Very Expensive Holidays', *Travel and Tourism Analyst*, No. 2, pp. 35–53

Wahab, S. 1975, *Tourism Management*, Tourism International Press, London

Walsh, R.G., Sanders, L.D. & McKean, J.R. 1990, 'The Consumptive Value of Travel Time on Recreation Trips', *Journal of Travel Research*, vol. 29 no. 1, pp. 17–24

Walther, Carl 1984, 'Airline Deregulation & its Implications for the U.S. Travel Industry', in: McIntosh R.W. & Goeldner C.R. (eds), *Tourism*, 4th edn, Wiley, New York, pp. 443–457

Wanhill, S.R.C. 1986, 'Which Investment Incentives for Tourism?', *Tourism Management*, vol. 7 no. 1, March, pp. 2–7

Waters, Somerset R. 1989, *Travel Industry World Yearbook—The Big Picture*, vol. 33, Child and Waters, New York

White, K.J. and Walker, M.B. 1982, 'Trouble in the Travel Account', *Annals of Tourism Research*, vol. 9, pp. 37–56

Williams, George 1993, *The Airline Industry and the Impact of Deregulation*, Ashgate Publishing, Aldershot UK/ Brookfield Vt, USA

Witt, Christine A. & Witt, Stephen F. 1990, 'Appraising an Econometric Forecasting Model', *Journal of Travel Research*, vol. 28 no. 3, pp. 30–34

Witt, Stephen F. 1992, 'Tourism Forecasting: How Well Do Private and Public Sector Organisations Perform?', *Tourism Management*, vol. 13 no. 1, pp. 79–84

Witt, Stephen F. & Martin, C.A. 1987, 'Econometric Models for Forecasting International Tourism Demand', *Journal of Travel Research*, vol. 25 no. 3, Winter, pp. 23–30

Wolff, Carlo 1993, 'The Bed Tax Dilemma', *Lodging Hospitality*, vol. 49 no. 2 February, pp. 34–36

Woodside, Arch G. and Lysonski, Steven 1989, 'A General Model of Traveller Destination Choice', *Journal of Travel Research*, vol 27 no. 4, Spring, pp. 29–37

World Tourism Organisation 1980, *Role and Structure of National Tourism Administrations*, WTO, Madrid, Spain

World Tourism Organisation 1983(a), *The Framework of the State's Responsibility for the Management of Tourism*, WTO, Madrid, Spain

World Tourism Organisation 1983(b), *Appraisal and Social Value of Investments in Domestic Tourism*, WTO, Madrid, Spain

World Tourism Organisation 1993, *Economic Review of World Tourism*, WTO, Madrid, Spain

World Travel and Tourism Council 1992, *Travel and Tourism—the WTTC Report*, WTTC, Brussels

Zegg, R. 1987, *Arbeitsplatz Hotellerie*, ed. Paul Haupt, Berne, Switzerland

Index of Names

Index of Subjects